Henry Caswall

The American Church and the American Union

Henry Caswall

The American Church and the American Union

ISBN/EAN: 9783744660891

Printed in Europe, USA, Canada, Australia, Japan

Cover: Foto ©ninafisch / pixelio.de

More available books at **www.hansebooks.com**

THE AMERICAN CHURCH

AND

THE AMERICAN UNION

LONDON
PRINTED BY SPOTTISWOODE AND CO.
NEW-STREET SQUARE

THE

AMERICAN CHURCH

AND THE

AMERICAN UNION

BY

HENRY CASWALL, M.A.

D.D. OF TRINITY COLLEGE, CONNECTICUT:
PREBENDARY OF SARUM : VICAR OF FIGHELDEAN :
AND LATE PROCTOR IN CONVOCATION FOR THE DIOCESE OF SALISBURY

LONDON
SAUNDERS, OTLEY, AND CO.
66 BROOK STREET, HANOVER SQUARE
1861

Preface.

HE Author of this work, though a native of England, removed to America in the year 1828, while yet in early life. Having received Holy Orders at the hands of an American bishop in 1831, he gained his clerical experience in various parts of the United States and Canada. At the same time he had the pleasure of forming the acquaintance of many persons eminent in Church and State, and of a large proportion of the writers whose works are quoted in the following pages.

Returning to this country in 1842, he obtained a Private Act of Parliament removing the legal disabilities attached to his American Ordination, and during the last nineteen years has enjoyed many opportunities of observing the operations of the Church at home. Although never an admirer of the political institutions of the United States, he has always felt an affectionate regard for the American Church, and rejoices in every occasion of making it favourably known in England. He has kept up a constant correspondence with his old friends beyond the Atlantic, and gladly welcomes them to his home when they visit the land of their ancestors.

The publication of the present volume has been suggested by the difficulties now existing between the North and the South. For the personal narrative of the author, and for more definite information respecting the social and religious condition of the English race in the New World, the reader is referred to "America and the American Church;"* "The City of the Mormons;"† "The Prophet of the Nineteenth Century," † and "The Western World Revisited." ‡ The last-mentioned book contains the narrative of a deputation on which the Author was sent with others to America in 1853, by the Society for the Propagation of the Gospel in Foreign Parts.

FIGHELDEAN:
  May 11, 1861.

* Published by Mozley.
† Rivingtons.
‡ J. H. and James Parker.

Table of Contents.

a

THE AMERICAN CHURCH

AND THE

AMERICAN UNION.

CHAPTER I.

THE CHURCH AND THE COLONIES.

SETTLEMENT OF NORTH AMERICA DUE TO THE REFORMATION. — EARLY
COLONIAL CHARTERS. — VIRGINIA AND THE SOUTHERN GROUP OF
COLONIES.—PENNSYLVANIA AND THE MIDDLE GROUP.

OMMUNITY of origin and of language
are among the strongest ties which can
exist between nations. As Englishmen,
therefore, it is impossible for us to avoid
feeling an interest in a people so closely
connected with us as those of the United States of North
America. Notwithstanding diversities of government,
of climate, and of geographical position, that people
must still be regarded as the enterprising portion of
ourselves, whose mission it has been to level the forests
and cultivate the wildernesses of the West, and to extend civilisation and religion from the Atlantic to the
Pacific, from the Great Lakes to the Gulf of Mexico.

In proportion too as we identify ourselves with the system of Christianity which grew out of the English Reformation, we shall be interested in tracing the fortunes of that branch of the Anglican Church which has now existed more than two centuries and a half in the New World. We shall notice its advancement from small beginnings, in the midst of formidable difficulties; we shall sympathise with it in its calamities; and we shall rejoice in the present wide diffusion of principles which we believe to be identical with primitive truth. Remembering that the population of the United States already exceeds thirty-two millions; that it embraces the largest English-speaking community in the world; that it doubles itself usually within a quarter of a century, and that its future influence on mankind, for good or evil, must be of the most important character — we shall heartily desire that the trials of the great republic, whatever they may be, may conduce to the permanent establishment of all that is safe, sound, and ennobling in politics and in religion.

North America was made known to the English at the close of the fifteenth century. Two Venetian mariners, John Cabot and his more celebrated son Sebastian, were authorised by Henry VII. to undertake new discoveries, towards which the king contributed the expense of fitting one ship at Bristol, while the merchants of that city and London added three or four small vessels, freighted with suitable commodities. On the 24th of June, 1497, they discovered Newfoundland, whence they sailed down to Cape Florida: being the first navigators who had seen the great continent of the West. No settlement, however, was attempted; and it is probable that the English government religiously respected the Papal grant which assigned to the Spaniards the lands lying above a hundred leagues westward of the Azores.

The settlement of the English race in America is mainly due to our great religious movement of the sixteenth century. In that century our Church took its present form : not by the substitution of a new society in place of an older one, but chiefly by the removal from its own system of certain additions to the faith made during the last thousand years. The clergy being represented by the Convocation, and the laity by the Sovereign and the Parliament, the piety, the learning, the good sense and the power of the nation were brought to bear on the great religious questions of the age. Under God, we thus retained the ancient landmarks of doctrine, discipline and worship, and rejected the modes of association and belief which appeared to be unauthorised by the original documents of Christianity. We retained the Episcopate, the Creeds, and Liturgical worship, while we rejected Purgatory, Images, and Transubstantiation, and cast off our allegiance to the Pope. Having done this, we felt no scruple in forming colonies in those wide and productive regions on which the eye of English enterprise had already fixed itself. Our national life had acquired new vigour in that age of theological inquiry and geographical discovery, and with the ascendancy of the Reformation,

England began to lay the foundation of her maritime superiority.

The great navigators of the time of Elizabeth, full of courage and the spirit of romance, ventured upon the wide and stormy Atlantic in vessels so small that at the present day they would be deemed hardly suitable to a voyage across the Channel. Their main objects were the discovery of gold and of a North-West passage to Eastern Asia. Under a patent obtained by Raleigh, two vessels sailed in 1584, and arrived at the country now known as Carolina, but which, together with the entire coast from the thirty-fourth to the forty-fifth degree of latitude, was named by the queen, Virginia, as a record of herself. The vegetation of that southern clime struck the beholders with admiration; and the Indians showed kindness and gave a friendly welcome to the English. In the following year a larger expedition was sent forth. The adventurers landed on the island of Roanoke, but the settlement proved unsuccessful. The capital of North Carolina now bears the name of Raleigh, in honour of the brave but unfortunate adventurer; and the potato and tobacco were among the first gifts of America to Europe.

James I. favoured the designs of those active men who aimed at the enlargement of his dominions, and with that view divided Virginia into two districts, called respectively North and South Virginia. The king formed two companies for planting colonies within their limits. He granted the southern district to a company resident in London, denominated the London

Company; and the northern to an association of merchants and others in the west of England, known as the Plymouth Company. The present States of Virginia and North Carolina were comprised within the limits of South Virginia, while Northern Virginia embraced New England, so named by Prince Charles, afterwards Charles I. The superintendence of the whole colonial system was confided to a council in England appointed by the king; while the local administration of each colony was intrusted to a council residing within its limits, to be named by the council in England.

The principles of popular liberty had already made great progress in the mother-country; and generally, as the colonies came into being, they were chartered as bodies politic and corporate, with the privileges of the most favoured corporations at home.* It was long before they ceased to be considered otherwise than as trading associations, entitled indeed to make their own bye-laws, but not constituting a government distinct from that of the mother-country. It was taken for granted, if not specially ordered, that the religion of the colony was to be that of the Church of England. Kindness to the aboriginal tribes was enjoined, with the use of all proper means for their conversion.

It was in May, 1607, that the newly reformed worship of our Church was first heard on the banks of that noble Virginian stream, denominated, after the reigning monarch, James River. The emigrants had found a

---

* New York Review, 1838.

delightful country, which seemed to them an earthly paradise, abounding in beautiful mountains and valleys, and in productive land. As members of the English establishment they had been required by their sovereign to provide for the preaching of the Gospel among themselves and the neighbouring Indians. They were accompanied by Robert Hunt, a wise and pious clergy-man, and soon, among their own hastily constructed huts, they erected a temporary building for the performance of Divine worship. This frail edifice eventually gave place to a more durable church, the ruins of which may yet be seen on the deserted site of Jamestown.

Notwithstanding this auspicious beginning, the early years of the colony of Virginia abounded in misery and discouragement. The settlers had left England with expectations of great and speedy gains, and the labour of felling the woods appeared enormous to a party consisting rather of broken gentlemen, tradesmen and serving-men, than of hardy and industrious labourers. Many of their number were killed by the Indians, and many died of disease. In 1610, the few who survived had resolved on returning to England, when the opportune arrival of reinforcements under the new captain-general, Lord De La Warr, changed their plans, and induced them to remain. In the course of a few years the Jamestown settlement had sent forth vigorous off-shoots into the neighbouring districts, in which churches were built and ministers stationed.

In 1613, Powhatan, the chief of the surrounding Indians, became the fast friend of the colonists, through the marriage of his daughter, Pocahontas, with John Rolfe, one of the settlers; a connection to which some of the best Virginian families trace their origin.

The English were now determined to establish an exclusive right of territory up to the forty-fifth degree of latitude, and accordingly Captain Argall was sent from Virginia with a naval force against the French settlements commenced in Acadia, now Nova Scotia. He succeeded, for the time, in enforcing the English claim, and on his return visited, with the same object, the new Dutch trading establishment within the present port of New York.

Thus far the colony had been governed by martial law, which was vigorously administered by Argall as deputy-governor, but, in consequence of the complaints of the people, a new governor was sent out in 1619. An Assembly was now constituted, composed of the governor, his council, and two representatives from each of the boroughs. At its first meeting, this legislature fixed the payment of the clergy at 200*l.* annually in maize and tobacco, the principal articles of their produce. A hundred acres in every borough were set apart as glebes, and application was made to the Bishop of London for a supply of " pious, learned, and painful ministers ; " " a charitable work," says the Bishop of Oxford, " in which he readily engaged." The people of England and the Virginia Company itself showed a commendable zeal for the firm establishment of religion in this new dominion. Money was freely given for founding a college, building churches, and supplying them with communion-plate.   The colonists were especially urged by the Company to educate well-disposed Indians, so that they might become instruments in the conversion of their countrymen.   The general treatment of the aboriginal race was mild and friendly, contrasting favourably with that which was afterwards adopted in the northern colonies.   Jealousies, however, arose, and the savages concerted a plot to murder the colonists, which so far succeeded, that only eighteen hundred survived out of nearly three thousand.   The loss was soon made up by emigration from England, but a spirit of deadly hostility had arisen on the part of the white men towards the Indians, and the former purposes of mercy were apparently forgotten.

In 1624, the Virginia Assembly provided "that there should be an uniformity in the Church as near as might be to the Canons of the Church of England, and that all persons should yield a ready obedience to them upon pain of censure."   It also required that a burial-ground should be enclosed, and a house or room set apart for divine service in every plantation, and declared that every colonist should attend public worship, under a penalty.

The great mistake was that the authorities of that age did not see the importance of supplying a young colony like Virginia with the oversight of a Bishop of its own.   Had Virginia in the seventeenth century commenced her career like British Columbia in the nineteenth, under the Christian guidance of a conscientious and energetic spiritual ruler, the course of events might have been far happier than it proved in fact. In the absence of a chief pastor, the clergy were almost independent of all ecclesiastical rule, and cases of delinquency among them were not met by needful discipline. Young men who desired to become ministers of Christ, were obliged to undertake a perilous and expensive voyage to England in search of ordination. The Confirmation of the young, with all its great advantages when rightly undertaken and performed, was utterly unknown. And, finally, the people, equally with the clergy, suffered from the want of that stimulus to good works which the presence of a really good Bishop is found to supply.

In many respects, however, the Church in Virginia, such as it was, worked decidedly well. It is certain that religious affairs were administered with mildness, and with a freedom from fanaticism which differed widely from the temper of the North. In 1624, the Crown resumed its grant, and Virginia became a royal colony, in which new character it was conspicuous for its attachment to the King as well as to the Church. When the great rebellion commenced in England, Virginia continued loyal, and many of the expatriated cavaliers fled to it as a refuge in which they were certain to meet with sympathy. Even when obliged to succumb to Cromwell's arms, the colony stipulated for the use of the Book of Common Prayer for one year ensuing, for the continuance of ministers in their places, and for the payment of their accustomed dues and agreements. Sixteen months before the Restoration in England, Charles II. was proclaimed in Virginia, and among the earliest business brought before the colonial legislature was the revival of the Church, ten clergymen alone remaining at the close of the Commonwealth. Provision was accordingly made for the building and due furniture of churches; for the canonical performance of the Liturgy; for the ministration of God's word; for a due observance of Sunday; and for the baptism and Christian instruction of the young.

Although the religion of the country was thus restored, the people were alarmed by new restrictions on their trade, by which Parliament sought to promote the interests of English commerce and navigation. A duty of five per cent. was charged on all merchandise exported from or imported into any dominions of the crown. Soon afterwards came the Navigation Act of Charles II., by which it was decreed that no merchandise should be imported into the plantations but in English vessels, navigated by Englishmen. On the other hand, tobacco, and other staple articles of American produce, were to be sent exclusively to England. The Assembly remonstrated in vain against these enactments, and in 1676 a rebellion broke out, headed by one Bacon. The governor, Berkeley, notwithstanding the popularity which he had enjoyed, was unable to maintain tranquillity, and fled to a distant part of the colony, where he collected some forces. Jamestown was burnt, and both parties laid waste whole districts as it served their purposes. The death of Bacon occasioned the dissolution of his faction, when severe punishments were inflicted on the ringleaders, and the body of the insurgents submitted to the governor on condition of receiving a free pardon. Under the succeeding administration, peace was concluded with the hostile Indians, and wealth and population rapidly increased. At the time of the Revolution in 1688, which placed William and Mary on the throne of England, the number of inhabitants amounted to sixty thousand.

Having thus dwelt at some length on the early history of Virginia, we may now briefly consider the remaining members of the group of southern colonies. As Virginia had been named from Queen Elizabeth, so Maryland, formerly a part of Virginia, derived its appellation from Henrietta Maria, the queen of Charles I. It was granted by that king in 1632 to Sir George Calvert, afterwards Lord Baltimore, to whom, though a " popish recusant," was intrusted the licence to found churches according to the ecclesiastical laws of England. The first successful settlement was made by about two hundred gentlemen of rank and fortune, chiefly Romanists, who landed on the Potomac River in 1633. The Roman Catholics claim that the " rights of conscience were first fully recognised in Maryland."* In 1635 the primary Assembly was convened, and in 1639 the people secured for themselves the tranquil exercise of

---

* Coit's Puritanism, p. 21.

the Roman Catholic religion. Trinitarians alone were tolerated by the Constitution, and in 1649 a law was passed mulcting all who should speak reproachfully against the Blessed Virgin or the Apostles. But the rapid growth of the Church of England in this colony effectually prevented any lasting predominance on the part of the Romanists.

In Maryland, as in Virginia, there were Indian hostilities and a rebellion, during which the governor fled. While the power of Cromwell continued, Romanism was placed under legal disabilities; but at the Restoration a tolerant government was again established, and Huguenots from France, and various sects from Holland, Sweden, and Finland, found protection in the colony. Lord Baltimore died in 1675, after a supremacy of more than forty-three years, and the commercial metropolis of Maryland commemorates his name. The proprietary government did not, however, satisfy the people. It was accused of favouring Popery: a Protestant ascendancy was determined upon in England, and, in 1691, King William constituted Maryland a royal province.

In 1702, a law was passed by the Maryland Legislature, which provided that every congregation and place of worship, according to the usage of the Church of England, was to be deemed a part of the Established Church. Every minister presented, inducted or appointed by the governor, was to receive forty pounds of tobacco per poll, to be collected by the sheriff. The English acts of toleration were extended to Quakers and Protestant dissenters, under certain regulations; but Roman Catholics were excepted from an indulgence of which in America they had been the first to show an example.

Carolina was named from our Charles I., or perhaps still earlier, from Charles IX. of France, under whom a settlement of French Protestants was attempted on this coast. It was originally a single province, the separation into North and South not being effected before 1728. No permanent settlement was made in Carolina until after the Restoration, the charter to the Earl of Clarendon, and seven others, being granted in 1663. The proprietors claimed all the country now comprised in the two Carolinas and Georgia, and extending westward to the Pacific Ocean. They commissioned Berkeley, the Governor of Virginia, to establish a government over this territory, and accordingly he visited the colony, instituted a General Assembly, and appointed a Governor. They also engaged the celebrated Mr. Locke to frame for them a constitution and a body of laws, which should be worthy of enduring through all ages. This curious scheme, then considered a masterpiece of statesmanship, attempted to connect hereditary wealth and political power, so as to secure the people against the republican tendencies which already showed themselves in other colonies. But the philosopher's model of an aristocratic state, with its orders of nobility and graduated rank, did not comport with the humble settlements of a new country, and it was never brought into successful action. By its ninety-sixth article it was declared that "the religion of the Church of England, being the only true and orthodox, and the national religion of all the king's dominions, was also that of Carolina." The public maintenance of the clergy was to be provided by the Legislature, and indulgence to form congregations was accorded to all. The charter gave to the Earl of Clarendon and others the right of patronage, and the advowson of all churches, chapels, and oratories, dedicated according to the ecclesiastical law of England. In 1682, St. Philip's Church was erected at Charleston, the capital of the colony, and in 1704, parishes were established and endowed by the Assembly. The planters built churches at their own expense, and sometimes provided glebes and parsonages.

The settlement of Georgia was projected in England as late as 1732, with a view to the accommodation of poor people in Great Britain and Ireland, and for the further security of Carolina. The benevolent James Oglethorpe and others proposed to raise a fund for conveying poor debtors, petty criminals, and other indigent emigrants, to this part of America free of expence. Their generous project was encouraged by a grant from Parliament and by letters-patent from George II., in honour of whom the new province received its name. A corporation was formed for settling the colony, and Savannah was founded by Oglethorpe himself, who, with a hundred and twenty emigrants, arrived there in 1733. Two years afterwards, Darien was settled by a company of Highlanders, and in 1736,

Oglethorpe, who had returned to England, brought over with him three hundred additional emigrants. They were accompanied by the celebrated John Wesley, then a missionary of the Society for Propagating the Gospel, who, after remaining nearly two years in America, returned to England. After Wesley left Georgia, the almost equally well-known George Whitfield arrived in the colony. He travelled through the American settlements soliciting subscriptions for the establishment and maintenance of an Orphan House in Savannah, which is still in existence.

The persecuted Protestants on the continent of Europe had been offered an asylum in Georgia, and many accepted the offer. A large number of Moravians came over, and built a village, which they called Ebenezer. When, in 1738, it was proposed to introduce negro slavery, as in the other colonies, Oglethorpe opposed the measure, as being contrary to the Gospel, and to the fundamental laws of England. The Moravians demonstrated that "whites" could labour in that southern climate, and the value of the raw silk raised by them soon amounted to 10,000l. a year. It was also said that the introduction of slaves would starve the poor labourers for whose sake the colony was founded. In 1743, Oglethorpe gave up his connection with the colony. Slavery was then introduced, and even the Moravians agreed with Whitfield in thinking that slaves "might be employed in a Christian spirit." * In

* M. Murray, p. 175.

1752, the trustees of Georgia surrendered their charter to the king, and the settlement became a royal colony, after which it advanced rapidly in wealth and population.

The Southern Colonies ultimately presented, on the whole, a uniform aspect in reference to their social condition. From an early time slavery existed among them, and in the first instance, the slavery of white men, not only criminals, but emigrants and political prisoners. Conditional servitude, under covenants, had been coeval with the first settlement of Virginia. The poor emigrant was bound to render to his American employer the full cost of his transportation. This led to a species of traffic in those who could be persuaded to embark. The speculation proved so lucrative that numbers soon took part in it, since men might be imported at a cost of *eight* pounds, who could afterwards be sold in the colony for *forty*. So established became this evil, that white men were purchased on shipboard as horses are purchased at a fair. This, under the rule of the Commonwealth, was the fate of the royalist prisoners of the battle of Worcester.*

But white slaves could not be had in sufficient abundance to bring into cultivation the wide tracts of the south adapted to the cultivation of tobacco, rice, sugar, and cotton. In the summer of 1620, a Dutch man-of-war sailed up James River, and landed twenty negroes, who found ready purchasers. For some time

* Bancroft, i. p. 175

this new trade continued chiefly in the hands of the Dutch, though discouraged by the laws of Virginia. But the blame does not rest in any especial manner on the people of Holland. Considerations of pecuniary gain prevailed with us over the dictates of justice, and it was resolved by England that her colonial possessions should be cultivated by the people of Africa. In carrying this bold design into effect, religion was forced into alliance with avarice, and the convenient principle was enunciated that Christians possessed the right to reduce the unbaptized to slavery, with a view to the propagation of the faith. The expedient of African servitude, thus devised and supported, rapidly gained favour, and negroes soon became a most profitable item of Christian commerce. Although Maryland, Virginia, and Carolina early took alarm at the dangerous increase of the African population, and passed laws restricting the importation of negroes [*], companies were constantly forming in England for the furtherance of the nefarious traffic. Finally, by the treaty of Utrecht, England engaged to act the part of a slave-merchant to the other nations of Christendom. This treaty, ratified under Queen Anne, bound us to import into the western world 144,000 negroes, in the course of thirty years, over and above the "assortments" of the ordinary merchants. It is calculated that during the century previous to the American Revolution, we did, in fact, import into America and the West Indies nearly three

[*] Bancroft, iii. 410.

C

millions, besides a quarter of a million purchased in Africa, and thrown into the Atlantic on the passage.*

In the southern colonies, therefore, there was comparatively little social equality, and the means of general education having been but scantily provided, the inhabitants, to a great extent, had lost the sense of its necessity. Nearly half the population, and, in some districts, more than half, consisted, at an early period, of negro slaves. There was also a large body of white slaves, or indented servants, and their descendants. In the back settlements of the Carolinas and subsequently in Georgia, there was a greater mixture of races than in Virginia, a large proportion of the people being recent immigrants, not only from England, but from Ireland, Scotland, Switzerland, and Germany. In their religious ideas and establishments these southern colonies differed greatly from the others† : the Church of England being, with few exceptions, the Church of the people. The Roman Catholics of Maryland were but a handful, certainly not more than an eighth of the population ; the Dissenters, once numerous in the Carolinas, conformed more or less to the Establishment ; and, perhaps, in no part of the British dominions were the doctrines and discipline of the Church more generally acquiesced in than in Virginia. Not that there was any special Church zeal, for there was little or nothing to call it forth ; but there was a general spirit of acquiescence, undisturbed by doubts or questionings, such as

* Bancroft, iii. 412.   † Church Review, Jan. 1852.

perhaps cannot readily be pointed out elsewhere. The Virginians, at the head of the slave colonies, had a landed gentry, who maintained, as far as possible, the usages of English society. But, on the whole, the people lived in the simplicity which naturally pervades the habitations in the wilderness. In 1671, a royal governor said, "I thank God there are no free schools nor printers, and I hope we shall not have them these hundred years; for learning has brought disobedience and misery and sects into the world, and printing has divulged them and libels against the best government. God keep us from both!" Travelling was performed by water, or on horseback through winding paths in the forest. There were no bridges, and rivers had to be crossed by fording, or by swimming. The houses were generally built of logs, and often with mere shutters to close the windows instead of glass. A collection of habitations in Virginia was rarely to be seen in the early times; and Jamestown had but a church, a court-house, and eighteen buildings. At this period, the people, being widely scattered, rarely met in large numbers, except for public worship.

The group of middle colonies, New York, New Jersey, and Pennsylvania, which then included Delaware, are next to be considered.

Manhattan Island, on which New York now stands, and the spacious bay adjoining, were discovered in 1609 by Henry Hudson, an Englishman in the employ of the Dutch East-India Company. Advancing up the river, now known by his name, he passed through the

c 2

magnificent scenery of the Highlands, and sent forward a small boat as high as the spot where Albany now stands.   This region was claimed by the Dutch as the discoverers, and, in 1614, they commenced a trading establishment on Manhattan Island, and another at the highest point attained by Hudson on the river. In 1627, the Dutch settlers proposed a treaty of friend-ship with the Pilgrims of the Plymouth colony, but their deputies, though well received, were informed, as Argall had already informed them, that the English had prior claims to the country on the Hudson.   After this, they came in collision with the Massachusetts settlers, who had secured possession of their discoveries on the Connecticut.   They had difficulty also in subduing the Swedes and Finns, who, under the protection of the Swedish government, had   settled   in   the   territory claimed   by   Holland, then   known   as   New   Sweden, and now constituting the State of Delaware, so named from the great river which commemorates the adven-turous Lord De La Warr.   They had bloody battles with the Indians, and   might have   been   annihilated, but for the mediation of Roger Williams, the founder of the   Rhode   Island   settlement.   They   continued, however, to gain ground as a colony of Holland, until, in 1664, Charles II. determining to   enforce the En-glish claim, granted   to   his   brother, the   Duke of York, the whole territory from the Connecticut River to the Delaware.   An English   fleet   accordingly   proceeded to Manhattan Island, and the Dutch   governor, finding resistance useless, consented   to   a   capitulation.   The settlemént on the island, previously called New Amsterdam, was henceforth known as New York, while the settlement one hundred and sixty miles up the river, heretofore Fort Orange, was denominated Albany. The colonists were not dissatisfied with the change; very few returned to Holland; and though afterwards, during fifteen months, the mother-country was again in possession of the colony, in 1674 it was finally transferred to England, and remained more than a century under British rule. The members of the Dutch Church long retained much influence in New York.

In 1683, the Duke of York conceded various liberties to the people, and the governor was instructed to call an assembly of their representatives. On his accession to the throne in 1685, James II. retracted these liberties, imposed new taxes, and forbade the existence of a printing-press in the colony. At this period, New York, which now boasts a million of inhabitants, contained less than four thousand, and the whole province under thirty thousand. Luxury was unknown, waggons were used instead of carriages, and the inhabitants depended on home-made cloth for their apparel. There were few merchants, few servants, and very few slaves. Fifteen or twenty vessels traded yearly to the port of New York, bringing English manufactures, and carrying, in return, the productions of the soil, chiefly wheat, timber, and tobacco, as well as furs procured from the Indians.

In 1684, the governors of New York and Virginia received at Albany the deputies of the five Indian nations, the Mohawks, Oneidas, Onondagos, Cayugas, and Senecas, and formed with them a treaty of peace and friendship which proved highly valuable in the wars of the following century. But New York now had its religious troubles. Although the members of the Church of England were not much more than a tenth of the population, their influence was prominent in the council, and awakened the dissenters to jealousy. Those of the old Dutch establishment had many points of sympathy with Anglicanism; but the English and Scottish Presbyterians and Puritans were decided in their animosity. Still the Church of England succeeded in obtaining a partial establishment, and under the authority of Queen Anne, a small piece of ground adjoining the city was given to Trinity Church, which has since become a valuable endowment. Busy streets now cover what was once a meadow, and the property is estimated at more than seven millions of dollars. Under an act of the Assembly, churches were erected in various places, and in 1761 the number of church-people in the province of New York was reckoned at twenty-five thousand, or a quarter of the population.

The tract between the Hudson and the Delaware had already been conveyed to English proprietaries, under the name of New Jersey, and had been partly settled by Quakers and by Puritans from New England. The proprietaries, in order to encourage the growth of population, allowed of a representative government, with freedom from taxation, and perfect liberty of conscience. They promoted, however, the slave-trade, by offering a bounty on the importation of every able-bodied negro. In 1683, considerable numbers of Scottish Covenanters escaped, or were expelled from, their native land, and settled in New Jersey, where they readily combined with the Puritans and Quakers in advancing the prosperity of the country. Many from England, who had taken part in Monmouth's rebellion, also joined them, some as transported criminals, and others as fugitives from the severity of the law. Thus, from various causes, the population rapidly increased, and, in 1738, amounted to forty thousand. Early in the century, St. Mary's Church was built at Burlington, which was at one time designed to be made the residence of a bishop. Notwithstanding the diverse origin of the first settlers, sixteen thousand, or nearly a sixth of the population, were claimed by the Church of England in 1761.

On the western side of the Delaware, the important colony of Pennsylvania was established in 1682, by William Penn. Having friends high in authority, he obtained, in discharge of a debt due from the crown, a grant of land extending over five degrees of longitude, and three of latitude, of which himself and his heirs were constituted proprietaries. New Sweden, now the State of Delaware, was esteemed a part of the province of the Duke of York, but Penn, by the payment of a stipulated sum, and after much negotiation, obtained possession of the title. He established within his province freedom of conscience, with equal liberties to persons from all countries. The first settlers were

Quakers, a sect whose abhorrence of forms became itself a most egregious formality. The constitution framed for his colony by Penn, was designed " for the support of power in reverence with the people, and to secure the people from the abuse of power. For liberty without obedience is confusion, and obedience without liberty is slavery." He confined capital punishment to the crimes of treason and murder, and made the prison, not so much a place of punishment as a house of reformation, where offenders might be reclaimed by judicious treatment and instruction.

His next step was to make a treaty of peace and friendship with the natives. At a place a little north of where Philadelphia now stands, he met a large company of them, and so affected their hearts that they promised to live in love with him and his children as long as the moon and the sun should endure. This treaty was faithfully kept, and Pennsylvania, during seventy years, was free from the stain of Indian blood, by which other colonies were so fearfully defiled. Penn, however, admitted the lawfulness of negro slavery, and lived and died a slaveholder.[*]

Philadelphia ˜was founded in 1683, and soon contained six hundred houses. In a representative assembly held the same year, the frame of government prepared by Penn was adopted, and remains substantially in force at the present time. After the return of their great legislator to England, the influence of Quakers in the colony rapidly diminished, and persons who had no

[*] Bancroft, ii. 401.

connection with their society as rapidly increased. Indeed, whatever may be their amiable qualities, their
want of Sacraments, and of an outward Church system,
has disqualified the Quakers, on both sides of the
Atlantic, for the diffusion and maintenance of their
own principles. It was expressly provided in the original charter, and readily conceded by Penn, that whenever twenty inhabitants requested a minister of the
Church of England to reside among them, he should be
allowed to do so without molestation.* Accordingly,
in 1695, the first place of Church worship was built in
Philadelphia, and a clergyman was appointed. Several
considerable congregations were afterwards established,
and many hundreds of the Quakers gladly received
baptism. The Swedes and German Lutherans in the
colony readily coalesced with the Church, and were
reckoned as its members. Altogether it was considered that, in 1761, sixty-five thousand persons might
be considered as belonging to her fold within the
province of Pennsylvania, which was nearly a quarter of
the entire population.

In all these middle colonies, notwithstanding the
settlements formed by other nations, the English race
greatly preponderated, and seemed destined, eventually,
to absorb the rest.

* Anderson's Colonial Church, ii. 605.

CHAP. II.

THE CHURCH AND THE COLONIES
(*continued*).

ORIGIN OF PURITANISM.—THE PILGRIM FATHERS.—SETTLEMENT OF THE
NORTHERN GROUP OF COLONIES.—INTOLERANCE OF THE PURITANS.—
BLUE LAWS OF CONNECTICUT.—PERSECUTION OF CHURCHMEN, QUAKERS,
BAPTISTS, ETC.—DEATH OF KING PHILIP.—PROSPERITY OF NEW
ENGLAND.—WITCHCRAFT IN MASSACHUSETTS.

HE most remarkable of the new communities planted along the coast of the Atlantic, were those established in the cold and bràcing climate of New England. As the Puritans by their vigour and determination of character have left a permanent and definite stamp on the mind and manners of America, it may be well if we look back upon the causes in which their peculiar principles originated.

The old Roman Catholic establishment of England, notwithstanding its outward power and splendour, became more and more inadequate to meet the deep want of inward religion which was felt by many earnest minds after the time of Wiclif. Those who were sensible of this want, needed the counsel of well-instructed ministers of Christ to regulate their zeal and direct their efforts. But the ecclesiastical authorities of that day, unable to sympathise with them, sought rather to crush them by every means in their power. Thus the personal religion of multitudes came to be separated from the public religion of the nation ; and during a hundred and fifty years a leaven was working among the people, the effect of which was to make them loathe as their worst enemies those who should have been their pastors and their guides. *

The Reformation unchained the public mind ; and private judgment, with all its benefits and all its dangers, came into almost unlimited exercise. The troubles of Mary's reign served to prevent the outbreak of serious divisions : but with the accession of Elizabeth, and the consequent safety of the reformed party, the true state of things began to appear. It was plain that the affections of the people had been to a great extent separated not only from the Church of Rome, but from all that external organisation which had been designed originally to nourish and sustain faith and devotion. Fearing to be learners lest they should be led astray, men had constituted themselves teachers, and had abandoned the very principle of obedience. The Reformed were now manifestly divided among themselves. With one party the authority of the Church, the succession of the ministry through the episcopate, and other important truths, went for nothing, because they had been seen in the hands of those who

* Bishop of Oxford's " American Church," p. 47.

taught many things contrary to the Gospel. Because they had themselves attained a sense of their individual responsibility, they forgot that God had made express provision for the union of individuals in a visible body upon earth. Because many things connected with the outward fabric of religion had been abused to super- stition, they were for destroying the entire structure, and tolerating nothing but what they themselves judged to be absolutely commanded in the written Word of God. This was Puritanism.

On the other hand, those by whom the existing re- formed institutions were upheld, had of course the law on their side, as well as the most considerable part of the nation. Their object had been, as I have already remarked, not to destroy, but to cleanse the ancient Church of England; not to establish for them- selves a new communion, but to continue members of that association which had existed in this country since its first conversion to the faith. In consequence of this principle, they wisely retained not only the essentials of the Catholic Church, but many things sanctioned by ancient usage and not contrary to Scripture. This was English Churchmanship.

During the reign of Mary, when many earnest men of both parties sought refuge on the Continent, cir- cumstances had strengthened the influence of the Puritans, and given definiteness to their system. In Switzerland they had received a hearty welcome, and those who desired a rigorous austerity of discipline and worship, were confirmed in their prepossessions by the stern simplicity then prevailing among the republican countrymen of Zuinglius and Calvin. After Elizabeth came to the throne, while many of the more peaceable Puritans continued in the Establishment, the bitter non-conforming party assailed their rulers with a coarseness of invective which was calculated to give the greatest possible provocation. Those who sat at the helm of Church and State, desired that the people of England should enjoy, if it were possible, the great blessing of union in the reformed doctrine and worship. Could they indeed have accurately foreseen all the desolating effects of religious division which we now behold — could they have foretold the scepticism, the indifference, and the obstacles to Christian education which follow in its train — they might well be excused if they had put forth more vigorous, and at the same time wiser efforts than they actually did to suppress the evil at its first appearance. As it was, the statesmen of that day adopted a course which under the circumstances was considered expedient, and allowed the arm of the law to fall heavily on a party which aimed at the mastery, and which abhorred the very idea of simple toleration. That they did not resist the Puritans merely on religious grounds, is proved by the kindness with which the quiet Protestant refugees from the Continent were always treated, though often differing equally with the Puritans from the established system. The contest was one which conciliation could never settle, as its object was, on one side, self-defence, and on the other, extermination. But perhaps the theological opponents of

Puritanism could have desired nothing better than that which actually took place, namely, that its professors should obtain an opportunity of reigning unchecked in a distant land, where their system could attain its full development. Future ages would thus learn that the substance of religion decays when its forms and outward framework have been destroyed, and that unwarranted separation, by continually producing new schisms, ultimately becomes its own punishment.

Much sentimentalism has been expressed in regard to the "Pilgrim Fathers," as if they were innocent victims of persecution driven to seek in a howling wilderness "freedom to worship God" in their own way. The truth is, that having been defeated in their first attempts to crush the Church of England, many of the Puritan faction preferred emigration to submission. Although in those days emigration was not free, as at present, the members of one of their congregations near the Humber managed to escape to Holland, where they resided twelve years and enjoyed the utmost religious freedom. But the struggle for bread was hard; they could not feel at home among the Dutch; and they turned their thoughts to the New World, where they hoped to see no superior, and at the same time to improve their temporal circumstances by engaging in the fur trade and the fisheries. Accordingly they sent two of their number to obtain the consent of the King and of the London Company to their settlement in Virginia. The company gave them some encouragement, but James I. would only give them an informal promise of connivance or neglect.

The Pilgrims now met with a fresh difficulty. They had not sufficient capital for the execution of their plans, and only obtained it by a kind of mortgage of their labour for the next seven years. They arranged that a part of their body should first proceed across the Atlantic, the weaker members being left to follow.

After many delays, a hundred and one of their number sailed from Plymouth in the "Mayflower," a small vessel of a hundred and eighty tons. They were carried more to the northward than they intended, and, after a boisterous voyage of sixty-three days, anchored in the harbour of Cape Cod, the most barren and inhospitable part of the New England coast. This place was not calculated for a settlement, and, after further search, they discovered another harbour, which they named Plymouth, in grateful recollection of the port from which they had sailed. On the 11th of December (O.S.), 1620, in the depth of winter, they landed on Plymouth Rock, having first voluntarily formed themselves into a body politic. In the following spring, when their numbers had been reduced to fifty by privation and disease, they concluded a treaty of friendship with Massasoit, one of the Indian princes, from whom the province of Massachusetts is supposed by some to have derived its name.

At the end of ten years, the population of the Plymouth colony did not exceed a few hundreds, but they had extended their settlements to various places, and one of them as far east as the Kennebec River in Maine. In the absence of a colonial charter, they had adopted a republican mode of government, the governor being elected by the people and his authority restricted by a council of five assistants.   For eighteen years the legislature was composed of all the men of the plantation; but afterwards, the increase of population and the extension of territory led to the introduction of the representative system. In 1623, under the English Plymouth Company, already mentioned, Sir Ferdinando Gorges took a patent for the country between the Merrimack and Kennebec Rivers, extending from the sea to the St. Lawrence.   In consequence of this, the towns of Portsmouth and Dover were settled, both within the present limits of New Hampshire.   Four years subsequently, a body of the emigrants, residing to the northward of Plymouth, concluded a treaty with the Plymouth Company, for the purchase of the territory between Charles River and the Merrimack, and extending three miles south of the former and north of the latter.   In 1628, Salem was founded by John Endicott on the coast within these limits, and in 1629 a charter was obtained from the Crown confirming the grant of the Plymouth Company. By it the association became a corporation, with the title of the "Governor and Company of Massachusetts Bay in New England."   The officers were to be a governor, deputy-governor, and eighteen assistants; the latter to be elected by the corporation.   No law was to be made in opposition to any law of England.   In the following year Boston was founded, and soon afterwards the persecuting spirit of Puritanism unfolded itself.

The people of Massachusetts Bay, rapidly increasing by emigration, now claimed and exercised nearly all the powers of an independent State. They deliberately set at nought many of the laws of England, in direct opposition to the terms of their charter. The laws which they enacted on the subject of religion were contrived and executed with so much rigour, that, in the words of a New England writer, "the persecution which drove the Puritans out of England might be considered as great lenity and indulgence in the comparison." *   "This people," says another author, "who in England could not bear being chastised with rods, had no sooner got free from their fetters than they scourged their fellow-refugees with scorpions." One of their own number left the settlement from detestation of their uncharitable conduct. "I fled from England," he said, "to escape the tyranny of my lords the *bishops*, but I was glad to flee away again to escape the tyranny of my lords the *brethren*." Amusements of nearly all kinds were viewed by these harsh enthusiasts with extreme aversion, and were forbidden and punished equally with vices and crimes. In England, those who neglected to attend their parish church were fined a shilling; but in Massachusetts, five shillings, and in the older Plymouth settlement, *ten* shillings was not too severe an imposition on those who failed to attend a meeting-house.† He who denied "the country's power to compel any one to attend congregational worship," was fastened in

* Judge Story.
† Coit's Puritanism, pp. 220, 221.

D

the stocks. He who kept Christmas, or any other holyday of the Church of England, must pay the same penalty as for slighting the puritanical conventicle. He who reproached a magistrate or minister, or circulated a heterodox book, must pay five or ten pounds according to circumstances. As women were less disposed than men to be silent under pecuniary impositions, there was an express provision on their account, namely, that their tongues should be kept fast in a *cleft stick*.

By the year 1640, the settlers of Massachusetts Bay were four thousand in number. Through their industry and enterprise, scarcity had yielded to abundance, rude huts had given place to well-built houses, and no less than fifty towns and villages had been established. Commerce, as well as agriculture, engaged attention, and the principal exports were furs, lumber, grain, and fish. Ship-building had commenced at an early period, and in 1643 the manufacture of cotton, imported from Barbados, was taken in hand, provision having already been made for linen and woollen manufactures.

The neighbouring territory of Connecticut was occupied by persons of the same sentiments and character with those of Massachusetts. The Connecticut River had been discovered, as I have already mentioned, by the Dutch, who made a station at the place now known as Hartford. In 1635, the English enforced their claim to the territory by erecting a fort at the mouth of the river, and in the same year sixty persons emigrated from Massachusetts and formed a settlement. In the following year, a government was organised under a commission from the parent colony, and the population continued to increase, though exposed for some time to the hostility of powerful tribes of Indians. In the first instance they formed three distinct settlements, Newhaven, Saybrook, and that under the government of Massachusetts. In 1662, these settlements were consolidated into one province under a charter of Charles II., and with the name of Connecticut.

The laws passed by the Newhaven dominion at an early period of its history were printed on blue paper, and are known to this day as the "Blue Laws." They serve to give an idea of the character and manners of the people, and the following are some of the most remarkable of them, as given by Hutchinson : —

" No one shall be a freeman or give a vote, unless he be converted and a member in full communion of one of the churches allowed in this dominion. Each freeman shall swear by the blessed God to bear true allegiance to this dominion, and that Jesus is the only king. No Quaker or dissenter from the established worship of this dominion, shall be allowed to give a vote for the election of magistrates or any officer. No food or lodging shall be allowed to any Quaker, Adamite, or other heretic. If any person turns Quaker he shall be banished, and not suffered to return but on pain of death. No one shall run on the Sabbath day, or walk in his garden, or elsewhere, except reverently to and from meeting. No one shall travel, cook victuals, make beds, sweep houses, cut hair, or shave on the Sabbath day. No woman shall kiss her children upon the Sabbath or fasting day. The Sabbath shall begin at sunset on Saturday. No one shall read common prayer, keep Christmas or saints' days, make minced pies, dance, play cards, or play on any instrument of music except the drum, trumpet, and Jew's-harp. Every male shall have his hair cut round according to a cap."

In 1642, by the request of the people of New Hampshire, that territory was annexed to Massachusetts on equal terms. Not having been settled by Puritans, the system of Massachusetts, requiring that " church members" alone should participate in the administration of the government, was not applied to New Hampshire. In the following year a confederation was effected, embracing the several governments of Massachusetts, Plymouth, Connecticut, and Newhaven, under the title of "The United Colonies of New England." The object of this voluntary alliance, thus foreshadowing the United States, was mutual protection against dangers at home or abroad; the local government being carefully reserved to each. Two commissioners were appointed from each colony, who were to meet annually for deliberation. Rhode Island and Maine were not admitted into this union, on account of differences in religious opinion as well as in civil administration. Maine had been granted to Sir Ferdinando Gorges in 1639, and had been regarded as a Church of England colony. In 1651 it was incorporated with Massachusetts, on the understanding that the members of the Church of England residing in it should not be disturbed in the enjoyment of their religious liberty. Even as early as the reign of Charles II. fears were entertained in England that through the instrumentality of the confederacy of New England, the people were aiming at independence.

The importance of general education was early seen by these New England republicans, though neglected in the southern and, comparatively speaking, in the middle colonies. Among the early settlers were many educated men, and a large proportion of them were members of the University of Cambridge. An American Cambridge was founded near Boston, where Harvard College was established in 1636. In 1647 a law was passed in Massachusetts requiring the establishment of a public school in every township containing fifty families, and a school of a superior kind for preparing boys for college in every township containing a hundred families. The rest of the New England confederacy soon followed the example of Massachusetts in this respect, and colleges grew up almost simultaneously with the system of common schools.

There can be no doubt that a large proportion of the New England Puritans were persons of much practical wisdom, earnest piety, and strong personal religion. It is, however, only too evident that, as a community, they went beyond others in their fanaticism and bigotry. Their strict, and indeed Judaical, regulations respecting the Sabbath, opposed as they were to the ancient Church doctrine respecting the Lord's Day, produced in many minds an aversion to that which they professed to honour. The spiritual pride and hypocrisy which grew out of their system, tended to bring all religion into contempt. Cruelty to animals was among them a punishable offence, but cruelty to men seemed in many cases to be considered a virtue.

In regard to the Church of England, it was declared in the fundamental principles of the Newhaven settlement, "that all vicars, rectors, deans, priests and bishops, are of the devil;" and that "it is a heinous sin to be present when prayers are read out of a book by a vicar or bishop." * As might be expected, the overthrow of the Church of England during Cromwell's usurpation, was an occasion of prodigious exultation in Massachusetts and Connecticut. Some of the settlers returned to England with the object of taking part in the work of destruction. One of their number, the notorious Hugh Peters, once a minister in Salem, preached in England in favour of the murder of the king. After the restoration, the regicides met with great sympathy, and three of them, Goffe, Whalley, and Dixwell, found a safe refuge in New England.

Two brothers, John and Samuel Brown †, emigrated to Salem with several hundred others in 1629. They were in high repute with the governor and other officers of the Massachusetts Company at home,

---

* History of Connecticut, 1781, quoted by the Bishop of Oxford.
† Coit's Puritanism, p. 177.

for as yet the charter had not crossed the Atlantic. From these high authorities they had received recommendations certifying to their respectability, and to their sincere affection to the good of the plantation, together with an order for two hundred acres each in the first division of the public lands. One of these gentlemen held official rank under the charter both at home and in Massachusetts; and the other was a member of the council in the plantation. Yet it happened, unfortunately for them, that they claimed the same right to judge for themselves which the Puritans had exercised, and their judgment was in favour of the Church of England. They did not think that the first step in reformation necessarily consisted in utter separation from that Church, in throwing her most sacred rites and symbols to the winds, and treating her bishops and clergy as the offscouring of the earth. They found the Church and government of England assailed, not in the sermons only, but in the very prayers, of the Puritan ministers. They consequently withdrew from the public meetings, and contented themselves with quietly hearing the Prayer-book in a private dwelling. Endicott, who then had rule in Salem, accordingly summoned them before him as the leaders of a faction. They were denounced as "factious and evil-conditioned," and notwithstanding their position and their loud remonstrances, were forthwith sent home to England. Their names are perpetuated to this day by an inscription on a marble tablet in the Episcopal church of St. Peter at Salem, which commemorates their "intrepidity in the cause of religious freedom."

It may seem a strange thing that intelligent men and churchmen like the Browns should have selected Massachusetts, above all other places, for their residence. But the truth is, that the Puritans while in England, or leaving it, often made such professions of attachment to the Church and State, that straightforward persons might easily mistake their real objects. Among the passengers who accompanied the Browns on their outward voyage, was Francis Higginson, formerly a clergyman of the Establishment at Leicester, and afterwards one of the earliest of the Puritan ministers at Salem. As he saw the white cliffs of his fatherland sinking beneath the horizon, his natural feelings, with perhaps some qualms of compunction, rose within his bosom. He called his children and the other passengers to the stern of the ship to take their last sight of their native country, and made the following speech, which certainly does credit to his feelings: — " We will not say, as the Separatists were wont to say at their leaving England, — farewell Babylon! farewell Rome! But we will say, farewell dear England! farewell the Church of God in England, and all the Christian friends there!" * He concluded with a fervent prayer for the King, the Church and the State in England.

About the same time †, a large party of Puritan emigrants addressed, on the eve of sailing, a singularly

---

* Coit's Puritanism, p. 156.   † Ibid. p. 157.

loving letter to their brethren of the Church of England. "We desire," they said, "you would be pleased to take notice of the principals and body of our company, as those who esteem it an honour to call the Church of England, from whence we rise, our dear mother ; and cannot part from our native country, where she specially resideth, without much sadness of heart and many tears in our eyes; ever acknowledging that such hope and part as we have obtained in the common salvation, we have received in her bosom and sucked it from her breasts. We leave it not, therefore, as loathing that milk wherewith we were nourished there, but blessing God for the parentage and education ; and as members of the same body shall always rejoice in her good, and unfeignedly grieve for any sorrow that shall ever betide her; and while we have breath sincerely desire and endeavour the continuance and abundance of her welfare, with the enlargement of her bounds in the kingdom of Jesus Christ."

The celebrated Cotton Mather, one of the leading Puritan clergy of New England, admits the difficulty of reconciling this letter with the principles declared and the practice really followed. Governor Hutchinson remarks, in his "History of Massachusetts," "However problematical it may be what these settlers were while they remained in England, they left no room for doubt after they arrived in America." President Quincy, of Harvard University, plainly says that the Puritans had an "utter detestation of the English hierarchy, service, and discipline." Though compelled by circumstances *sometimes to conceal,* and *sometimes to deny,* this antipathy, it was, in truth, one of the master-passions in the hearts of those early emigrants, and constitutes a principal clue to their language, conduct, policy, and laws."

It was not, however, the members of the Church of England only who suffered from the violence and, we fear we must add, the duplicity of the Puritan party. Puritanism, with its doctrine of unlimited private judgment, was continually giving rise to new divisions which the Puritan rulers endeavoured by the severest measures to restrain. Some of the people embraced Quaker opinions, and these opinions were forthwith denounced as " a stinking * vapour from hell ; " while the members of the sect were described as " rogues and vagabonds." Quakers, as such, could be put in stocks and cages, tied to a cart's tail, or driven into the wilderness among wolves and bears. Their ears might be cropped and their tongues bored ; they might be sold as slaves, and finally hung and left unburied.† William Robinson, Marmaduke Stephenson, William Leddra, and Mary Dyar, being found guilty of Quakerism, the first three suffered death at Boston on the 27th of October, 1659, and the last soon afterwards. Baptists fared little better. Roger Williams, a young Puritan minister of disputatious spirit, professed Anabaptist opinions, and refused to hold communion with intolerance, which he declared to be " lamentably contrary to the doc-

* Coit, p. 308.　　　　　　† Coit, p. 311.

trine of Christ." His independence gave great offence
to the magistrates, and he was driven into exile in the
depth of winter. He took refuge with Massasoit, the
Indian chief, and finally, together with some of his
own party, established a settlement in the continental
portion of Rhode Island. He was a man of peace, and
by his influence with the Indian tribes, was enabled to
save the Dutch from extermination, as I have already
mentioned.

Soon after the expulsion of Williams, another party
arose contending for freedom of religious opinion.
Their founder was Anne Hutchinson, a woman of eloquence and ability; and her brother, John Wheelwright,
together with the celebrated Henry Vane, the younger,
at that time governor of the colony, favoured the new
doctrines. After a violent dispute, Anne Hutchinson
and her brother were exiled from Massachusetts. The
latter, with his friends, founded the town of Exeter on
the Piscataqua, and the former, with a considerable
number of followers, proceeded to Rhode Island, where
the insular portion of the district was assigned to them
as their abode. In 1644, through the influence of
Williams with the Long Parliament, the settlements were
incorporated as a colony, " with full power and authority
to rule themselves." In 1695, Cotton Mather describes
Rhode Island, continental and insular, as "a colluvies
of Antinomians, Familists, Anabaptists, Anti-Sabbata-
rians, Arminians, Socinians, Quakers, Ranters, and
everything but Roman Catholics and true Christians,
bona terra mala gens."

Again, another party headed by Samuel Gorton, following their own judgment, were adjudged guilty of death, and though this sentence was not executed, they were condemned to work like convicts, and wear irons on one leg till they could be conveniently banished. Even as late as 1700, a law, the penalties of which were perpetual banishment or death, was made against the followers of the Church of Rome. Indeed the bare toleration of different forms of worship was condemned as unquestionable sin. "I look upon toleration," said one of the influential Puritans in 1673, " as the firstborn of all abominations."

The aversion entertained to all symbols which could be in any way identified with Rome, was a strong feature in the Puritan character. Endicott, the first Puritan governor, even attacked the banner of his country, and caused the cross to be torn out of it, as a symbol of idolatry.* From a similar spirit the meeting-houses were built north and south, because the English churches stood east and west, and the windows of these strange structures were made square in opposition to the ancient pointed style. No prayer was used at funerals †, "lest it might in time introduce the customs of the English Church."

The principal end of founding the colonies of Massachusetts and Connecticut had been declared in the royal charter to be " the winning of the natives to the know-

---

* Coit, p. 248.   † Ibid. p. 495.

ledge and obedience of the only true God and Saviour. John Eliot, formerly a member of the University of Cambridge and a clergyman of the Church of England, was one of the very few who devoted themselves to the spiritual improvement of the aborigines. He gathered many of them into villages, taught them to read and write English, and induced them to adopt civilised habits. He prepared an Indian grammar, and published a translation of the whole Bible in the Massachusetts dialect. He taught the men how to cultivate the ground, and the women various arts of domestic industry. He instructed them in the principles of Christianity, while the simplicity of his life and manners, and the sweetness of his temper, won the affections alike of the emigrants and of the savages.

Yet the conversion of these unhappy people was generally neglected, while the Puritans took possession of their broad lands, either on the payment of merely nominal prices, or under the plea that the Lord had given the earth to be the inheritance of His saints. Instead of seeking by kindness and fair dealing to remove the suspicions which naturally arose on the part of the ancient inhabitants, they shed Indian blood without mercy, as the blood of Canaanites. The result was the same as with the wretched natives of Mexico and Peru, and it has been calculated that 180,000 of the red men came to an untimely end in Massachusetts and Connecticut alone. The following narrative will help to solve the question why the red man fades away at the approach of civilisation.

The aged chief, Massasoit, who had welcomed the pilgrims to New England, and afterwards given an asylum to the founder of Rhode Island, was succeeded, at his decease, by his son Philip, as chief over the confederacy of the Pokanoket Indians. As the villages of the English drew nearer and nearer to them, the natives found themselves deprived of their land by unfair though legal contracts, and crowded into narrow necks of country, in which they could be readily watched. Collisions took place in which some of the colonists lost their lives. A war broke out in which King Philip and his tribe, after being driven from their homes, succeeded in exciting the natives generally to adopt their cause. Town after town was burned by them, and during a whole year New England was kept in a state of constant alarm.

The Narragansett tribe was now declared by the commissioners of the united colonies to be accessory to these outrages, and accordingly their wigwams were set on fire, and the people who were receiving shelter during the winter were shot down if they attempted to escape. Men, women and children, "no man knoweth how many hundreds of them," were burned to death. Many of the survivors became suppliants for peace, but Philip refused to submit. At length his wife and only son were taken prisoners, and the unhappy chieftain exclaimed, "My heart breaks, now I am ready to die." Philip and his few remaining men were surprised in their encampment and slain, and his son, a child nine years old, the last of the family of the kind and friendly Massasoit, was sold as a slave into the island of Bermuda.

Eliot's converts, the "praying Indians," suffered cruel injustice. The colonists regarded them with suspicion, while the Indians looked on them as allies of the English. Some were killed, others were imprisoned, or driven from their settlements, and a blow was inflicted on the progress of Christianity among the natives from which it never recovered.

Their Indian wars, though doubtless sufficiently exciting, by no means diverted the attention of the Puritans from theology. "From the year 1650 to the Restoration," we are informed that "Massachusetts was chiefly employed in a business that, of all others, seems to have been most congenial to it; in preserving, by persecution, uniformity in opinion and discipline."* But power changed hands in England, and a voice from the throne came over the Atlantic, "as the roar of a New England sea-beach presaging an eastern storm."† The Puritans were compelled to hear from a source, "resentment against which was paralysed by the ague of apprehension," such language as this: — "That such as desire to use the Book of Common Prayer, be permitted to do so, without incurring any penalty, reproach, or disadvantage; it being very scandalous that any persons should be debarred the exercise of their religion, according to the laws and customs of England, by those who were indulged with the liberty of being of what profession or religion they pleased."

* Chalmers, quoted by Coit, p. 195.   † Coit, p. 201.

The Puritans were unable openly to oppose this sarcastic edict of the merry monarch. But, by means of evasions and postponements, they kept up a contest till 1684, when the charter itself became a nullity under the sentence of an English court. Resistance now became fruitless ; and Dudley, the Royal President, with an Episcopal clergyman in his train, entered the capital of Massachusetts. Andros, appointed in 1686 Governor-general of the colonies north of Maryland, showed an arbitrary disposition, and a spirit of resistance was aroused, which exhibited itself in open insurrection. The news of the Revolution of 1688 reached America in April 1689, and was the signal for wide-spread rejoicings.

With the exception of the painful effects of religious bigotry, New England at this time presented a bright picture of colonial happiness. In Connecticut the government was exercised by a community of intelligent farmers; and for a long time there was hardly a lawyer in the land.* In those days of simplicity the best house required no fastening but a latch lifted by a string ; and bolts and locks were unknown. The fields, the hills, and the rivers, supplied the settlers with food, and their clothing was the result of domestic industry in spinning and weaving. The state of things was not materially different in the other north-eastern colonies, where the neat and thriving villages already excited admiration. Massachusetts possessed a widely extended

* M. Murray, p. 111.

trade; commerce had increased; and such was the prosperity of the country that after the great fire in London large contributions were sent to the sufferers from their transatlantic brethren. The population of New England is supposed to have amounted, in 1675, to 55,000, of which the government of Massachusetts comprised about one half. The recent enforcement of the English Act of Uniformity had doubtless contributed to swell the amount; but independently of emigration it has been found in America that natural increase alone suffices to double the inhabitants within a quarter of a century. In the course of fifteen years after its first settlement, New England received from the parent country 21,200 persons, and never afterwards derived any considerable accessions from beyond the seas.

In the year 1691, " King's Chapel " was founded in Boston for Church of England worship, under the charter of William III. Yet, for many years, the churchmen of New England had a severe struggle for bare existence.* In an address to the king, the rector and wardens of this chapel complained, in behalf of the congregation, that they had been injured and abused, their church daily threatened to be pulled down, the minister hindered in the discharge of his duty, and excessive taxes charged upon them to support a disloyal party, " which, under pretence of the public good, desired nothing but destruction to the Church and to the whole country." At Stratford, in Con-

* Coit, p. 207.

E

necticut, a new congregation endured barbarous cruelty, As they claimed exemption, under English law, from payments in support of Puritanism, one of the church-wardens and a vestryman were seized at midnight, and hurried off eight miles to the gaol, where they were confined without fire or lights, until, after three days of suffering, they paid the sums demanded. At the same time it must be recollected that, although the only offence of these men lay in their religion, the Puritan establishment was in no way recognised by the laws of England. In other parts of New England, wherever churchmen ventured to show themselves as such, they were compelled to suffer every kind of insult and annoyance at the hands of the dominant party. Little more than a hundred years ago, an old man, long a member of the Church of England, was publicly whipped for not attending meeting; and the intolerant spirit which prompted this and similar acts was by no means extinct even in the present century.

Not long after the introduction of organised church-manship into Massachusetts, a new cause of excitement appeared. In New England, as in the kindred religious communities of Scotland, the belief in witchcraft had fastened itself with peculiar tenacity on the elements of religious faith. In the memorable year 1688, as Bancroft informs us, the daughter of John Goodwin, a child of thirteen years, charged a laundress with having stolen linen from the family. An Irishwoman named Glover, the mother of the laundress, rebuked the false accusation, and the girl, to secure revenge, became bewitched. The infection spread, and three others of the same family, the youngest a boy of less than five years old, soon succeeded in equally arresting public attention. They would affect to be deaf, then dumb, then blind, or all three at once: they would bark like dogs, or purr like so many cats; but they ate well and slept well. The renowned Cotton Mather went to prayer by the side of one of them, and the child lost her hearing till the prayer was over. What was to be done? The four ministers of Boston and the one of Charlestown assembled in Goodwin's house, and spent a whole day in fasting and prayers. In consequence, the youngest child was delivered from the possession. But it was concluded that if the ministers could by prayer deliver a possessed child, there must have been a witch, and the affair was prosecuted with vigour. Glover, the supposed culprit, when questioned, exhibited great bewilderment, and made strange answers in her native Irish dialect. One woman testified that six years before she had heard another woman say that she had seen Glover come down her chimney. It was plain that the prisoner was a Papist. She had never learned the Lord's prayer in English; she could repeat the paternoster fluently, but not correctly. Accordingly the Puritan ministers and Goodwin's family had the satisfaction of seeing her condemned as a witch and executed.

The possessed girl, however, obtained no relief, and Cotton Mather invited her to his house, eager at the same time to obtain a knowledge of the world of spirits, and to confute the "Sadducism" of the times. By a series of experiments he found that the devil would permit her to read in Quaker or Popish books, or the Book of Common Prayer; but a prayer from Cotton Mather, or a chapter from the Bible, would throw her into convulsions. His vanity was further gratified; for the bewitched girl would say that the demons could not enter his study, and that his own person was shielded by God against blows from the evil spirits.[*]

The first governor of Massachusetts, appointed under the new charter of 1691, was Sir William Phipps, a native of New England, who had gained wealth and distinction by his enterprise with the diving-bell in raising treasure from a Spanish wreck. He is described by Bancroft as dull and headstrong, and in religious matters a victim to superstition. Mather had procured the appointment of one Stoughton as deputy-governor, and the whole of the governor's council were friendly to the interests of Puritanism. Mather now thanked God that "the set time to favour Zion" had come; and accordingly proceeded with all his energies to stir up the people in a wild crusade, not only against witchcraft itself, but against all who should be bold enough to assert that witchcraft was a delusion. One poor old woman of Salem, who bore the hated name of "Bishop," was said to have the power, through her spectre, of inflicting tortures. "She gave a look," says Mather, "towards the great and spacious meeting-house of Salem, and immediately a demon, invisibly

* Bancroft, iii. p. 77.

entering the house, tore down a part of it." She was found guilty, and under the authority of Phipps and his council, was hanged, protesting her innocence. At its next session the court condemned five more women, all of blameless lives, and all declaring their innocence to the last.

It was now hinted that confession was the only avenue to safety for the accused. The gaols were soon filled, for fresh accusations were necessary to confirm the confessions. Six persons who had been convicted agreed in denouncing a seventh, who was accordingly seized and hanged. Some would make no confession till after torture; and as the Anabaptists were unpopular, they were often denounced by the accused. One man of eighty, refusing to plead, was pressed to death. Within five months after Phipps assumed the reins of government, twenty persons had been executed for witchcraft, and fifty-five tortured or terrified into penitent confession.* With accusations, confessions increased; and with confessions, accusations were multiplied.

The deputy-governor continued to act in the matter with unabated zeal, though embarrassed by some more enlightened persons who regarded the executions as judicial murders. Cotton Mather continued eager " to lift up a standard against the infernal enemy," and prepared his narrative entitled " The Wonders of the Invisible World," in order to promote a pious thankfulness

* Bancroft, iii. p. 94.

E 3

for the execution of justice. For this book he received the approbation of the President of Harvard College, the praises of the governor, and the gratitude of Stoughton.*

The following extracts will give some idea of this remarkable literary curiosity† : —

" The New Englanders are a people of God settled in those which were once the devil's territories ; and it may easily be supposed that the devil was exceedingly disturbed. The devil, thus irritated, immediately tried all sorts of methods to overthrow this poor plantation. Wherefore the devil is now making one more attempt upon us. . . . An army of devils is horribly broke in upon the place which is the centre, and after a sort, the firstborn of our English settlements, and the houses of the good people are filled with the doleful shrieks of their children and servants, tormented by invisible hands with tortures altogether preternatural. . . . More than twenty have confessed that they have signed a book which the devil showed them, and engaged in his hellish design of bewitching and ruining our land. . . . Yea, that at prodigious witch-meetings the wretches have proceeded so far as to concert and consult the methods of rooting out the Christian religion from this country, and setting up instead of it perhaps a more gross diabolism than ever

* Bancroft, iii. p. 95.

† " The Wonders of the Invisible World ; being an Account of the Tryals of several Witches lately executed in New England." By Cotton Mather. 4to. London, 1693.

the world saw before. . . . These monsters of witches . . . each of them have their spectres or devils, commissioned by them to be the engines of their malice. By these wicked spectres they seize poor people about the country with various and bloody torments. . . . The people thus afflicted are miserably scratched and bitten, so that the marks are most visible to all the world, but the causes utterly invisible. And the same invisible furies do most visibly stick pins into the bodies of the afflicted, and scale them, and hideously distort and disjoint all their members. Yea they sometimes drag the poor people out of their chambers, and carry them over trees and hills for divers miles together. A large portion of the persons tortured by these diabolical spectres are horribly tempted by them . . . to sign the devil's laws in a spectral book laid before them, which two or three of these poor sufferers, being by these tiresome sufferings overcome to do, they have immediately been released from all their miseries, and they appeared in spectre then to torture their former fellow-sufferers."

After this follows an account of the trial, condemnation and execution of one George Burroughs, a preacher of Salem. "He was accused by nine persons for extraordinary lifting, and such feats of strength as could not be done without a diabolical assistance. . . . There were now heard the testimonies of several persons who were most notoriously bewitched, and every day tormented by invisible hands, and these all now charged the spectres of George Burroughs to have a share in their torments. . . . It was remarkable, that whereas biting was one of the ways which the witches used for the vexing of the sufferers, when they cried out of George Burroughs biting them, the point of the teeth would be seen on the flesh of the complainers, and just such a set of teeth as George Burroughs', which could be distinguished from those of some other men. . . . Others of them testified that in their torments George Burroughs tempted them to go unto a sacrament, unto which they perceived him with the sound of a trumpet summoning of other witches, who quickly after the sound would come from all quarters. . . . Several of the bewitched gave testimony that they had been troubled with the apparition of two women, who said that they were George Burroughs' two wives, and that he had been the death of them. . . . He was a very puny man, yet he had often done things beyond the strength of a giant. A gun of above seven foot barrel, and so heavy· that strong men could not steadily hold it out with both hands, there were several testimonies given in by persons of credit and honour that he made nothing of taking up such a gun behind the lock with but one hand, and holding it out like a pistol at arm's length."

Poor George Burroughs is said to have made faltering and inconsistent answers at his trial. But his worst offence seems to have been that he declared before the court "that there neither are nor ever were witches; nor that the having made a compact with the devil, can send a devil to torment other people at a distance." This opinion wounded the self-love of the judges, for it made them the accusers and judicial murderers of the innocent.* The jury found him guilty, and he was hanged, after fervently repeating the Lord's Prayer and asserting his innocence to the last.

The people now began to think that, if these trials proceeded, no one was safe. The excitement rapidly abated, and Cotton Mather attempted to persuade others that he had not been specially active in getting up the delusion.† He had encouraged it in order to check the growing spirit of " Sadducism," but when it died away it left men infinitely more disposed to scepticism than before.

I have dwelt to some extent on the harsh temper and strange inconsistencies of the Puritans, in the hope of correcting some misapprehensions respecting them. Their virtues have been abundantly celebrated by their own writers, and it would be unjust to withhold due praise from their industry, frugality, intelligence and enterprise. Their descendants now constitute perhaps one third of the population of the United States, and can scarcely be estimated at less than ten millions of souls. In forming a proper judgment of the American people, it is therefore of the first importance that not only the lights but the shades of Puritan character should receive their full share of attention.

In the year 1761, the population of Massachusetts was estimated at a quarter of a million, and that of all

---

* Bancroft, iii. p. 97.   † Ibid. p. 98.

New England at 435,000.   Such had been the progress
of the Church in the face of opposition, that her fold now
embraced nearly a tenth part of the New-Englanders,
or about forty thousand.   The causes which led to this
remarkable reaction will be explained in another
chapter.

It is to be noticed that just before the conclusion of
the century, viz. in 1697, William Penn, improving on
the idea suggested by the New England confederacy,
proposed an annual Congress of all the provinces on the
continent of America, with power to regulate commerce.*
It will be seen how Franklin in the following age took
up the idea, gave it a definite form, and endued it with
vitality.

* Bancroft, iv. p. 125.

CHAP. III.

THE CHURCH AND THE COLONIES

(*continued*).

FORMATION OF THE AMERICAN CHARACTER. — SLAVERY. — ANTIPATHY BETWEEN NORTH AND SOUTH. — RISE OF THE SOCIETY FOR PROPAGATING THE GOSPEL. — PROGRESS OF THE CHURCH IN NEW ENGLAND. — APPROACHING INDEPENDENCE OF THE COLONIES. — HOSTILITIES IN AMERICA. — COLONEL WASHINGTON. — CONGRESS OF ALBANY. — DEFEAT OF BRADDOCK. — WAR WITH FRANCE. — REVERSES OF THE BRITISH. — THEIR FINAL SUCCESS. — THE ACQUISITION OF CANADA AND THE VALLEY OF THE MISSISSIPPI.

IN the former half of the eighteenth century, infant America already exhibited most of the features of character which we behold in a more developed state at the present time. As a general rule, aristocracy had little or no root in the soil. In the south, indeed, the landowners, dwelling apart and surrounded by their black and white dependents, occupied a position in some measure corresponding with that of country gentlemen in England. But in the middle, and especially in the northern, colonies, nearly every man was engaged in the labours of agriculture or trade. Here the manners of the people were, to a great extent, those of the industrious classes in the "old country," with the addition of the acuteness and independence which grew out of their new circumstances. Questions of politics and government deeply interested them. The first emigrants had been accustomed to take part in public affairs, even before they left England. They had been engaged in elections, in trials by jury, in matters involving freedom of the person and of speech. They had carried their habits of thinking and acting on these subjects to the new country, which afforded many opportunities for their exercise. Monarchy was, in a great measure, an abstraction; a wide and stormy ocean intervening between the sovereign and his western subjects. No Prince of Wales traversed the wilds, diffusing, as he went, agreeable notions of royalty. There were few objects on which the natural loyalty of the heart could fix itself, although no doubt some of the colonial governors did their best to represent absent majesty. The government of the country, so far as it practically affected the daily life of the people, was conducted by a class of persons who, with all their shrewdness and common sense, were no more calculated to awaken feelings of veneration than the managers of the trading corporations from whom they had politically descended. Slavery was, in 1754, proportionately more diffused than at present; the northern and middle colonies being involved in it as well as those of the south, and the slaves being a sixth of the whole population, instead of an eighth as in 1860. Even at that period there was a "fugitive slave law," which allowed persons pursuing fugitive coloured slaves to wound or even to kill them.* With the exception of the position of the African race, the general aspect of things must have resembled that which prevails in Canada, New Brunswick, or Nova Scotia. It might have been predicted that if such colonies should by any event be separated from the mother-country, they would almost necessarily become a republic, or a collection of republics, the elements of that system of government being alone at hand and available. It was plain, also, that if such a commonwealth should come into being, the religious divisions of the people would render a national establishment impossible.

There were strong antipathies, political as well as religious, between the North and the South, which, together with diversity of interests, would evidently place great difficulties in the way of a general and permanent legislative union. A new and important element in society was also now at work, which, though contributing to the diffusion of intelligence, assisted in giving point to all matters of controversy. With the eighteenth century the periodical press began to exercise its influence, and the first American newspaper, the "Boston News-Letter," was commenced in 1704. Another paper was set on foot in 1719, and in the same year a third appeared in Philadelphia. The "New England Courant" was next published by James Franklin in 1721, assisted by his brother Benjamin as an apprentice. The talents of the latter contributed

* Bancroft, ii. p. 193.

greatly to the success of the paper, until, wishing for
greater liberty of the press than was permitted in New
England, he quitted that country, and commenced his
remarkable career at Philadelphia.

While the North still remained essentially Puritan
and republican, the South continued to pray fervently
for the king according to the liturgy.   But dissenting
opposition had so far prevailed with the government of
England, that, notwithstanding the earnest petitions of
churchmen, bishops were still withheld.   As a necessary
consequence the Church continued weak, while, virtually,
every form of sectarianism was encouraged.   Episcopal
ordination formed no part of the system of the Congregational, Presbyterian, Quaker, Dutch-reformed, or
Baptist sects, which, consequently, were able to multiply
their ministers without restraint.   Many well-disposed
young men, originally members of the Church, being
unable to bear the cost of a journey to England, received dissenting ordination, and assisted in weakening.
that mother whom they would otherwise have sustained.   Of those who crossed the Atlantic to receive
the imposition of the Bishop of London's hands, a fifth
part died at sea or by disease.   Many of the English
clergy sent out to the southern colonies were men of
little or no reputation, who disgraced their sacred calling by their conduct, while at the same time they were
beyond the reach of effective discipline.   For a whole
century the most earnest and piteous entreaties for
bishops crossed the Atlantic, but the mother-country,
from a narrow and mistaken policy, continued deaf to

the wishes of her most loyal children. The Church, therefore, remained in an incomplete state, and was denied the liberty of expansion allowed to all other religious bodies. We need not, therefore, be surprised to learn, that when, in 1745, it was decided that the English Act of Toleration extended to Virginia, Presbyterianism arose and flourished in that colony.* The same was the case elsewhere; and before the Revolution the Church found herself in a minority, even in places where she had formerly reigned supreme.

Other nations had not been so supine as England in establishing their Church in their colonies. As early as 1649, the Spanish Church in America is estimated to have had 1 patriarch, 6 archbishops, 32 bishops, 346 prebends, 2 abbots, 5 royal chaplains, and 840 convents, besides a vast number of parish priests and missionaries. † But circumstances, as the Bishop of Oxford reminds us ‡, had led England to neglect in this respect her duty to her transatlantic dominions. The first colonies of conformists were settled by private adventurers, and their continued existence was long doubtful. They had no sooner gained some strength than the king resumed the charters he had given, and they fell under the influence of courtiers who felt no interest in the extension of the Reformed Church. Then followed the troubles of King Charles's reign, and the overthrow of

---

* Hoffman, p. 21.
† Bishop of Oxford's "American Church," p. 148. ‡ Ibid.

the altar and the throne. Charles II. was a concealed Papist, and James II. an avowed one; after which the temper of those who conducted public affairs under the reign of William III. prevented the friends of episcopacy from taking the necessary steps. Indeed, the sending of bishops into colonies, some of which had been founded by dissenters, would have been most distasteful to that large party at home which William sedulously courted. Queen Anne's accession promised better things; but when the appointment of four American bishops appeared certain, her death frustrated the hopes of churchmen. In the reign of George I. further discouragements followed; early neglect had made the line of duty more difficult than ever, and the great object remained unaccomplished.

The Bishop of London was considered, in virtue of his office, the bishop of the colonies.* This authority seems to have originated, not in any express law or order, but in the request made by the Virginia Company with regard to the appointment of their first clergy. As early as 1685, Dr. Blair acted as the bishop's commissary in Virginia. He zealously discharged his office during fifty-three years, and succeeded in establishing "William and Mary" College, the second institution of the kind founded in the country, Harvard College, near Boston, being the first. Subsequently Dr. Bray was appointed commissary in Maryland, where the mass of people were now Protestants, and

---

* Bishop of Oxford's "American Church," p. 135.

where the Church of England had obtained almost the position of an establishment. He commenced his labours in 1700, and displayed a zeal and an activity which under God would have wrought great results had he been a colonial bishop. He met with great opposition, and his stay was but short; nevertheless, the Church made some progress, and a large majority of the colony, now increased to 30,000, was considered to belong to her communion. The opposition of the legislature defeated the efforts of the succeeding commissaries to restore discipline, and in consequence the Baptists and other dissenters extended their influence in the colony.

Commissaries were also appointed for several other colonies: namely, Johnson for South Carolina in 1707; Vesey for New York in 1713; and Henderson and Wilkinson for Maryland in 1716. But a new and important ally had now come into the field in the Society for Propagating the Gospel, an institution which, like the Society for Promoting Christian Knowledge, owed its existence in a great measure to the labours of Dr Bray. In the language of the charter, it was established, " for the receiving and managing of such funds as might be contributed for the religious instruction of his Majesty's subjects beyond the seas; for the maintenance of clergymen in the plantations, colonies and factories of Great Britain; and for the general propagation of the Gospel." In the words of an American writer, Judge Hoffman, "the story of its abundant labours and countless blessings is a proper theme for the historian; and when from the altars of the American

F

Church the utterance of praise and prayer arises in the stately and flowing language of the liturgy of Edward, let us remember that chiefly to that Society we owe the inappreciable gift." *

The Society was careful in the choice of its missionaries, who were generally men of excellent character, and well acquainted with the principles of their own Church and the right way of defending them. In the first instance it deputed the Rev. George Keith (a convert from Quakerism, who had formerly resided in Pennsylvania), to travel over and preach in the several governments in British America. He sailed from England in 1702, and in two years returned home and gave an account of his labours.†

He went over all the colonies between North Carolina and the river Piscataqua, in New England, extending eight hundred miles in length. He preached usually twice on Sundays, besides week days, the people generally showing a good disposition to profit by his teaching. His labours were most successful in Pennsylvania, the Jerseys, Long Island, and New York. He found a numerous congregation of Church people at Philadelphia, where more than five hundred Quakers had been baptized. Mr. Keith himself and his associate baptized in the course of this journey at least two hundred persons of that sect. In Pennsylvania there were now two Church of England congregations, besides

* Hoffman, p. 25.
† Humphrey's " History of the Society for the Propagation of the Gospel."

that in Philadelphia. At Burlington, in New Jersey, he met with good success, and was the means of strengthening a congregation lately formed. The " Foxian Quakers," seceders from the old party, in many places allowed him to address their meetings, but appeared, in their zeal for the inward light, to be fast losing all sense of Christianity. Often, instead of showing him kindness, they used much reviling language towards him, and continued "obstinately attached to their own notions." In various parts of New England he found, not only many people well affected to the Church who had no clergymen, but several of the Puritan or Congregational ministers desirous of episcopal ordination, and ready to embrace the Church worship. In concluding his narrative, Mr. Keith represented to the Society the want of a great number of ministers for a people dispersed over such large countries. The Society proceeded to act according to his recommendations as far as the slender means of a voluntary association at that date would permit.

There are some who imagine that clergymen appointed to new stations among persons of English descent ought to be regarded as chaplains or parochial clergy rather than as "missionaries." It should, however, be borne in mind that although such pastors may be engaged rather with white men and nominal Christians than with absolute pagans, their difficulties are often not less than those of the propagators of Christianity among Hindoos or Africans. Bishop Berkeley, who spent several years of his valuable life in America, says : — " There was but little sense of religion, and a most notorious corruption of manners, in the English colonies settled on the continent of America." Half the people of South Carolina were living " regardless of any religion," and the same might no doubt be said with truth of other colonies. The aboriginal inhabitants in many districts had been nearly destroyed, not only in war, but by the diseases and vices introduced by Europeans. Those who had taken possession of their wide lands, so far as they had any religion at all, were divided into various sects and parties, many of which regarded the Church of England with extreme bitterness and hostility. There were deep forests for the missionaries to penetrate, there were wide rivers and swamps to be crossed, long and painful journeys to be undertaken. These earnest men were often exposed to the extremes of an American climate without ade-. quate shelter, and while bearing witness to the truth they often met with rude contradiction and abuse. A large party in Massachusetts, headed by Mayhew, a bitter Puritan, sought to excite the public mind against them as the agents of a society which had no legal right to appoint missionaries in the villages and seaports of New England. Yet they persevered with the spirit of martyrs, and met with a degree of success for which America has good reason to bless their memories. In 1725 they had increased to 36, in 1750 to 70, and the largest number ever maintained by the Society in the old colonies was 101. It is computed that one of their number, the Rev. C. Hall, baptized not less than ten thousand persons.*

In reading over the abstracts of the Society's proceedings above a century ago, we are struck by the amount of labour performed, and of substantial good accomplished. The negroes and the remnants of the Indian tribes received an equal share of attention with the settlers of European origin. The Rev. Mr. Auchmuty, for example, the Society's catechist in the city of New York, informs his employers in 1750 that he had baptized 25 negro infants and 8 adults. So also the Rev. Mr. Ogilvie, of Albany, states that "besides reading prayers and preaching twice on Sundays, he read prayers and catechised on Wednesdays near 50 white children; and as many negroes appeared desirous of instruction, he catechised them on Sundays in the afternoon after - Divine service. On the 5th of June he went up to the Indians with the interpreter of the province, and was met by two of the principal sachems, who congratulated him on his arrival, and expressed great thankfulness to the Society for sending him to them." In the same annual report I find the following notice: — "The Society desire their friends in America to be so just to them, when any person appears there in the character of a clergyman of the Church of England, but by his behaviour disgraces that character, as to examine as far as may be his letters of orders, his name and cir-

* S. P. G. Report, 1750.

cumstances, and to inspect the public list of the names of the missionaries of this Society, published annually with the abstract of their proceedings; and the Society are fully persuaded it will appear that such unworthy person came thither without their knowledge. But if it should happen that any such should come thither from them, they entreat their friends in America, in the sacred name of Christ, to inform them, and they will *put away from them that wicked person.*"

The labours of a charitable society, England's oldest missionary society now in existence, gave a character to the American Church which it had failed to derive from the establishments of the south. Although bishops were still withheld, encouragement appeared in a quarter where it might have been little expected. The Puritans in New England actually began to turn to the Church in considerable numbers. They had found by, experience the evils of their own system, and some of their best men, after careful study, now desired to build upon the old foundations which their forefathers had abandoned. Rhode Island, too, distracted by religious divisions, became a scene of most successful labour to our missionaries.

In 1723 a treatise favourable to episcopacy was published by a Mr. Checkley in Massachusetts. For this he was arrested as a libeller and a disturber of the public peace. He was obliged to pay a fine of 50*l.* and bound over in recognisances for six months. But during the same year several distinguished Puritan divines, Cutler, a rector of Yale College in Connecticut, Brown, a tutor in the same establishment, and two of the neighbouring ministers, declared for episcopacy, an event which filled the minds of the Independents with "apprehension and gloom." The celebrated Cotton Mather, who still retained great influence among the Puritans, attempted to induce the legislature of Massachusetts to assemble a large convention to ascertain what might be "the most evangelical and effectual expedient to put a stop unto these or the like miscarriages." Checkley however succeeded, notwithstanding many hindrances, in obtaining holy orders from the Bishop of Exeter in 1739. In the sixtieth year of his age he commenced his career as missionary in Rhode Island, where he did valuable service during fourteen years. Sixteen years before that date, Cutler and one of his companions, Johnson, had been ordained to the priesthood in England, Brown having fallen a victim to the small-pox after coming to this country. Cutler received a doctor's degree in England, and settled in Boston, where he maintained to the last the standard of the faith, amidst incessant persecutions. Johnson laboured patiently and earnestly for half a century among the oppressed churchmen at Stratford, in Connecticut, with the exception of nine years, during which he presided over King's College at New York. Through his efforts churchmen continued to increase in numbers, though obliged to pay heavy taxes for the support of Puritan preachers, and for the erection of Puritan meeting-houses. Opposition did not extinguish the principles of the Anglican Reformation, which advanced with a progress all the more certain because it was the result of sober examination and sincere conviction.

Many an honest farmer, many an intelligent tradesman or mechanic, now recognised in the Reformed Catholic Church a " pillar and ground of truth," and wondered at the madness of his ancestors who had destroyed the peace of England because they would not, as Southey says, kneel at the communion, tolerate the surplice, or use the finest liturgy that was ever composed. Mr. Johnson was enabled to write : — " We see the success of our labours in the frequent conversion of dissenting teachers in this country, and the good disposition towards the excellent constitution of our Church growing amongst the people wherever the Society have settled their missions." One of Johnson's converts was a learned Congregational divine, Mr. Beach, who, with a large proportion of his flock, came over to the Church, and was afterwards ordained in London as one of the Society's missionaries. Before the outbreak of the Revolution, there were in Connecticut alone seventy-three Church congregations, three more than Virginia itself possessed in 1722.

There were even endowments in New England, some of which the Church retains to the present day. When, in 1741, New Hampshire with Vermont came under the government of Wentworth, a loyal churchman, it was determined that some provision should be made for the Church out of the wild and unoccupied lands in

Vermont then about to be surveyed. Accordingly the country was divided into grants or townships of about six miles square, in each of which one seventieth part, or about 330 acres, was reserved for "the first settled minister of the Gospel," one share of equal size for the Church of England, and a third for the Society for Propagating the Gospel. Although 114 of these grants were made, the surveyors, being hostile to the Church, exerted themselves to render ecclesiastical property as useless as possible. They sometimes managed that the glebe allotments and those for the Society should overlap or cover one another; and often the share of the Church was placed, with a perverse ingenuity, at the bottom of a lake or marsh, amidst barren rocks, or on the side of a precipice. Still there was of course some good land, and a considerable quantity not altogether worthless.

But while the missionaries of the Society were at work and the Church was advancing in favour and prosperity, political affairs gave indications of approaching changes. As early as 1701, a public document declared that the independence desired by the colonies was notorious. In 1703 it was said: — "Commonwealth notions improve daily, and if they be not checked in time the rights and privileges of English subjects will be thought too narrow." In 1705 it was stated in print that "The colonists will in process of time cast off their allegiance to England, and set up a government of their own." "Some great men professed their belief of the feasibleness of it, and the probability of its

some time or other actually coming to pass." * As
a general rule, however, this tendency towards independence was rather an instinct than a desire. The
colonists looked round on the wide territory which as
yet they had but partially occupied. They saw its
vast rivers and lakes, its capacious harbours, its fruitful
soil, and they perceived its capability of maintaining
a population far greater than that of England. Know-
ing the rate of their increase, they considered that in
the course of a hundred years they would be numerically stronger than the mother-country, and that the
dependence of a continent on a remote island must
therefore sooner or later terminate.

As time advanced, circumstances contributed to give
additional clearness to their half-formed ideas. The
restrictions imposed by the laws of England on their
commerce and manufactures were plainly an obstacle
in the way of their prosperity. In some minds there·
was a constant fear lest the Church party should succeed in completing the fabric of American episcopacy
and should get up an aggressive hierarchy. The colonial governors by no means fulfilled the wishes of
the people. Although dependent for their allowances
on the votes of the respective colonies, they were often
entire strangers to the people whom they had been
sent to govern. In many cases they had accepted
office in America merely to retrieve their broken
fortunes, and it was asserted that their desire for the

* Bancroft, iii. p. 108.

public good was commonly made subordinate to motives of self-interest.

Boston contained twenty thousand inhabitants in the middle of the century*, and as the management of its affairs devolved on the people assembled in town-meeting, it already constituted a democracy by itself. Here Mayhew taught in reference to the Stamp Act proposed in England for the colonies, that if the common safety and utility would not be promoted by submission to government, disobedience would become a duty. At the same time New Jersey was in a state of disaffection and manifested a disposition to revolt †; while the " House of Burgesses " in Virginia was in " a republican way of thinking." A few years afterwards the members of both houses in New Hampshire, now a colony by itself, are described by their governor as being commonwealth men; and in North Carolina the governor complained that the republican assembly would not submit to his instructions.

Different plans were proposed for meeting this growing spirit of insubordination. Some were for overawing the colonial assemblies by military power; while others proposed to render the governors independent of colonial supplies, and dependent only on the Crown. In America the idea began to gain ground that an American constitution and parliament ought to be established, from which the defects of the English system of government should be excluded. In England

---

* Bancroft, iii. p. 39.   † Ibid.

the question was asked, "When have colonies a right to be released from the dominion of the parent state?" There were thoughtful persons who replied, "Whenever they are so increased in numbers and strength as to be sufficient by themselves for all the good ends of a political union."* As it seemed probable that this state of things was near at hand in our American colonies, it was even proposed in 1756 that the Duke of Cumberland should be appointed their sovereign, and that they should be made independent at once.

Hitherto the grand obstacle in the way of their independence was their want of union, arising from the circumstances of their early settlement and the antipathies existing between North and South. But the progress of events now taught the people how to combine, and showed them the actual amount of their strength.

The power of France in America was at this time, considerable. The French had settled Quebec in 1608, and their missionaries and fur traders had explored the great West. From Canada they had pushed forward their settlements and military stations to the Lakes, to Illinois, and to Michigan, and thence descending the Mississippi, they had laid the foundation of New Orleans in the region afterwards denominated from their sovereign, Louisiana. The territory claimed by France was twenty times as large as that of the English colonies, and covered four-fifths of the North

* Bancroft, iv. p. 181.

American continent. Over this vast extent there roamed numerous tribes of Indians, generally in alliance or at peace with France ; while those denominated the "Five Nations" were almost the only allies of England. The French in America were in number little more than a twentieth of the English, and in 1735, when we counted above a million of colonists, they could reckon only 52,000. But their influence over the savage tribes rendered them dangerous neighbours, and long prevented our people from forming settlements beyond the ridge of the Alleghany or Apalachian mountains. To dispossess France of her American possessions was an object popular alike with the Virginians and the New Englanders. If this point could be gained, the savage tribes would be less formidable, and the English race would be enabled to settle quietly in the magnificent region watered by the Mississippi and its branches, and covering a million of square miles.

Aware of this feeling on the part of the English, the French conceived the design of erecting a chain of forts connecting Canada with Louisiana. In pursuance of this plan they erected a fort within the territory claimed by Virginia in the valley of the Ohio, and committed various aggressions on the English who had already attempted settlements in the neighbourhood. Complaints were made to Governor Dinwiddie, of Virginia, who laid the subject before the Assembly, and sent an envoy to the French commander on the Ohio, demanding a reason for his hostile proceedings in a time of peace, and requesting him to withdraw his troops. This envoy was none other than the celebrated George Washington, at that time (1753) twenty-one years of age. The distance was above four hundred miles, and much of the route was through a wilderness occupied by hostile Indians. The journey occupied six weeks, and was performed partly on horseback and partly on foot, with an interpreter, a guide, and four attendants. On his way, Washington came to the place where the Alleghany river, by its confluence with the Monongahela, forms the Ohio. At once he foresaw the destiny of the place. The land at the " Fork," as it was called, had the command of both rivers, and the flat, well-timbered land around lay convenient for building. Hence he proceeded to Fort Le Bœuf, and, after encountering many perils, brought back a message from the French commander to the effect that he acted under orders, that he was responsible only to his general, then in Canada, and that he proposed to seize every English intruder within the valley of the Ohio.

This answer led to forcible measures for the expulsion of the French from the disputed territory. The Ohio Company, founded in 1749 under royal authority, agreed to build a fort at the Fork, in accordance with Washington's advice, and the work was commenced early in 1754. The French, however, attacked the post, and, having compelled the English to withdraw, completed the fortification and named it " Du Quesne," from the governor of "New France," as the vast French possessions in America were then denominated.

Washington, now a lieutenant-colonel, was sent again to the West to cooperate with troops already assembled there. While on the way with a detachment of forty men, he encountered and defeated a party of French. But as the British forces approached Fort Du Quesne, they were attacked by a superior force of French and Indians, and, after a contest of nine hours, terms of capitulation were agreed on. The French consented to return to their fort, and the English were allowed to retreat quietly to Virginia. In the whole valley of the Mississippi, and from Quebec to New Orleans, no standard floated but that of France.*

The British government now perceived that their occupancy of the western country must either be abandoned or maintained by the sword. Preparations were immediately made in England for active warfare, and the Secretary of State wrote to the governors of the different American colonies recommending united action, and urging them to secure the friendship of the Indian tribes known hitherto as the "Five," but, after the admission of the Tuscaroras, as the "Six Nations."

Accordingly, in the summer of 1754, there assembled at Albany a "Congress" of commissioners from all the northern and middle colonies, Virginia being represented by the lieutenant-governor of New York. A treaty was effected with the Six Nations, and a committee chosen

* Bancroft, iv. p. 121.

to form a plan of perpetual union.   In this committee
the celebrated Benjamin Franklin appeared, and it was
his scheme which was finally adopted.   The seat of the
proposed federal government was to be Philadelphia,
where delegates chosen by their respective legislatures
were to assemble from all the colonies.   A president of
this council was to be appointed by the Crown, with
power to place a negative on the proceedings.   The
delegates were to be not fewer than two, nor more than
seven, from every colony, according to the proportion
of the respective contributions.   Each colony was to
retain its domestic constitution, while the federal
government was to regulate the relations of peace or
war with the Indians, affairs of trade, and purchases of
lands not within the bounds of particular colonies, to
raise soldiers, to equip vessels of war, and levy taxes.
The members were to be elected triennially, and
the council was to meet once a year.   After much
debate, this measure, in which we may see the germs
of the present confederacy, was adopted by the commissioners.

We are told that as Franklin descended the Hudson
on his way to New York at the close of the Albany
congress, the people thronged about him to welcome
him; and he who had first entered their city as a run-
away printer's apprentice, was revered as the mover of
American union.[*]

The system, however, was acceptable neither to

* Bancroft, iv. p. 125.

the American people nor to the government at home. The colonies were too much attached to their individual liberties to allow of an overruling central power, while in England the plan appeared to be a certain step towards American independence.

A plan of union was now proposed in England.* A certain and permanent revenue was to be raised, the amount of which was to be determined by a meeting of commissioners, one from each colony. In electing the commissioners, the council of each colony, though appointed by royal authority, was to have a negative on the votes of the assembly, and the royal governor was to have a negative on both. Seven commissioners were to be a quorum, and a majority of these, with the king's approbation, were to control the continent. The executive department was to be held by a commander-in-chief, who was to draw for his expenses on the treasuries of the several colonies. This plan, as might be expected, was still less acceptable to the colonists than the former, and it was never carried into effect. Both schemes having failed, it was now resolved to carry on the war by British troops, with such reinforcements as could be raised in the colonies, the population of which now amounted to a million and a half.

Early in 1755, although war had not been declared between France and England, General Braddock was sent to America with a considerable force to protect the frontier. The governors of the several provinces

* Bancroft, iv. p. 166.

G

were convened to make arrangements for the campaign. It was decided that three expeditions should be undertaken: one against Fort Du Quesne, commanded by Braddock, aided by the provincial militia of Virginia and Maryland; another against Forts Niagara and Frontenac, situated at the two extremities of Lake Ontario; and a third against Crown Point and Ticonderoga, two strong French stations about fifteen miles apart, near the southern extremity of Lake Champlain.

Having appointed Washington his aide-de-camp, Braddock, after many delays, set out with twenty-two hundred men, and pursued his march through the woods and over the mountains in the direction of Fort Du Quesne. He had often been warned against surprises; and now Washington, who was familiar with the mode of French and Indian warfare, requested to be permitted to search the forest in advance with his Virginian rangers. But Braddock, who had 'been educated in the art of war as taught in Europe, haughtily rejected the advice of a provincial officer, and the result was that which might have been expected. While marching in advance with twelve hundred troops, and within a few miles of the fort, he was attacked, after crossing the Monongahela, by an unseen foe concealed by rocks, trees, and underwood. After a contest of three hours Braddock fell mortally wounded, the greater part of the officers and men were killed, and the remainder took to flight. Washington, whose life had been wonderfully preserved, rallied the provincial troops, and, after burying the unfortunate general, retreated to the eastward. The French and Indians now had the complete ascendency, and the English settlements west of the mountains were abandoned.

The two northern expeditions, though less disastrous, were both unsuccessful. That against Niagara, under General Shirley, was delayed by heavy rains and other causes until the season became too far advanced to proceed. A fort was however built at Oswego, on Lake Ontario, and garrisoned with 500 men. The force designed for the capture of the fortress at Crown Point was composed of provincial troops under General Johnson from Connecticut and New Hampshire, who, together with their Indian allies, amounted to thirty-four hundred men. After meeting with some ill success, the American forces succeeded in defeating the enemy, but the capture of Crown Point and Ticonderoga was not accomplished.

Meantime the people of Massachusetts had raised nearly eight thousand men, and attacked the French settlers of Acadia or Nova Scotia. These quiet and amiable people lived happily in the district which they had occupied before the landing of the Pilgrims, and where they had received Argall's hostile visit in 1613.* Although by the treaty of Utrecht, Nova Scotia had been conceded to Britain, they neither took the oath of allegiance to the King of England nor ceased to consider themselves Frenchmen. By extraordinary efforts of industry they had created a little Utopia in a country

---

* See p. 7, above.

possessing few natural advantages, and their numbers had increased to sixteen or seventeen thousand. But they were Roman Catholics and unwarlike, and their Puritan invaders, acting under high authority, had determined on their utter dispersion. Some fled to Quebec, others took refuge in the forests, but nearly seven thousand of them were driven on board ships and scattered among the English colonies from New Hampshire to Georgia. Their villages were burnt, their farms laid waste, and their country was reduced to a solitude.

Up to this time, notwithstanding the hostile proceedings of the colonies, England and France had remained at peace. But, in the spring of 1756, war was declared, and in the summer the British and colonial forces in America again experienced bitter reverses. The fort lately built at Oswego was taken by the French, and the breaking out of small-pox rendered it necessary to disperse the provincial troops which had been assembled. In the following year, a naval expedition, which proved unsuccessful, was undertaken against Louisburg, on the island of Cape Breton. Fort William Henry, on Lake George, defended by a garrison of nearly three thousand men, and covered by an army of four thousand under General Webb, fell into the hands of the enemy and was demolished. The French, with forces numerically far inferior to our own, everywhere gained the advantage. The lakes between the Hudson river and Canada were in their possession, as well as the great lakes Ontario and Erie, and the rivers Ohio and Mississippi.

It was therefore most justly apprehended that they would make good their claim to the whole region west of the Alleghany mountains and Lake Champlain, and confine the English settlements to the borders of the Atlantic. The colonists were becoming dissatisfied, attributing their losses to mismanagement on the part of English officers, and to the subordinate position which the provincial officers were made to occupy notwithstanding their superior local knowledge. Already John Adams, then a poor young schoolmaster at Worcester in Massachusetts, was meditating on the growing union of the colonies, on their resources, and on their advancing population. He reckoned that, if only the French could be put down, the Americans would soon be so powerful that all Europe could not subdue them. In less than thirty years from that time, John Adams was himself the envoy of independent America to the King of Great Britain.*

The British government was now seriously alarmed; and William Pitt having been placed at the head of a new ministry, it was hoped that past losses would be repaired. In the summer of 1757, General Abercrombie, commander-in-chief of the British forces in America, was at the head of fifty thousand men, of whom twenty thousand were provincials. Great efforts were made to induce the colonists to unite for the common safety, and treaties of alliance were formed with various Indian tribes whose friendship hitherto had

* Bancroft, iv. p. 216.

G 3

been doubtful. The British fleets blocked up the ports of France, or captured at sea the men and stores designed for Canada. The brave but unhappy Canadians were thus cut off from intercourse with their mother-country, while British America was not only powerful in itself, but strengthened by an unbroken communication with England. Three expeditions were again under-taken: one against Louisburg, another against Crown Point and its neighbour Ticonderoga, and the third against Fort Du Quesne. In the siege of Louisburg, at which General Wolfe became conspicuous, fourteen thousand men, twenty ships of the line, and eighteen frigates were engaged for nearly two months, when the fortress was surrendered, and the trophies were sent home to be deposited in St. Paul's Cathedral.

For the attack on Ticonderoga and Crown Point, both on Lake George, there assembled an army of above fifteen thousand men. Of these more than half were provincials, comprising six hundred New England rangers, dressed like woodmen, each armed with a fire-lock and hatchet, with a powder-horn under his arm and a leather bag for bullets at his waist; while every officer was provided with a pocket-compass as a guide in the forests. There were also Puritan chaplains, who preached to the regiments of citizen-soldiers a renewal of the days when Moses sent Joshua against Amalek. The regular troops exceeded six thousand, and Aber-crombie commanded the entire force.

Notwithstanding these great preparations, the attack on Ticonderoga was unsuccessful, and the general was obliged to withdraw before a French force far inferior to his own, commanded by the brave and generous Montcalm. A detachment of his army, however, proceeded under Bradstreet, a provincial officer, against Fort Frontenac, adjoining the present site of Kingston, on Lake Ontario, which fell into their hands and was destroyed.

As for Fort Du Quesne, the opinion had long prevailed that the frontiers could not be freed from the dreadful visits of the Indians in connection with the French until the enemy were driven from this important post. Accordingly an army of eight thousand men was placed under General Forbes, Virginia sending nineteen hundred under her beloved Washington. Pennsylvania, notwithstanding her Quaker origin, was fired with unusual military ardour. Benjamin West, afterwards the celebrated painter, joined the expedition; and Anthony Wayne, a boy of thirteen, and subsequently distinguished in American annals, raised for the expedition twenty-seven hundred men. When the army had arrived within ninety miles of the fort, a reconnoitring party of eight hundred troops was met by a body of French and Indians and utterly defeated. Washington, who pleaded " a long intimacy with these woods," * was now sent forward with a detachment of provincials. The garrison at the fort, consisting of only five hundred men, saw the hopelessness of resistance, and, setting fire to their buildings, escaped down the Ohio to the French

---

* Bancroft, iv. p. 310.

G 4

settlements on the Mississippi. On the following day, Nov. 25th, 1758, the flag of England was waving on the ruined bastions, and the place, then named Fort Pitt in honour of the great minister, is now known as Pittsburgh, the Birmingham of America. Washington then resigned his commission, after receiving from the officers who had served under him assurances of regret for the loss of " such an excellent commander, such a sincere friend, and such an affable companion." Soon afterwards he married a lady of large property, and lived for some years on his estate at Mount Vernon, discharging his duties not only as a member of the Virginia legislature, but as a sincere churchman and a vestryman of two parishes. He became known as a man of sound judgment, exact integrity, and strict justice, and though a slave-owner and naturally irritable, yet self-constrained and forbearing. Without being himself learned, he advocated the promotion of learning; and though not a fluent orator, he spoke to the purpose and readily commanded attention. He farmed his large estate of several thousand acres with economy and profit; he rose early, kept his own accounts, exercised liberal hospitality, and received all the respect due to a plain and honest country gentleman.

In 1759, the year after Washington's retirement, bold measures were taken, and the three strongest holds of the French were attacked, Quebec, Niagara, and Ticonderoga. The forts at Ticonderoga and Crown Point were deserted on the approach of the British forces under General Amherst. Fort Niagara was taken by General Sir William Johnson, and the garrison of that important post, which had secured the communication between Canada and Louisiana, were carried prisoners to New York. General Wolfe, with an army of eight thousand men, proceeded against Quebec, and, after meeting some checks, finally succeeded in conveying his troops unobserved to the heights of the citadel. In the engagement which followed, Wolfe himself fell in the very moment of victory. The gallant French general Montcalm was also mortally wounded, and five days afterwards Quebec surrendered. In the following year Canada became a British province.

Unbounded triumph and exultation now pervaded England and America. Henceforth the great West was to be in the hands of the Anglo-Saxon race, to which the capture of Quebec was nothing less than the opening of a continent.

CHAP. IV.

THE CHURCH AND THE COLONIES

(*concluded*).

ENGLISH PLAN FOR TAXING THE COLONIES.—THE "STAMP ACT" CON-
GRESS.—BOSTON OCCUPIED BY THE KING'S TROOPS.—PROGRESS OF
DISCONTENT.—SERMON OF THE BISHOP OF ST. ASAPH.—CANADA PRO-
PITIATED.—CONGRESS AT PHILADELPHIA.—BATTLE OF LEXINGTON.—
CONGRESS PETITIONS FOR REDRESS. — EXPEDITION TO CANADA. —
DECLARATION OF INDEPENDENCE.—CHARACTER AND PROGRESS OF THE
REVOLUTIONARY WAR.—SURRENDER OF LORD CORNWALLIS.—ACKNOW-
LEDGMENT OF INDEPENDENCE. — CONSTITUTION OF THE UNITED STATES.
—SUFFERINGS OF THE LOYAL CLERGY DURING THE WAR.—CONFISCA-
TION OF CHURCH PROPERTY AND RUIN OF THE CHURCHES.

HEN the war with France was thus
brought to a successful termination, the
colonists were not only strongly attached
to the mother-country, but more united
among themselves than at any former
period of their history. The expenses of the contest
had, however, been enormous, and it was thought in
England that the Americans, now rapidly increasing
in wealth and population, ought to be required to
sustain a portion of the burden.

In 1760, the year after the capture of Quebec,
George III. came to the throne, and in the following

year William Pitt, the tried friend of America, resigned his power. Four years afterwards a bill was carried through Parliament imposing additional duties on the trade of the colonists, and it was also resolved that stamp duties should be imposed on all their law documents, leases, contracts, bills of sale, notes of hand, newspapers, and pamphlets. The Americans, on the other hand, set forth that by their early charters the rights of English subjects had been secured to them, and that among those rights none was more valued than that which secured them from taxation, unless by their own consent expressed through their representatives. It was also urged that the domestic governments in America were supported wholly at the expense of the colonists, that they had already paid their full proportion of the war expenses, and that, considering their means, their burdens were actually greater than those of the people of England. The Stamp Act Bill, however, became a law in 1765, and immediately a flame of indignation pervaded America. A congress of delegates, representing nine provinces, and known as the Stamp Act Congress, assembled at New York, and, after declaring their view of colonial rights, appointed special agents to represent their case to the authorities in England. At the same time, with the view of defeating the measures of Parliament, it was resolved that American manufactures should be encouraged, and that, if possible, all business should be suspended in which the obnoxious stamps would be required.

A change of ministry favoured the views of the colonists, and, on the recommendation of William Pitt, the Stamp Act was repealed. The joy of the Americans was, however, damped by an assertion put forth by Parliament of its abstract right to bind the colonies in all cases whatsoever. Fresh indignation was aroused when an indirect tax was levied upon them by an enactment requiring them to furnish quarters for the king's troops at their own expense. Under the new ministry additional duties were imposed, and strict measures were adopted for the collection of the revenue. Hostile feelings were now violently excited, and the colonial press took an active part in awakening a spirit of resistance. The governors, being appointed by the Crown, rendered themselves particularly obnoxious to the people by the support which they gave to the Acts of Parliament. The legislature of Massachusetts resolved on addressing a circular to the other colonial assemblies urging the importance of united action in all efforts to obtain redress. The ministers at home, fearing that union would give additional strength and confidence to the disaffected party, directed the Governor of Massachusetts to call on the legislature to rescind their resolution respecting the circular. The assembly, by a large majority, refused to agree to this order, and was accordingly dissolved.

Finding that remonstrances were unavailing, the people again resolved to encourage domestic industry, and to purchase no articles of foreign growth or manufacture but such as were absolutely indispensable. In consequence of riotous proceedings interfering with the collection of revenue, four thousand royal troops occupied Boston in the latter part of 1768, and Parliament petitioned the king that persons accused of treason in Massachusetts during that year might be sent to England for trial.

The Assembly of Virginia now came to the rescue of Massachusetts, and passed resolutions re-asserting the right of the colonists to exemption from parliamentary taxation, and further declaring that to send persons to be tried in places beyond the sea, where they could not produce witnesses or have a jury from their own neighbourhood, would violate the rights of British subjects. These resolutions were forwarded to the other legislative bodies, and their concurrence was earnestly solicited. The governor now dissolved the assembly, but the members met again in a private house, and unanimously passed agreements unfavourable to the importation of goods from abroad. In the course of a few weeks this example was followed by most of the southern colonies.

In 1770, an affray took place between the troops and the populace of Boston, in which, after enduring much provocation, the soldiers fired and killed four of the mob. Meanwhile English commerce began to feel the effects of the non-importation agreements, for in a single year the exports to America fell from two millions and a half sterling to about a million and a half. The new ministry under Lord North prevailed on Parliament to withdraw the duties, as discouraging to English manufactures, but to retain the duty on tea, by way of asserting the right of the mother-country to the taxation of her foreign possessions.

The Americans, however, were now united in contending against this very principle, and although they recommenced a brisk trade in other foreign articles, they agreed to consume no tea. In 1772, some of the people of Rhode Island burned a revenue cutter, and were shielded from punishment by their fellow-countrymen, notwithstanding a reward of 500*l*. offered for their apprehension. The British Government, conceiving that, during the present excitement, certain law officers of Massachusetts were too dependent on the colony, now placed those gentlemen in an independent position by granting them liberal salaries out of the colonial revenue. Upon this the opposite party appointed committees of correspondence, and in 1773, at the suggestion of the legislature of Virginia, the several colonial assemblies nominated similar committees, by means of which an interchange of sentiments was kept up by the disaffected throughout the provinces. Resistance to the British Parliament completed that which the war with French Canada had begun, and the thirteen colonies, which formerly had known less of one another than of the parent State, were now a united people.

In February, 1773, during the progress of these events, a sermon was preached by the Bishop of St. Asaph before the Society for Propagating the Gospel, which contained some apposite allusions to the state of affairs. " Perhaps," said the eloquent prelate, " the annals of history have never afforded a more grateful spectacle to a benevolent and philosophic mind than the growth and progress of the British colonies in North America. We see a number of scattered settlements growing by degrees under the protection of their mother-country, who treated them with the indulgence due to their weakness and infancy, into little separate commonwealths. Placed in a climate that soon became fruitful and healthy by their industry, possessing that liberty which was the natural growth of their own country, and secured by her power against foreign enemies, they seem to have been intended as a solitary experiment to instruct the world to what improvements and happiness mankind will naturally attain when they are suffered to use their own prudence in search of their own interest. . . . The colonies have not only taken root and acquired strength, but seem hastening with an accelerated progress to such a powerful state as may introduce a new and important change in human affairs. Descended from ancestors of the most improved and enlightened part of the old world, they receive, as it were by inheritance, all the improvements and discoveries of their mother-country. And it happens fortunately for them to commence their flourishing state at a time when the human understanding has attained to the free use of its powers and has learned to act with vigour and certainty. They may avail themselves not only of the experience and industry, but even of the errors and mistakes of former days. . . . May the wise and good on both sides, without inquiring too curiously into the grounds of past animosities, endeavour by all prudent means to restore the old public friendship and confidence which made us great, happy, and victorious."

At this crisis, however, when wisdom and prudence were most necessary, a step was taken by Benjamin Franklin, then agent in London for Massachusetts, which added fresh fuel to the flame, and threw new difficulties in the way of reconciliation. By some means, said to be not the most honourable, he obtained possession of some letters, which he promptly despatched across the Atlantic to Boston.

These letters had been written by the Governor of Massachusetts and others to their correspondents in Parliament, and stated that the opposition was confined to a few, and that more vigorous and coercive measures ought at once to be taken. They added that the people in the colonies ought to be deprived of the power of appointing colonial magistrates, and that all the high officers of every description should be made dependent for their salaries on the Crown. The people were now exasperated, and when in the following winter some vessels laden with tea arrived in Boston harbour, a company of seventeen men, disguised as Indians, boarded the vessels, and threw the tea into the water.

In 1774, the aspect of affairs threatening an appeal to arms, the home government took measures for securing the attachment of the conquered Canadians. Extensive powers were conferred on a Canadian Legislative Council, the members of which were to be nominated by the king; a perfect equality was established between the Roman Catholics and the Protestants, the privileges of the clergy were secured, and the existing French laws were confirmed. As for the rebellious port of Boston, the authorities removed the custom-house to Salem, and by the Boston Port Bill forbade the loading or unloading of merchant-vessels until good order should be restored, and compensation made to the East India Company for the tea which had been destroyed. Four vessels of war were stationed in the harbour to enforce these enactments. The appointment to all important offices was given to the king, and it was provided that all persons indicted for offences committed in aiding the magistrates might be removed to another country, or to England, for trial.

Boston, hitherto prosperous and improving, was now in a situation of great distress. But the other colonies sympathised with Massachusetts, and gave assurances of support, and the first day of June, when the new Act of Parliament went into effect, was observed throughout the provinces, by common consent, as a public and solemn fast. The people generally concurred in the proposition for holding a congress, in order to concert measures for the preservation of their rights. Deputies were accordingly appointed by all the colonies except Georgia, and the assembly took place on the 5th of September, 1774, at Philadelphia. They agreed in promising support to the people of Massachusetts, in recommending contributions for their relief, and in passing resolutions against all commercial intercourse with England until their grievances should be redressed.

This meeting gave a tone and character to the struggle which followed, and might be considered as the first decided pulsation of a national life distinct from that of the parent State. Fifty-five delegates were present, among whom were some of the most eminent persons of America. They had the eloquence of Patrick Henry, the Virginian, and of the New-Englander, John Adams. They had the plain sense of Roger Sherman, of Connecticut, and the tranquil energy of the southern gentleman, George Washington. Among them were persons of refinement and polish, as well as of rude simplicity and stern enthusiasm, but the prevailing state of mind was that of firm determination to maintain what they believed to be their rights. Some of them may have been insincere in the professions which they now made of attachment to the king, and in disclaiming a wish for independence. A few of the leaders of the party may have been merely acting a part which they considered politically expedient; but it is certain that as yet the people of America were not generally prepared for the steps which were subsequently taken, and that conciliation on the part of the mother-country would, for the time, have satisfied their wishes.* It is worthy of note that on the 7th of September the meeting of the Congress was opened with prayers according to the Liturgy, and that one of the psalms for the day, " Plead thou my cause, O Lord, with them that strive with me," was regarded almost as an oracle from heaven.

* Bancroft, vii. chap. ii.

The resolutions of this Congress being published in England enlisted much feeling in behalf of the Americans, and their old friend William Pitt, then Earl of Chatham, strongly commended the dignity, firmness, and wisdom with which the Americans had acted. On the other hand, George III. declared that the New England governments were in a state of rebellion, and that blows must decide as to their independence or their subjection. The crisis was now rapidly approaching. The colonists were embarked in a common cause, and throughout the cities and villages of America companies of volunteers were organised, gunpowder was manufactured, and measures were taken to obtain all kinds of military stores. Many persons, however, for various reasons, took the part of England in the controversy, and many on the popular side still hoped that a resort to arms might be averted by the adoption of conciliatory measures by Parliament. The abstract justice of their claim seems to be now admitted, our present colonies occupying the same favourable position in regard to the mother-country for which the Americans in vain contended. Happy indeed would it have been for both parties if, on either side, the point in dispute could have been conceded, and, at the same time, provision made for an ultimate peaceable separation. Long years of bloodshed would then have been averted, enormous expenses saved, and the growth of bitter animosities, which have scarcely yet entirely died away, prevented.

On the 19th of April, 1775, some British troops were

sent from Boston to destroy a quantity of military stores which had been collected at Concord, about eighteen miles to the westward. While on their way they found about seventy provincials under arms, and on parade, at Lexington. Major Pitcairn rode up to them and said, "Disperse, rebels; throw down your arms and disperse;" but as the provincials did not obey the order, they were fired upon, and seven of their number were killed. The British finally effected their object, but on their return they were attacked wherever an opportunity presented, and before the close of the day sixty-five of them had been killed, nearly two hundred wounded, and twenty-eight made prisoners. Soon afterwards the important fortresses of Crown Point and Ticonderoga were surprised by the provincials, and surrendered without firing a gun.

On the 10th of May, the Congress again assembled at Philadelphia, and petitioned George III. for a redress of grievances, at the same time deciding on further preparations for defence. They organised an army, and at the suggestion of John Adams unanimously appointed Washington, then a delegate from Virginia, commander-in-chief. At this time the population of the thirteen colonies amounted to about two millions six hundred thousand, of whom half a million were negroes.

On the 17th of June, the Americans having formed an entrenchment on Breed's Hill, in sight of Boston and near another height known as Bunker Hill, were attacked by the British, who, after losing a thousand men, obtained the advantage.

In the following autumn, Washington sent a detachment of his troops into Canada, with the view of securing the co-operation of the people of that colony, many of whom were favourable to the American cause. But the soldiers, too independent and undisciplined to obey their own officers, cheated the Canadians, and treated their religion with contempt. They took Montreal, but failed at Quebec, and after nine months were driven from the province, having made enemies of the people instead of friends.

About this time Thomas Paine, an emigrant from England, and a notorious infidel, published, at Franklin's suggestion, a strongly-written book, entitled "Common Sense," in which kingly authority was denounced, and George III. especially pronounced a malevolent tyrant. The book had an immense circulation, and from this time the very principle of monarchy was execrated by many who hitherto had only desired the enjoyment of their rights as British subjects.

During the winter, the American arms prevailed in South Carolina, and in March, 1776, Washington gained possession of Boston. On the 4th of the following July, after long hesitation and several fruitless petitions to the king, Congress took a decided stand in favour of separation, and the celebrated Declaration of Independence was proclaimed from the State House in Philadelphia. In this declaration it was set forth as self-evident "that all men are created equal; that they are endowed by their Creator with certain inalienable rights; that among these are life, liberty, and the pursuit of happiness; that, to secure these rights, governments are instituted among men, deriving their just powers from the consent of the governed; and that whenever any form of government becomes destructive of these ends, it is the right of the people to alter and abolish it." The document proceeded to assert that the conduct of George III. had proved his object to be the establishment of an absolute tyranny over America, and concluded by proclaiming the United Colonies free and independent States, and dissolving all political connection with Great Britain. It is worthy of remark that the facts stated in this declaration in proof of the tyrannical objects of the king were of recent occurrence, being generally subsequent to the outbreak of the existing quarrel. The flourishing condition and growing population of the colonies certainly proved that, on the whole, the rule of England had been far from destructive of the ends of government, though sometimes harsh and sometimes unwise. But, under the present excited state of feeling, the declaration expressed the sentiments of the multitude, and in support of it the members of Congress pledged to each other " their lives, their fortune, and their sacred honour."

The events of the revolutionary contest must be noticed but briefly in this place, since to mention them in detail would require a volume. It was a civil war between Englishmen, for, though fought in America, each party found encouragement on both sides of the Atlantic. Like the civil war of the preceding century, it was in a great measure free from the reproach of wanton cruelty and unnecessary violence. There was none of that inhuman ferocity which made the first French revolution so hideous, none of that gloating over human gore which, after the lapse of seventy years, it is appalling to contemplate.

The first year of the war closed with great discouragement to the Americans. Their armies were defeated, New York was taken from them, and many of their troops deserted to the British side. As the enemy advanced, Congress retreated from Philadelphia to Baltimore, where they found themselves without the means of obtaining a revenue adequate to the necessities of the country. Under these circumstances they invested Washington with dictatorial powers for six months, recommended a day of fasting and humiliation, and sent an embassy to France in the hope of inducing Louis XVI. to attack the West Indies. Rhode Island was taken by the British, and in England it was believed that the rebellion was effectually crushed; but a victory gained by Washington at Trenton, in New Jersey, raised the spirits of the provincials, whose army was again enlarged by accessions from the militia.

In the following year, 1777, Benjamin Franklin was in France vainly soliciting open assistance and an acknowledgment of American independence. Arms were, however, privately sent over, and the Marquis de la Fayette, then a young man of nineteen, devoted himself personally to the American cause, and landed at Charlestown in the spring. The battle of Brandywine Creek followed, in which the Americans were defeated by Lord Cornwallis. Washington and his army retreated, and Philadelphia was occupied by the British in the following September.

A plan had been formed by the British in the mean time for sending an army from Canada to the Hudson River, by way of Lake Champlain and Lake George, in order to recover possession of Crown Point, Ticonderoga, and other important posts. General Burgoyne was placed in command of the army, and was joined by many Indians of the Six Nations. After taking Ticonderoga and gaining various other advantages, Burgoyne was forced to surrender with an army of 6000 men to General Gates at Saratoga.

The forts on the lakes now fell into the hands of the revolutionists; many who had been considered "Tories" joined the popular party; and France acknowledged American independence. In the autumn of this year a form of confederation between the thirteen provinces having been proposed by the provisional Congress was adopted by the several provincial legislatures. The new confederacy was entitled "The United States of America," each of which was bound to the others for the security of their joint liberties. Each State was to retain its sovereignty and every right   expressly surrendered to the United States. The powers of Congress were defined by the Articles of Confederation. A national flag was adopted, thirteen stars and as many stripes representing the combined republics. In England the apprehension of a French war led to a proposal that the original demands of America should be granted for the sake of peace. But the proposal came too late, and the provincials refused to treat until the British armies should have been removed from their territory and their independence acknowledged.

In the following year, 1778, the treaties with France were ratified by Congress; war broke out between France and England, and although Washington's army was in the greatest distress through the want of food and clothing, the prospects of the revolution brightened. Considerable numbers of those who had hitherto declared themselves royalists went over to the popular side, and the British evacuated Philadelphia, concentrating their forces at New York. Attempts were now made by intriguing persons to remove Washington from the chief command, but without success. A Prussian officer was employed to discipline the hitherto raw troops, whose efficiency was, in consequence, much increased. In the mean time the mass of the people suffered greatly from the devastating effects of the war. Marauding parties of royalists on the one hand, and provincials on the other, were constantly employed in plundering and burning barns, mills, and private dwellings. Privateers were fitted out in the American ports, and the notorious Paul Jones in the next year alarmed even the coasts of England and Scotland by his depredations. On the other side, the beautiful district of Wyoming, in Pennsylvania, was devastated by royalists and Indians, men, women, and children being cruelly destroyed by the remorseless

savages.   In the latter part of this year the principal
seat of the war was in the Southern States, where the
loyal party was still powerful.   South Carolina was
composed in a great measure of " Tories," and after a
battle near Savannah, in which the Americans were defeated, the whole of Georgia came under British authority.   The slaves, not being identified with American
interests, manifested great willingness to aid the royal
cause.   During the contest many of them were induced
to enlist in the British army by the king's proclamation
of freedom to all slaves of rebel masters who should join
the royal standard.   After the war a number of them
were carried to Nova Scotia, where allotments of
land were promised to them, " which it appears they
never received."*   From Nova Scotia they sailed for
Sierra Leone in 1791, in sixteen ships furnished by
government, and after some losses on the passage
more than eleven hundred remained to settle that important colony.

The year 1779 was unfavourable to the Americans
In the South, their troops with their French auxiliaries
were defeated, and the Polish officer Pulaski fell at
Savannah.   The British commanded the sea and the
navigable rivers, and by destroying magazines, capturing
ships, and attacking towns, kept the people in constant
alarm; while, at the same time, they prevented nearly
all communication between the North and South
They defeated the provincial forces on the Hudson

---

* Walker's "Church of England Mission at Sierra Leone," xxiv.

river and on the Penobscot, and ravaged the villages on the coast of Connecticut. At the end of the year, notwithstanding French assistance, it appeared probable that America would be obliged to yield to the supremacy of England. The credit of Congress had sunk so low that at this time thirty dollars of its paper money were considered no more than equal in value to a single dollar in silver.

The following year was little more favourable to the revolutionary party. Charleston, the capital of South Carolina, was taken by the British under General Clinton, who now proclaimed in the South a pardon for past offences on submission, and exemption from all taxation excepting by the colonial legislature. Many who had been deterred from taking any active part by the superior force of the Americans, now avowed themselves faithful subjects of King George. But when it was afterwards proclaimed that all who would not take an active part in settling and securing the king's government should be treated as rebels, many resumed their arms and joined the forces which Congress was raising for the recovery of South Carolina.

This army, under General Gates, finally came in conflict with the British, under Lord Cornwallis, at Camden, not far from Charleston. The Americans were totally defeated, but soon afterwards gained an advantage among the mountains in the west of North Carolina. Meantime Washington continued with his army in the neighbourhood of New York, attempting to restrain the incursions of the British. His situation was very trying, and he found it difficult to keep down the mutinous spirit which prevailed among his troops on account of their want of the common necessaries of life. In the autumn, Arnold, one of his generals, gave up the American cause, and entered the service of the king. A French fleet arrived in Rhode Island with six thousand troops under the Count de Rochambeau, but it was immediately blockaded by the British, under Admiral Arbuthnot. Little more was effected during the year, and after a general exchange of prisoners both parties went into winter quarters. The American army was again in a most wretched state, and officers were sent to seize provisions wherever they could, the only payment given being a certificate of the quantity and value of the articles taken.

The year 1781 began with a victory gained by the Americans at a place called " The Cowpens," near the line dividing North and South Carolina. Another deadly conflict took place near Guildford, in the former State, which resulted in the retreat of the Americans. Several battles were afterwards fought with various success, but, on the whole, the Americans, aided as they were with money and troops from France, were gradually gaining the advantage. Want of supplies obliged Cornwallis to draw back to Wilmington, whence, in the spring, he advanced to Petersburg in Virginia. As he considered it advisable to secure a strong post for communication with the fleet, he selected and fortified York Town, at the mouth of York River, which he occupied with all his force. He was there surrounded by the combined French and American forces by land, and blocked up by a French squadron on the Chesapeake. Every attempt to relieve him being frustrated, he was compelled, on the 19th of October, to surrender his naval force to France, and his troops, seven thousand in number, to the United States.

This event decided the contest, which had cost England a hundred thousand men and more than seventy millions of money. Early in the spring of 1782, hostilities were suspended, and John Adams having been appointed by Congress to conduct the negotiations, the independence of the United States was finally acknowledged, and a treaty of peace concluded in the following October.

Soon after the termination of the war it was found that the existing articles of confederation were insufficient for the purposes of a regular government. Congress had no power to make treaties with foreign nations which would be binding on the several States, and the trade between the States themselves was impeded by many restrictions. It was not to be thought that because the States had become independent of England, they were therefore independent of each other. Something was wanted which should supply the bond which had formerly existed in their common dependence on the mother-country. Accordingly John Adams, as early as 1783, suggested that Congress should effect a closer union of the States, and enlarge the powers of the general government. In 1786, on the suggestion of James Madison, of Virginia, a convention of dele-

gates met in Maryland, and laid before Congress a proposal for a General Convention for effecting such alterations as would meet the necessities of the case. The
proposal being sanctioned, a Convention met at Philadelphia in May, 1787, composed of the principal statesmen in the country. After four months' labour, the
new Constitution was drawn up, and was further examined and discussed by various state conventions and
by the people at large. Public opinion was by no
means unanimous in its favour, the party called "Federalists" supporting it, and those who objected to the
amount of power conferred on the rulers opposing it.
Ultimately all the States gave it their sanction, North
Carolina and Rhode Island being the last to acquiesce
in its provisions.

By this new Constitution* the general government
was made to consist of three departments, legislative,
executive, and judicial. The legislative department is
composed of a Senate and House of Representatives, collectively styled Congress. The former body is composed
of two members from each State, whether its population
be large or small, who hold their office for *six* years,
and are appointed by their respective legislatures. The
Senate confirms the appointment of officers nominated
by the President, and ratifies treaties. One-third of the
members go out of office every two years, and by this
arrangement a permanent character is given to the
Senate, which the other House does not possess. The

* M. Murray, p. 816.

members of the House of Representatives are elected by the people for *two* years, a prescribed number of inhabitants to each district being entitled to send one member. In the States where slavery exists, this required number is made up of slaves as well as free persons, five slaves being counted as three freemen; but since the slaves have no vote, the whites in those States have many more representatives in proportion to their number than in the free States. With the view of preventing the growth of an aristocracy, titles of nobility and the entail of estates were prohibited.

The executive of the government is the President. He is appointed by electors in the several States, chosen by the people, or by the House of Representatives in case no person should receive a majority of all the votes of the electors, those from each State having one vote collectively. He is elected for four years, but may be removed from office by impeachment in case of conviction of misconduct. He nominates, subject to confirmation by the Senate, all civil, military, and naval officers of the general government, and is commander-in-chief of all the land and naval forces. He ratifies treaties, subject to the approbation of two-thirds of the Senate. The President also has power to pass a veto or negative on such acts of Congress as he may disapprove, which acts may subsequently be passed and become laws by a majority of two-thirds in both Houses, without the concurrence of the President.

A Vice-President is elected at the same time and in the same manner as the President, to fill that office in case it should become vacant by death or any other cause.

In Congress is vested the power to declare war, to raise and support armies, to provide and maintain a navy, to collect a revenue by direct taxes and duties, to regulate commerce, coin money, and, in general, to provide for the security and welfare of the nation. Both Houses must concur in supporting any bill before it can become a law.

The judicial department is vested in a Supreme Court and such district courts as Congress may establish. All questions arising under the laws of the United States come under the cognisance of these courts, as well as those concerning treaties, and cases arising between individuals of different States and between foreigners and citizens. The judges are appointed by the President, for life, and it is worthy of remark that in seventy-two years, since the adoption of the present constitution, there have been but four Chief Justices of the United States.

The functions of Congress extend to affairs of a general nature, and must not be considered as identical with those of the British Parliament. The legislation, which principally affects the daily life of the people, is carried on in the several State legislatures, much in the same way as it was formerly conducted in the colonial assemblies. Each of the States has its House of Representatives, usually elected annually. It has its Governor and Senate, chosen by the people, and occupying a position analogous to that of the Governor and Council anciently nominated by the Crown. It has also its Supreme Court and its judges, appointed in various ways, according to the traditions of the several communities.

We have now traced the progress of the American Union from its first rudiments in the humble New England confederacy. We have seen the primitive idea gradually developed in the abortive plan of the Albany Congress, in the Stamp Act Congress at New York, in the more authoritative assembly of 1774, in the revolutionary government formed at Philadelphia in 1776, in the Articles of Confederation of 1777, and finally in the constitution which has retained its hold on the great mass of the American people to the present time. That constitution, whatever may be its defects, is the result of past history; not an attempt to realise a beautiful theory, but an adjustment of the actual facts, the conflicting interests, and the established principles of a previous condition.* In all this, religious persons in America believe they see the hand of a guiding and controlling Providence.

Leaving the new government thus established with George Washington at its head, we must now direct our attention to the fortunes of the Church during the period of fearful excitement which I have briefly described.

As the Revolution approached, the clergy in the South found themselves more and more under the

* Church Review, Jan. 1859.

I

domination of the people, while at the same time there was a general spread of sectarianism. At an early period the vestries in Virginia had gained the right of induction, and had often availed themselves of their power to keep the rectory vacant, while they employed some person to officiate during their pleasure upon a miserable stipend. Actions of this kind now became more and more common. In Maryland, laws were passed by the provincial assembly subjecting the clergy to the jurisdiction of laymen. Justices of the peace, as well as dissenting ministers, took upon themselves to perform marriages, where formerly the licence to do so was restricted to the ministers of the Establishment. Influenced by the eloquence of the celebrated Patrick Henry, the law courts in Virginia decided against the clergy, in a great case involving the payment of their lawful dues. In 1771, not only the laity, but the clergy themselves in that colony, had become indifferent to the question of an American episcopate. Four clergymen even protested against the project, and received for their protest the thanks of the legislature. Many worthy persons feared that, under existing circumstances, bishops would be little more than political tools in the hands of the British ministry.

When the Revolution broke out, snares were sometimes artfully laid with the view of entrapping the clergy, and they were expected to take part in public services and fasts, some of which were probably designed not so much to seek the favour of Heaven as to arouse the people against the lawful authorities.

On the day after the arrival of the news of the Boston Port Bill, the Virginian House of Burgesses being in session, a resolution was introduced and adopted fixing a day of fasting, humiliation, and prayer. The infidel Jefferson, afterwards President of the United States, was a member of this assembly, and gives the following account of the spirit in which he bore his part of the performance : —

" No example of such a solemnity had existed since the days of our distresses in the war of '55, since which a new generation had grown up. With the help of Rushworth, whom we rummaged over for the revolutionary precedents and forms of the Puritans of those days, preserved by him, we cooked up a resolution, somewhat modernising the phrases, for appointing the 1st of June, on which the Port Bill was to commence, for a day of fasting, humiliation, and prayer, to implore Heaven to avert from us the evils of civil war, and to inspire us with firmness in support of our rights, and to turn the hearts of the king and parliament to moderation and justice." *

There can be no doubt that while the Puritan preachers were declaiming on such texts as " What portion have we in David ? " " To your tents, O Israel ! " the general influence of the Church was in favour of loyalty. Yet in the South, where the decay of zeal and piety in the Church had been most conspicuous, there were many among the clergy who felt little

* Jefferson's Works, quoted in the " New York Review."

scruple in absolving themselves from their sworn allegiance. About one-third of those in Virginia joined the Revolution, and some of them even gave up their clerical character and became officers in the army. A better course was taken by a respected young clergyman, William White, of Pennsylvania, who, having adopted the popular cause from a belief in its justice, was appointed to the responsible post of Chaplain to Congress.

Yet the hatred of the Church, instinctively felt by the bulk of the revolutionists, was not appeased by the adhesion to their cause of even such clergymen as White, and such laymen as Washington. The Anabaptists of Virginia, having obtained popularity by their ready concurrence in the war, first obtained from the legislature a position of equality with the Establishment, and next prevailed on the same body to repeal former laws in favour of the Church. The effect of this act was to stop the incomes of most of the clergy and to drive them from the country. The churches were now abandoned, congregations were broken up, and divine ordinances were maintained only in an occasional way by a few zealous pastors, who itinerated as missionaries with that pious object.

To the northward of Pennsylvania, the clergy, without exception, considered themselves bound to abide by their oaths of allegiance, and consequently endured a persecution which displayed the bitterness of political and theological rancour combined. The sufferings which they endured, and the insults heaped upon them, were innumerable. One of their number who refused to pray for Congress was barbarously murdered. Another was dragged at a horse's tail and rendered insane for life. Mr. Beach, the venerable pastor, whose conversion from Puritanism has been mentioned, on being ordered to cease praying for the king, replied that "he would do his duty and preach and pray for his sovereign till they cut out his tongue." One of the revolutionary generals informed the Rev. Mr. Inglis, of Trinity Church, New York, afterwards Bishop of Nova Scotia, that, on a certain day, "General Washington would be at church, and would be glad if the prayers for the king and royal family were omitted, or the word 'king' exchanged for 'commonwealth.'" Mr. Inglis took no notice of this message, and afterwards told Washington that it was in his power to close the churches, but not to make the clergy depart from their duty. With the object of overawing him, a hundred armed men were marched into the church while he was officiating; but he fearlessly continued the appointed service, refused to admit sectarian chaplains, and succeeded in maintaining the high ground which he had taken.

When American independence was finally recognised by Great Britain, the Society for Propagating the Gospel, in compliance with the terms of its charter, made no further allowances to the missionaries in the United States, and the northern clergymen were soon thrown entirely on the voluntary support of their people, who hitherto had only assisted the grants of the society. The endowments in Vermont, which the want of clergy had hitherto rendered unserviceable, were applied to purposes of education, and ultimately in Virginia an unjust sentence took away the remaining glebes and many of the houses of worship. Great numbers of people who formerly were considered members of the Church of England, had forsaken it in its evil day, and attached themselves to the popular sectarianism. Many of the loyalists, laity as well as clergy, had gone to reside in England, Nova Scotia, or Canada. Thus, both in the North and South, the Church was fearfully weakened, and in some places almost annihilated. The churches were in ruins, or closed, or deserted; there was no centre of unity, and not a shadow of ecclesiastical government existed.

CHAP. V.

THE CHURCH REVIVED.

CONDITION OF THE CHURCH AFTER THE REVOLUTION.—DENMARK OFFERS
LUTHERAN ORDINATION.—CONSECRATION OF BISHOP SEABURY.—FOR-
MATION OF THE GENERAL CONVENTION.—ADMISSION OF THE LAITY.—
REVISION OF THE LITURGY.—THE "PROPOSED BOOK."—REMONSTRANCE
OF THE ENGLISH BISHOPS.—ELECTION AND CONSECRATION OF BISHOPS
WHITE AND PROVOOST.—INTERVIEW WITH GEORGE III.—FORMATION OF
THE HOUSE OF BISHOPS.—FINAL ADOPTION OF THE PRAYER-BOOK.

HOSE who regard the Church as merely
a function of the State must think that
our communion in America ought to
have come to an end simultaneously
with the prostration of those powers
by which it had been hitherto in some measure
supported. But there was in it a principle of independent life which quickly showed itself. The
storm passed away, and the labourers returned to
their work. After the recognition of independence
by England, the clergy who had been loyal to the
king and parliament could pray with a good conscience for the President and Congress, though the
old ties between Church and State did not exist. Whatever might have been their opinions as to the Revolution,
they could now unite with their people in measures
for the good of their common country. Separation

from England having been accomplished, their attachment to the king during the recent contest was no longer a just occasion of suspicion or maltreatment. Many of the refugees returned, and found less difficulty than might have been expected in co-operating with those of their brethren who had adopted the popular cause. Yet the whole number of the remaining clergy was very small, and certainly was considerably below two hundred. Even in this remnant there were divisions of opinion affecting the very essence of churchmanship. In the Northern States, the absence of an establishment and the reaction against Puritan congregationalism had led the clergy and their people to set a high value on all the strong and distinctive peculiarities of the Church as opposed to dissent. In the South, where the Church in former times had been taken for granted and her authority little questioned, attention had been less directed to the real foundations on which her authority rests, and too many were radically unsound in their views, not only of episcopacy and the sacraments, but of other important parts of the Christian scheme. Some of the more zealous of the Virginian clergy had even assisted in building up the rival system of Methodism, which then professed communion with the Establishment. After the Revolution, however, Dr. Coke, appointed by Wesley superintendent of that connection in America, assumed to be a bishop, and ordained one Asbury as his colleague. The Methodists consequently became a separate sect, contrary to the protestations of their founder. It might be questioned whether the somewhat discordant materials which existed in the Church itself could ever be brought into union ; and, in short, the same difficulty was to be surmounted in ecclesiastical affairs which the States had successfully encountered in politics. We shall now consider the constructive process by which, under Divine Providence, the desired result was accomplished.

I have already mentioned the Rev. William White as having become chaplain to Congress in the darkest days of the revolutionary struggle. At the close of the war he was the sole remaining clergyman in Philadelphia, where his presence contributed to turn aside the angry jealousy with which the Church was regarded. Washington himself was his friend, and a regular worshipper at his church. At one time, perceiving the ministry of the Church " gradually approaching to annihilation " while no prospect appeared of obtaining a bishop, he had proposed a scheme for uniting the American congregations in a Convention, and, on behalf of the whole body, committing to a clerical president a power of conferring a kind of provisional ordination. Most happily this dangerous idea never came into effect, and, after the acknowledgment of independence, Dr. White's main object was to gather together the scattered members of the Church, with a view to a joint application to the mother-country for the consecration of bishops.

Soon after the cessation of hostilities, several young gentlemen of the South, who had been educated with a view to holy orders, embarked for England, and applied to Dr. Lowth, then Bishop of London, for ordination. An obstacle at once appeared. The laws of England forbade the ordination of those who could not take the oath of allegiance to the king. The bishop was therefore obliged to apply for a special Act of Parliament allowing him to dispense with this requirement in cases like that now before him. While the success of his application was doubtful, John Adams, once the New England schoolmaster, and now the American minister at the Court of St. James, mentioned to the Danish minister, then in London, the case of the American candidates. This led to a kindly intended offer on the part of the Lutheran bishops in Denmark, who declared their willingness to ordain the young men, on condition of their subscribing such Articles of the Church of England as are purely theological. But, as Parliament consented to Bishop Lowth's request, the questionable Danish episcopate was not employed, and the ordinations finally took place under the same episcopacy with which America had been connected from the beginning.

It was, however, very plain that the American Church could not remain dependent on the good offices of a prelate residing in a land which was now foreign. It became more than ever desirable that it should have bishops of its own, and as separation from England had removed the political objections, the scheme was again taken up with a view to practical measures. Here, however, a difference of opinion manifested itself. In Connecticut it was thought that nothing ought to be attempted in the way of organisation until a bishop had been obtained, while, in the Middle States, it was considered that the first step should be the formation of an association under which the churches might act as a body, the old medium of connection through the Bishop of London having been destroyed. Soon after the ratification of the treaty of peace, the clergy in Connecticut assembled again in a voluntary Convention, as they had been accustomed to do in the colonial times, and elected as their bishop Dr. Samuel Seabury, lately a missionary of the Society for the Propagation of the Gospel. The election was easily accomplished; but the main point was, of course, the *consecration*, to which, as yet, the way was by no means open. The well-instructed friends of Seabury firmly believed in a succession transmitted from a source coeval with Christianity itself. They held that as truly as all men are descended from the first parents of mankind, so truly the bishops of the Church Catholic are descended from the original pastors of the Christian world. They knew that by the law of nature every man had his two parents, and that in order to prove a succession of men from Adam to the present time, it was by no means necessary to trace every particular link of the chain. So, in like manner, they were satisfied that, by the constant law of the Church, every true bishop had his ecclesiastical progenitors in the bishops who consecrated him, and that the successive steps, connected as they are with various lines of descent, might safely be taken for granted.

It was hoped that consecration might be obtained in England, and accordingly Dr. Seabury sailed for this

country, bearing a certificate of his election, together
with letters from America earnestly requesting the
boon which during a century and a half had been
asked in vain.   But he arrived here at an unfavourable
time, the relations between this country and her late
colonies being new and uncertain, and the government
fearing * " lest any apparent interference on their part
should stir up the jealousy of new-born independence."
The see of Canterbury was then vacant, and the Archbishop of York was unable to take measures for the
consecration of an American citizen without the authority of Parliament.   As it was evident that, at all
events, a long delay was unavoidable, Dr. Seabury, following the advice of Dr. Berkeley (son of the great
Bishop Berkeley), the late Dr. Routh of Magdalen
College, and other sound divines, proceeded to Scotland,
where he applied for consecration to the bishops of
the " Scottish Episcopal Church," a communion which
had maintained a true succession, though long trodden
down by established dissent.   He produced a copy of
the recent law of Connecticut, enabling episcopal congregations to transact their own ecclesiastical affairs,
and proved that the number of those congregations in
that State now exceeded seventy, and composed a body
of nearly 40,000 persons.   After overcoming several,
difficulties, Dr. Seabury was solemnly consecrated at
Aberdeen, on the 14th of November, 1784, by the
Bishops of Aberdeen, Ross, and Moray.   Subsequently

* Bishop of Oxford's "American Church," p. 196.

to the consecration, he signed, on behalf of the Church in Connecticut, certain articles which might serve as a basis for permanent fraternal intercourse between the Churches in Scotland and America, and engaged to favour the introduction into America of the Scottish communion service. In the beginning of the summer of 1785, he was again in Connecticut, and soon afterwards entered on the duties of his new office. He met with no disrespect; but the Puritan ministers seemed rather alarmed, and, in order to neutralise his influence, gave one another the title of bishops, which formerly they had reprobated.

In 1783, the Church in Maryland assembled in Convention, and declared that she " possessed the right to preserve and complete herself as an entire Church, agreeably to her ancient usages and professions, and that the churches, chapels, glebes, and other property formerly belonging to the Church of England, belonged to that Church and were secured to it for ever."

In the mean time the clergy of the Middle States had pursued their separate plan. A few of them having met, in May 1784, at Brunswick in New Jersey, in order * to renew a charitable society, it was determined to hold a larger meeting in New York, with the view of agreeing on some general principles of union between all the episcopal churches in the United States.

About the same time the clergy and laity of Pennsylvania assembled and agreed to certain fundamental

* Bishop White's " Memoirs of the Episcopal Church," p. 11.

principles favourable to the independence of the American Church, the continuance of the former doctrines and worship, the ministry of bishops, priests, and deacons, and the enactment of general canons or laws by a representative body of the clergy and laity conjointly. Resolutions of a like nature were adopted in Maryland in the summer of 1784, and in Massachusetts in the following September. In South Carolina a tardy consent to apply for the episcopate was clogged with a condition (now long since abandoned) that no bishop should reside within her borders. In the South generally, there was far too much of this unreasonable jealousy, which grew out of the general prostration of authority. It was evident that the Church needed some leading person who (like Washington in the State) should, by patience, wisdom, and moderation, combine men of various parties in a general alliance. Such a man the Church now found in the friend of Washington, William White.

In October, 1784, the meeting proposed by the more informal assembly at Brunswick took place at New York. It consisted of fifteen clergy and eleven laymen, from New York, New Jersey, Pennsylvania, Delaware, Maryland, and Virginia. These gentlemen agreed in recommending the following principles of ecclesiastical union * : —

First. — That there shall be a General Convention of the Episcopal Church in the United States of America.

* Bishop White's "Memoirs of the Episcopal Church," p. 66.

Second.—That the Episcopal Church in each State shall send deputies to the Convention, consisting of Clergy and Laity.

Third.—That associated congregations, in two or more States, may send deputies jointly.

Fourth.—That the said Church shall maintain the doctrines of the Gospel as now held by the Church of England, and shall adhere to the liturgy of the said Church as far as shall be consistent with the American Revolution and the constitutions of the respective States.

Fifth.—That in every State where there shall be a bishop duly consecrated and settled, he shall be considered a member of the Convention *ex officio*.

Sixth.—That the clergy and laity, assembled in convention, shall deliberate in one body, but shall vote separately; and the concurrence of both shall be necessary to give validity to every measure.

Seventh.—That the first meeting of the Convention shall be at Philadelphia, on the Tuesday before the feast of St. Michael next; to which it is hoped and earnestly desired that the episcopal churches in the several States will send their clerical and lay deputies, duly instructed and authorised to proceed on the necessary business herein proposed for their deliberation.

There was in Connecticut and elsewhere a strong prejudice against Dr. White's favourite measure, the embracing of the laity in a scheme for ecclesiastical legislation. But from what he had read of primitive usage, Dr. White considered * that in very early times,

* Memoirs, p. 76.

when the Christian people in every city (with the surrounding district) were an ecclesiastical commonwealth, the body of the people had a considerable share in the determinations of the church. From the fifteenth chapter of the Acts of the Apostles, he gathered that the decree of the council at Jerusalem was accompanied by the consent of the laity. Hence he argued that the people might lawfully give by representation the same sanction which they gave originally in a body. If, then, the principle of lay representation were lawful, the propriety of adopting it ought to be determined by expediency. That it was expedient he judged first from its being a natural consequence of the principle of following the Church of England in all the leading points of her doctrine, discipline, and worship. " We could in no other way," he says, " have had a substitute for the parliamentary sanction to legislative acts of power. Such a sanction is pleaded for by Mr. Hooker and others, as rendered proper by the reason of the thing and the principles of the British constitution. . . . Bishop Warburton says : — ' There was no absurdity in that custom which continued during the Saxon government and some time after, which admitted the laity into ecclesiastical synods; there appearing to be much the same reasons for laymen sitting in Convocation, as for churchmen sitting in Parliament.' "

A second reason for a lay element in synods was found in the great doubt which existed as to the practicability of commending episcopacy to the people in any other way. " The prejudices," says Dr. White, "of even some of the members of our own Church against the name, and much more against the office of bishop, and, added to this, the outcry which had been made on former occasions by persons of other denominations, that not spiritual powers only but civil also were intended, rendered it very uncertain whether we could accomplish the design without engaging in the measure such a description of gentlemen as might give it weight, and show to the world that nothing inimical either to civil or to religious rights was in contemplation."

A third and equally cogent argument, as stated by the same writer, was the following: — " Without the order of laity permanently making a part of our assemblies, it were much to be apprehended that the laymen would never be brought to submit to any of our ecclesiastical laws in such points as might affect the interests or the convenience of any of them, which it is evident might happen in very many cases: for instance, admission to the communion and exclusion from it. And they would have the principles and the practice of England to plead in their favour."

On the 25th of September, 1785, the first General Convention, as previously arranged, assembled in Philadelphia. Members were present from New York, New Jersey, Pennsylvania, Delaware, Maryland, Virginia, and South Carolina. Connecticut was not represented; and Bishop Seabury declined to attend, fearing the adoption of dangerous measures, and disliking especially the admission of the laity. The principal subjects which came before the meeting were the general con-

K

stitution of the proposed union, the formation of a
common liturgy, and the obtaining of an American
episcopate. "Never," says the Bishop of Oxford, "had
so strange a sight been seen before in Christendom as
this necessity of various members knitting themselves
together into one by such a conscious and voluntary act.
In all other cases the unity of the common episcopate
had held such limbs together.   But this common bond
we had left wanting in our colonies, and it was the want
of this which had thus dismembered their communion."   The measures which were now adopted, though
without precedent and open to grave theoretical objections, were probably the wisest which could have
been chosen under the circumstances, and in fact resulted in the complete union of the American Church.
The times were, in many respects, exceedingly unpro-
pitious.   In regard to politics the people were in an
angry and unsettled state; and having lately overthrown
the ancient authority of the sovereign, they were about
to revise the articles of their political confederation,
and to form a new constitution for the United States.
In regard to Church affairs, the standard of doctrine in
England was by no means elevated, and latitudinarian
ideas were generally fashionable.   It could not be
expected that deeper principles should prevail in
America, where the sects were in the ascendant, and
French infidelity was already exerting a powerful
influence.   Yet this was the period in which our
brethren were under the absolute necessity of settling
their form of worship and their mode of Church

government. All might have been lost, but through Divine mercy much was saved and much was gained. The moderate and conciliatory course of Dr. White, as president of the Convention, contributed more than any other earthly cause to this happy consummation.

At this meeting most of the articles of union were ratified which had been proposed in the informal meeting at New York in the preceding year. An ecclesiastical constitution was likewise framed, which was made to agree as closely as possible with the new constitution of the country. It was arranged that as every State had its own civil legislature, so in every State the churchmen should have their separate Convention. In like manner, as the American nation had its Congress, the American Church was to have its triennial General Convention, consisting of a clerical and lay deputation, four of each order, from the several States. It was also provided that when there should be a bishop, he should be a member of the Convention by virtue of his office ; that the clergy should be accountable to the ecclesiastical authority in the State only to which they should respectively belong; and that the engagement previous to ordination should be a declaration of belief in the Holy Scriptures, and a promise of conformity to the doctrines and worship of the Church.

In regard to the liturgy, it had been proposed at New York that only such changes should be allowed as had been made necessary by the altered political circumstances of the country. But the friends of liturgical revision, who should, in all reason, have waited for

the presence of the episcopate, thought the opportunity
too favourable to be lost, and a Mr. Page, afterwards
governor of Virginia, began by proposing to strike out
the first four petitions in the Litany, for the alleged
reason that the word "Trinity" is not found in Scripture.   This proposal did not ultimately prevail; but
discussions followed, more or less painful, on the Thirty-
nine Articles, on the doctrines of justification, predestination, and original sin, and on various rubrics and
liturgical expressions.   Great objections were alleged
against the Article in the Apostles' Creed, "He descended into Hell," as well as against the public use of
the Nicene and Athanasian Creeds.   Very unwisely, a
service was appointed for the 4th of July, as a thanksgiving for American independence, the effect of which,
had it been allowed to remain, would have been to alie-
nate from the Convention many who had been loyal
during the war. The result of the discussions was that a
"Proposed Prayer-book," having been hastily drawn up
and printed, was afterwards sent to the Church Conventions of the several States for their approval.   In
some of the proposed changes Dr. White heartily concurred, while others were carried in opposition to his
wishes and advice.

    There was much more agreement in regard to the
third and most important point, the obtaining of
bishops, and that too notwithstanding the sneer of the
worldly-wise Benjamin Franklin, who said that "men
would one day learn not to be dependent upon other
countries, but would make their own bishops for them-

selves." * It was resolved that, although Dr. Seabury's consecration was doubtless valid, the succession
should be sought from England rather than from
Scotland. Accordingly † the Convention addressed the
archbishops and bishops of England, stating that the
Episcopal Church in the United States had been severed
by a civil revolution from the jurisdiction of the
parent Church in England ; acknowledging the favours
formerly received from the Bishop of London in particular, and from the Society for Propagating the
Gospel ; declaring their desire to perpetuate among
them the principles of the Church of England in doctrine, discipline, and worship ; and praying that their
lordships would consecrate to the episcopacy those
persons who should be sent with that view from the
churches in any of the States respectively. A committee was appointed with various powers, among which
was that of corresponding with the archbishops and
bishops of England during the recess. The Convention
finally adjourned to meet in Philadelphia on the 20th
of June, 1786.

By some neglect the proposed alterations in the
Prayer-book were not communicated to the English
prelates, who were left to form their opinion of them
from private correspondence and public rumour.

The address was forwarded by the committee to John
Adams, the American minister in London, together

---

* From a sermon by the Rev. Dr. Shelton, of Buffalo.
† Bishop White's Memoirs, p. 14.

with certificates from the governors of several States, showing that no political objections now existed in America to the proposed consecrations. Mr. Adams was requested to deliver these papers to the Archbishop of Canterbury, and to forward the object of them as far as lay in his power. Though not himself a churchman, and though fully aware that he risked his popularity with the sects at home, this gentleman honourably performed his commission, and met his reward when afterwards he came to occupy the high position of President of the United States.

Early in 1786 an answer was received in America, signed by the Archbishop and eighteen of the bishops, in which those eminent persons declared their wish to comply with the request, but wisely stated that they must delay measures to that effect until they should have become fully acquainted with the changes intended by the Convention. The letter closed in the following words: " While we are anxious to give every proof not only of our brotherly affection but of our facility in forwarding your wishes, we cannot but be extremely cautious lest we should be the instruments of establishing an ecclesiastical system which will be called a branch of the Church of England, but afterwards may possibly appear to have departed from it essentially either in doctrine or discipline."

After this letter had been despatched, the " Proposed Prayer-book " was received by the two Archbishops, and underwent their careful examination. In a letter addressed to the Convention they stated that they saw

with grief not only various unnecessary verbal alterations, but the entire omission of two of the Creeds and
the mutilation of the third. Nevertheless they had
agreed on presenting a bill to Parliament, and hoped
soon to be enabled to consecrate for America. In the
mean time they earnestly exhorted the Convention to
restore the Apostles' Creed to its integrity, and to give
the other two Creeds a place in the Prayer-book, even
though the use of them were left discretional. They
also objected to an article in the constitution, which
seemed to degrade the clerical and even the episcopal
character, by making the clergy accountable to a mixed
lay and clerical assembly in the State to which they
might happen to belong. Hints were added as to the
care that should be taken in the choice of those who
were to be elected bishops, and the Convention was re-
minded that the credit of the English Church was
involved in that of her American daughter.

During the spring of 1786, the "Proposed Prayer-
book" was considered by Conventions in the several
States. Everywhere it proved a subject of controversy,
and appeared likely to endanger the union so aus-
piciously commenced. In New York nothing was decided on the subject, but the matter was kept open for
consideration. In New Jersey the book was rejected.
In Pennsylvania and Maryland some amendments were
proposed. In South Carolina it was received without
limitation. In Virginia it was adopted, but great objections were made to the rubric which still empowered
the minister to reject evil-livers from the Holy Com-

munion.   On the whole it was evident that, in regard to the Liturgy, the labours of the General Convention had thus far proved a failure.

After the receipt of the first letter from the English prelates, the General Convention assembled in Philadelphia on the 20th of June, 1786, under circumstances of considerable embarrassment.   The churches in the different States had given instructions to their delegates which greatly interfered with their freedom of action.   There were also the controversies respecting the proposed book, the objections made by some to the Scottish ordination of two clergymen in the Convention, and the demur expressed in the important communication from England.   It was now confidently predicted by her enemies that the Church would fall to pieces, but happily the difficulties were all surmounted.   The system of receiving instructions from the State Conventions of the Church was evidently so fruitful of discord, that it was forthwith abandoned.   The questions as to the proposed book were allowed to rest for the present, and the objections to Scottish ordination were met in a way calculated to obviate future difficulty with Bishop Seabury and his clergy.   The article in the constitution which would apparently make a bishop amenable to the laity was amended before the English objections to it arrived.   In regard to the only letter received from the English bishops, little more could be done at the time beyond repeating the application for the episcopacy, and reasserting the attachment of the Convention to the well-understood system of the Church.   As to the Liturgy, the Convention wrote, " We have made no alterations or omissions but such as our civil constitution required, and such as were calculated to remove objections. It is well known that many great and pious men of the Church of England have long wished for a revision of the Liturgy, which it was deemed imprudent to hazard, lest it might become a precedent for repeated and improper alterations. This is with us the proper season for such a revision. We are now settling and ordering the affairs of our Church, and if wisely done, we shall have reason to promise ourselves all the advantages that can result from stability and union."

Soon after the rising of the Convention the letter, already mentioned, from the two Archbishops was received by the committee. Shortly afterwards there came a letter from the Archbishop of Canterbury alone, enclosing an Act of Parliament just obtained, which authorised the solicited consecrations, but provided that no person ordained by bishops consecrated in virtue of this Act should thereby be empowered to officiate within the British dominions. On the receipt of the Act the committee summoned the Convention to reassemble on the 10th of October. At this meeting it appeared that there was a general desire to comply as far as possible with the wishes of the English prelates, and without debate it was resolved to replace the Nicene Creed in the Prayer-book, to stand after the Apostles' Creed, with permission to use either. The clause in the latter Creed, of the " descent into hell," occasioned much debate, but it was finally restored. On some minor points the Convention adhered to its former judgment, as well as on the liturgical employment of the Athanasian Creed, though the doctrinal statements of that formulary respecting the Trinity were fully admitted.

It appeared that Dr. White had been chosen bishop by the Convention of the Church in Pennsylvania, Dr. Griffith by that of Virginia, and Dr. Provoost by that of New York. The General Convention now signed the testimonials of these gentlemen, according to a form provided by the Archbishop of Canterbury, and Drs. White and Provoost soon afterwards embarked for England. Dr. Griffith was prevented by poverty from accompanying them, and as the Church in Virginia did not furnish him with the necessary means, he was under the necessity of resigning his appointment.

The election of Dr. Provoost proved equally unfortunate, but for a different reason. His orthodoxy and zeal were very questionable, and fifteen years after his consecration he retired from the duties of his office. He was elected mainly because it was supposed that his ultra-democratic opinions would induce the people to tolerate him the more readily in his episcopal character.

The two bishops elect sailed from New York on the 2nd of November, and, after a pleasant and speedy voyage of eighteen days, landed at Falmouth on the 20th. They met with various delays, and did not reach London until the 29th, when they made it their first business to call on Mr. Adams. By this gentleman they were introduced to the Archbishop of Canterbury;

who received them in the kindest manner, and promised to fix as early a date as possible for the consecration. Some days afterwards they waited on the Bishop of London, the learned Dr. Lowth, who was then in decaying health and near his decease. Dr. White also tried to have a conversation with John Wesley in reference to the design, then lately adopted, of withdrawing the Methodists in America from the communion of the Church. Wesley, however, treated him rather unceremoniously, and the desired interview never took place. Wesley's brother Charles was more courteous, and in a conversation with Dr. White expressed himself strongly against the proposed separation.

As the consecration was to be performed under the consent of the king, it was thought proper that the candidates should be presented at court. Accordingly the Archbishop took them to the palace in his coach, and the late chaplain of the "rebel Congress" was introduced to the sovereign whom the Declaration of Independence had denounced as a tyrannical despot. Dr. White * gives the following account of the interview :—

" While we were waiting in our places until the king should come to us in his passing from one to another, there occurred an additional instance of the attention of the Archbishop to the delicacy of our situation. ' When the king speaks to you,' said he, ' you will only bow;' adding, with a smile, ' When an Eng-

---

* Memoirs, p. 157.

lish bishop is presented, he does something more.' On being introduced to the king, I made this preconceived address, that 'We were happy in the opportunity of thanking his majesty for his licence, granted to his grace the Archbishop, to convey the episcopal succession to the Church in America.' The king made this answer, which I set down, to show the kindness of the archbishop : 'His grace has given me such an account of the gentlemen who have come over, that I am glad of the present opportunity of serving the interests of religion.' His majesty then asked Dr. Provoost whether the episcopal communion was not numerous in New York, and was answered by the doctor in the affirmative, with further thanks for the licence granted. The king then passed to the next in the circle, and after a little while we withdrew with the Archbishop."

On Sunday, February 4th, the consecration took place in the chapel of the Archbishop's palace at Lambeth, the congregation present consisting of very few persons in addition to the family and the house-hold. On the following day the new bishops left London, and after a journey of five days arrived at Falmouth. Here they embarked on the 17th, and after a voyage of seven weeks, including the whole of the stormy month of March, safely landed at New York on Easter Sunday, April 7th, thankful to God for their personal protection, and for the obtaining of the long-sought American episcopate.

The triennial General Convention assembled in July, 1789, Bishop White presiding, when it appeared that

Dr. Bass had been elected bishop of the Church in Massachusetts and New Hampshire. The Convention resolved that as there were already three bishops in America, including Bishop Seabury, those bishops were fully competent to consecrate other bishops, to ordain priests and deacons, and to govern the Church according to the canons. It was thought fit, however, to defer the consecration of Dr. Bass until the churches of New England should have united themselves with the general body. It was also determined that as soon as three bishops should be members of the Convention, the episcopal order should constitute a separate house, corresponding, in some measure, with the Senate of the United States, or with the Upper House of Convocation in England. It was arranged that either house should have the power of originating acts, and that the non-assent of the Upper House should negative all acts to which four-fifths of the Lower House did not still adhere. In order that the desired union might be accomplished, the Convention adjourned for two months, and met again on the 29th of September, when, to the joy of all sincere churchmen, Bishop Seabury appeared with several of the clergy from Massachusetts and Connecticut. The House of Bishops was accordingly formed, and the Convention proceeded to the enactment of such canons as existing circumstances required, the canons of the Church of England, which had never been more than partially binding in the colonies, being considered as abrogated by the separation between the two countries. Bishop Seabury gave up his opposition to the admission of the laity to synodical powers when he found that only *legislative* and not *judicial* powers were contemplated by the Convention. But unhappily, the rules of the Church of England respecting Matrimony and Divorce being considered as virtually abolished, the American Church was left destitute of any authoritative regulations on these important subjects. To this day the defect remains unsupplied, and the marriage laws of the several States, generally lax and inconsistent, seem practically the only rule. Hence divorces are too readily obtained, and the marriage of divorced persons and marriage with a deceased wife's sister, though hardly deemed respectable, are more frequent than could be wished.

The alterations in the Prayer-book now came under discussion, and the presence of Bishop Seabury proved to be of the utmost importance. The Lower House, recognising neither the authority of the " Proposed Book," nor of the English Prayer-book, undertook the perilous course of framing a new liturgy, and accordingly appointed committees to prepare a morning and evening prayer, a litany, a communion service, and other offices. The value of the House of Bishops was now seen, though consisting of only two members, Bishop Provoost absenting himself from the deliberations, and rendering himself troublesome alike to Bishop Seabury and to Bishop White. Representing, as they did, the two schools of theology prevailing in the Church, these two good men acted together harmoniously, the latter cheerfully resigning the pre-

cedency to the former by reason of his seniority in point
of consecration. The laity, then as now, generally
strengthened the hands of the bishops, and such proposals as might justly be considered rash and ill-advised
too often emanated from the ranks of the clergy. As
a body, there is no reason to doubt that the members
of the Convention acted from pure motives, and according to the best light which they had. Yet Bishop White
tells us that a bystander who had heard some of the
discussions made the following remark:—"When I hear
these things, I look back to the origin of the Prayer-
book, and represent to myself the spirits of its venerable
compilers ascending to heaven in the flames of martyrdom that consumed their bodies. I then look at the
improvers of this book in . . . . and . . . . and . . . .
The consequence is, that I am not sanguine in my expectations of your meditated changes in the Liturgy."

The two bishops, acting on a different principle from
the Lower House, determined to regard the English
offices as the basis of the work, and to discourage all
changes but those which were obviously necessary or
clearly expedient. All of the original was to remain,
excepting where definitely altered. In carrying out
this principle they were in some points obliged to yield,
while in others the Lower House gave way to their
suggestions. Hence the work jointly accomplished
was to a great extent the result of compromise. The
changes now made " show," says the Bishop of Oxford,
" the great peril of attempting to improve fixed and
ascertained forms; for they are marked by a tendency

to opposite extremes." Yet the American Prayer-book is substantially identical with that of the Church of England, and we have reason to be thankful that, under Divine Providence, the work of our Reformers passed safely through a trying ordeal, and commended itself to the religious feelings and convictions of independent America.

Dr. Bass was not consecrated at this time, since Bishop White considered himself bound to carry on the English line of consecration without the admixture of the non-juring element involved in Bishop Seabury's episcopate. It appeared to him, therefore, a necessary preliminary, either that the Archbishop of Canterbury should release him from this supposed engagement, or that another American bishop should be consecrated in England, three bishops being required by the ancient canons to consecrate a fourth. The difficulty was solved in the way last mentioned, for, in 1790, Dr. Madison, bishop elect of Virginia, was consecrated at Lambeth, and afterwards took part with Bishops White and Provoost in consecrating Dr. Claggett for Maryland, Bishop Seabury assisting in the imposition of hands. Dr. Smith was consecrated in 1795 for South Carolina (which had consented to admit a bishop), and Dr. Bass for Massachusetts in 1797. The Church system was now becoming more consolidated, and its subsequent progress will be traced hereafter. In the mean time it may be well to consider the liturgy, constitution, worship, and general arrangements of the American Church as they exist at present.

CHAP. VI.

LITURGICAL REVISION.

RULE OF THE CHURCH OF ENGLAND.—THE SAME RULE IN AMERICA.—
ENGLISH REVIEW OF 1689.—CHANGES CAUSED BY THE REVOLUTION —
BY A DESIRE TO IMPROVE — BY CONNECTION WITH SCOTLAND.

T may be important to notice that, in the alterations made in the Prayer-book, the American Church was only following a course which had been in a great measure marked out by the acknowledged principles and practice of the mother Church. The Church of England, in the Preface to her Prayer-book, has laid down as a rule that "the particular forms of divine worship and the rites and ceremonies appointed to be used therein, being things in their own nature indifferent and and alterable, and so acknowledged, it is but reasonable that upon weighty and important considerations, according to the various exigencies of times and occasions, such changes and alterations should be made therein, as to those who are in places of authority should, from time to time, seem either necessary or expedient." The practice of the Church of England has been in con-

formity with this principle. We find that "seeking to
keep the happy mean between too much stiffness in
refusing, and too much easiness in admitting, variations
in things once advisedly established, she hath in the
reign of several princes, since the first compiling of her
liturgy in the time of Edward VI., yielded to make
such alterations in some particulars as in the respective
times were thought convenient."

The last review of the English Prayer-book was made
in 1661, when, after various alterations and additions,
the book received its present form. A commission for
a further review was issued in 1689, shortly after the
accession of William III., and consisted of ten bishops
and twenty other divines, who assembled in the Jerusalem Chamber. The commissioners aimed chiefly at
conciliating the dissenters, and proposed a number of
sweeping alterations.   Some of them were as follows :—

> Non-conforming ministers joining the Church to
> be *conditionally* ordained.
> Chanting in cathedrals to be abolished.
> The Absolution to be read by Deacons as well as
> Priests.
> The Communion to be administered to persons
> while sitting in their pews, if they prefer it.
> The *Gloria Patri* to be used at the end of the last
> Psalm for the day, not at the end of each
> Psalm.
> The versicles after the Lord's Prayer to be said
> kneeling.

Sponsors and the sign of the Cross to be omitted if the parents should desire such omission.

The use of the Athanasian Creed to be left to the discretion of each minister.

The substitution of canonical for apocryphal lessons.

The removal of legendary saints' days from the calendar.

The revision of the Table of Lessons.

The omission of all high titles of the king or queen, such as " most religious," or " high and mighty," as well as of the supplication that the sovereign may " vanquish and overcome all his enemies."

Some of the proposed changes were no doubt defensible; but Convocation was determined not to sanction them, and the measure came to nothing.   The document containing the alterations as projected by the commissioners, though long kept private in the Lambeth library, became ultimately the basis of many modifications in the American Prayer-book.   It will be seen, however, that some of the most objectionable parts of the scheme found no favour beyond the Atlantic.

In their anxiety to commend the Church to the hearts and judgments of the American people, the members of the early General Conventions seem to have admitted three leading principles.*   The first was that the Revolution made some alterations necessary; the

---

* Church Review, Jan. 1859.

second, that the services might be safely and wisely shortened; and the third, that where words and phrases had lost their meaning, had ceased to convey truth to common minds, or had become associated with low ideas, they might sometimes be varied. The alterations finally decided upon may however be rendered more intelligible if arranged under appropriate heads.

Under the *first* head we may enumerate those which were occasioned by political circumstances. The forms of prayer for " Gunpowder Treason," King Charles's Martyrdom, the Restoration, and the King's Accession, together with the prayers for the Royal Family, were of course omitted. Even the thanksgiving for the American Revolution, substituted in place of them, was soon abolished, though at first it met with favour in some quarters. The prayer for the king after the third collect, with some alterations, became a prayer for the President. Kings, princes, and lords being associated in the public mind with lions and tigers and other savage beasts*, the words " High and Mighty King of kings, Lord of lords, the only Ruler of princes," were changed to " the High and Mighty Ruler of the universe." In the Litany, a petition for all Christian rulers and magistrates was substituted for those respecting the sovereign, the royal family, and the nobility. The prayer for Parliament was applied with little alteration to Congress, while the State Legislatures were unaccountably left unnoticed. In the prayer for

---

* See Jefferson's Works.

the Church militant, the petition for the king and council was changed to a prayer for all Christian rulers In the Articles, the twenty-first, thirty-sixth, and thirty-seventh, being political in their character, were set aside. In the Catechism, "honour and obey the king" was changed to "honour and obey the civil authority."

A *second* class of alterations consists of those which appear to have been suggested by the proposals of King William's commissioners of 1689.

Thus, the *Gloria Patri* was *allowed* to be omitted at the end of each Psalm, and was *required* to be used only at the end of the Psalms, the *Gloria In Excelsis* being permitted as a substitute. The versicles after the Lord's Prayer, previously repeated by the priest standing, were wholly set aside, and the Lord's Prayer in that place omitted. On the same principle it was provided that the Lord's Prayer should not be used more than once in the course of the morning or evening prayer. The hundredth Psalm was placed before *Benedicite,* and only the first four verses of the latter were retained. In the evening prayer *Magnificat* and *Nunc Dimittis* were omitted, and *Cantate Domino* and *Benedic Anima Mea* substituted. Parents were allowed to be sponsors to their own children, and the sign of the Cross was suffered to be omitted if the sponsors should express a wish to that effect, a case which has very seldom, if ever, occurred. The Athanasian Creed was removed from liturgical use, the Commination service was abolished, and the reference to Judas in the exhortation before the Communion struck out. In the exhortation at the Communion service, the whole passage respecting eating and drinking our own damnation, and the plaguing with divers diseases and deaths, was also expunged. The Apocryphal chapters were struck from the table of daily lessons, and the use of them was restricted to Saints' Days. The Calendar was altered by removing the names of all Saints for whose days a special service had not been provided. The arrangement of the Sunday lessons in general was changed. It was appointed that from Septuagesima to Easter, passages from the Prophets of a penitential character should be read; from Easter to Whitsunday, chapters from the Prophets appropriate to the season; and from Trinity Sunday to the twenty-second Sunday after Trinity, selections from the historical books. Lessons from the New Testament were specially appointed for every Sunday in the year. The petition for victory over enemies was laid aside in the prayer for the President, together with all words expressive of personal character in the chief magistrate, such as "most religious and gracious." In like manner, in the Burial service the words " *dear* brother" are changed into "deceased brother;" "in sure and certain hope of the resurrection," to " looking for the general resurrection;" while the sentence " as our hope is this our brother doth " is altogether omitted. No wish was however expressed to admit dissenting ministers by *conditional* ordination, as recommended in 1689. Chanting was *not* abolished, nor were deacons allowed to read the Absolution, nor was the communion suffered to be administered to persons in their pews, nor otherwise than according to the English rubric.

A *third* class of alterations must be ascribed to a wish to avoid mistakes growing out of the popular but incorrect associations attached to particular words.

There was, for example, the objection before noticed as to the words " *He descended into Hell.*" Although the wish of the English bishops was so far complied with, that these words were permitted to retain their former place in the Apostles' Creed, yet a rubric was prefixed allowing any churches to omit those words, or to use instead of them the words, " *He went into the place of departed spirits.*"

It must, however, be noted, that in the Baptismal service the question is, " Dost thou believe *all* the articles of the Christian faith as contained in the Apostles' Creed ? " In the Catechism the child is taught to rehearse the articles of his belief exactly as in the English book; and the same form is repeated in the Visitation of the Sick.

Many persons, not content with the doctrine of Scripture which teaches that Christ alone is our *High* Priest, denied that men could properly be priests at all. Even the word " priest," like. " prelate," had come to be vulgarly associated with all that is bad, repulsive, and disagreeable. Accordingly we notice, here and there in the rubrics, the substitution of " presbyter " for " priest," though generally the latter word remains as in the English book. A graver alteration is seen in the " Absolution " at the commencement of daily prayer, the title of which was altered to " Declaration of Absolution." The Absolution in the " Visitation of the Sick " was struck out, as well as the rubric requiring that the sick person "shall be moved to make a special confession of his sins, if he feel his conscience troubled with any weighty matter."

In the Catechism the words " verily and indeed taken and received " were changed to " spiritually taken and received." In the first exhortation before the Communion service, the words "discreet and learned," as applied to the minister, are omitted, as well as the subsequent reference to " the benefit of absolution." In the Ordinal, the words " Receive ye the Holy Ghost," and " whose sins thou dost forgive they are forgiven," &c., were allowed to remain; but any bishop was permitted to substitute another form, viz.: "Take thou authority to execute the office of a priest in the Church of God, now committed to thee by the imposition of our hands."

A *fourth* kind of alterations must be traced to certain ideas of delicacy and refinement which, though sometimes questionable, it was deemed proper to respect. In the *Te Deum*, the second half of the sixteenth verse was changed to " Thou didst humble thyself to be born of a Virgin." In the Litany the eighth petition begins with the words " From all inordinate and sinful affections." The Marriage Service, for a similar reason, was greatly abridged, and the public use of entire chapters of Holy Scripture, though sanctioned by the

Church of England, was abolished. The 127th Psalm was struck from the " Churching " service, and, to save the feelings of the person principally concerned, permission was given to omit the entire service and to substitute a short collect. But the American women have gone even a step beyond this, and have dispensed alike with the service and with the collect.

A *fifth* class of changes originated in a wish for improved grammatical accuracy. " Our Father *which* art in heaven " was changed to " Our Father *who* art in heaven; " as in England the expression in the Creed, "*which* was conceived," had already given place to the present form. " In earth " became " on earth," and " them that trespass," " those who trespass." Throughout the Liturgy, " them which " gave place to " those who." In the Apostles' Creed, " rose again " was altered to " rose," although the former has the sanction of the authorised version of Holy Scripture. Other variations of the same kind might be mentioned, the utility of which may be doubted, while it is certain that they confuse and annoy those who have been accustomed to the older form in England or the colonies.

A *sixth* kind of changes arose from a wish to shorten the service, which in America, considering the great extremes of heat and cold, is often more excusable than it would be in our temperate climate. In that new country, too, where the rural population is widely scattered, persons often come ten or twelve miles to church, and evening prayer frequently follows morning service with only an intermission of half an hour, in order to give the worshippers time to return home by daylight. Greater liberty, therefore, was necessary than in an old and thickly inhabited country like our own. I have already mentioned that the proposal to abolish the first four petitions in the Litany was unsuccessful. The latter part of that service, from " O Christ, hear us," to " We humbly beseech thee," was, however, bracketed, the minister being allowed to omit it at his discretion. The short Absolution in the Communion office was allowed to be substituted for the ordinary one in morning and evening prayer. The Nicene Creed might at any time be substituted for that of the Apostles; but in such cases it was omitted in the Communion service, so that the two are never read during the same morning prayer. The wish to abbreviate may also have assisted in promoting other changes, some of which have been noticed under different headings, such as the abolition of several repetitions of the Lord's Prayer in the same service. The omission of the words " Lighten our darkness " is accounted for by the curious reason that, in country places, evening prayer was often celebrated at one o'clock, in the full blaze of day.

A *seventh* class of alterations grew out of the early connection of the American Church with the Episcopal Church of Scotland through Bishop Seabury. These changes, in their theological bearing, savoured of a school very far from latitudinarian. The most noted instance in the Prayer-book is the approximation of the Communion office to that of the Scottish Episcopal Church. The prayers of Oblation and Invocation, omitted in the second Prayer-book of Edward VI., were restored to the place which they held in the first, and the prayer of consecration was shortened by the omission of the whole passage beginning "Hear us, O merciful Father," and ending with "His most blessed body and blood." The Baptismal Service remained unaltered, as in the English Prayer-book, the Church doctrine respecting regeneration being then little questioned.

Besides the changes mentioned above, there were some new services added. A form for the consecration of churches, similar to that which is commonly used in England, was set forth by authority of the Convention and printed in the Prayer-book. An office was adopted for the institution of ministers into parishes or churches, in which the minister returns public thanks for the Divine promise "to be with the ministers of apostolic succession to the end of the world." A form for the "Visitation of Prisoners" was adopted from the Irish Prayer-book, in which confession and satisfaction are required of the guilty person, and absolution is given by the priest. A form of prayer for families was abridged from the Family Devotions of Bishop Gibson, and inserted just before the Psalms. A form of thanksgiving for the fruits of the earth was appointed for the first Tuesday in every November, or on such other day as may be appointed by the civil authority. A prayer was set forth and required to be used in all the churches during the meetings of the General Convention. The two great commandments of our Lord were ordered to be read after the Ten Commandments.

Three sentences were prefixed to those at the opening of morning and evening prayer. A selection of Psalms, fixed portions of which might be used at discretion instead of the Psalms for the day, was also agreed upon. This was done partly with the design of shortening the service when it might be deemed expedient to do so, and partly to avoid the imprecations contained in several of the Psalms, which were regarded by some as hardly consistent with the objects of Christian worship. Two hundred and twelve hymns were, at a comparatively recent date, set forth by the Convention and published with the Prayer-book, and ultimately a modified selection from Tate and Brady was in like manner authorised. The Thirty-nine Articles were not finally established and printed with the Prayer-book until 1801. With some exceptions, already mentioned, they are almost word for word identical with those of England, and it is to be particularly noticed that the third article, on Christ's going down into Hell, is the same with our own. In the eighth article the mention of the Athanasian Creed is omitted. The heading of the twenty-first, "Of the Authority of General Councils," is retained, though the article itself is omitted. A note is appended to the *thirty-fifth,* suspending the order for the reading of the Homilies in churches. The thirty-sixth refers the authority of the Ordinal to the General Convention instead of Parliament. The thirty-seventh, on the "power of the civil magistrate," is as follows: "The power of the civil magistrate extendeth to all men, as well clergy as laity, in all things temporal, but hath no authority in things purely spiritual. And we hold it to be the duty of all men who are professors of the Gospel, to pay respectful obedience to the civil authority, regularly and legitimately constituted."

Bishop Seabury doubted the expediency of adopting the Articles, presuming that all necessary doctrine would be comprehended in the Liturgy. Bishop Madison, for different reasons, gave a very decided opinion against Articles altogether. Even now, the Articles are not subscribed as in England, according to the tenor of our thirty-sixth Canon; and the obligation of them rests solely on the promise made at Ordination. Nor are any persons required to give a plenary assent and consent to everything contained in the Prayer-book.

The history of American Liturgical Revision affords on the one hand a remarkable instance of the overruling providence of God; while on the other hand it furnishes a memorable example of the danger of hastily meddling with that which has been once settled by competent authority. The American Church itself is now so well aware of this danger, that it has bound itself by stringent regulations not to allow of further alterations until the proposed changes have been discussed during three years at least, and have been duly considered by the Conventions in the several States.

It is but fair to mention that some of the arrangements of the American rubrics and rituals harmonise with recent recommendations of several committees appointed by the revived Convocation of the province of Canterbury. Among these may be specified the admission of parents as sponsors; the permission of a third service, considerably abridged, though not actually printed in the Prayer-book; the adoption of an authorised hymnal; and the appointment of an annual thanksgiving for the fruits of the earth.

The Preface to the American Prayer-book asks the reader to consider the work " with a meek, candid, and charitable frame of mind." If it be really viewed in this spirit, there will be found no reason to doubt its orthodoxy, whatever disapproval may be felt in regard to some of its details. Though the daily offices, like those of the Orientals, are without the Athanasian Creed, yet all the doctrines of that creed are substantially taught and professed, and never more earnestly than at present. The eighth Article acknowledges the *Nicene* Creed, which also has its place in the service, and the first five Articles prove that the American Church is neither Nestorian nor Eutychian. " After fifty years," * says a distinguished American layman, " without the Athanasian Creed in the Prayer-book, we understand and love it, and were it now part of the book, it could not be stricken out. The laity would be the last to touch it."

I have already mentioned that the omission of the sign of the cross in baptism is never desired. To this may now be added, that the Apostles' Creed is almost

* Letter of " H. D. E." in the Church Review for 1859.

universally repeated as in England, and that the Psalms
for the day are usually preferred to the Selections. If
any doubt still remained as to the identity of the faith
of the American Church with our own, it ought to be
fully set at rest by the memorable declaration prefixed
to the Prayer-book: "This Church is far from intending
to depart from the Church of England in any essential
point of doctrine, discipline, or worship, or further than
local circumstances require."

CHAP. VII.

ECCLESIASTICAL ARRANGEMENTS.

CHURCH LEGISLATURES INDEPENDENT OF THE STATE.—ADMISSION OF THE
LAITY.—PAROCHIAL ORGANISATION.—ENDOWMENTS.—POSITION OF THE
CLERGYMAN.—DIOCESAN ORGANISATION.—THE DIOCESAN CONVENTION.—
THE STANDING COMMITTEE.—THE BISHOP.—EPISCOPAL MAINTENANCE.—
ELECTION OF BISHOPS.—ECCLESIASTICAL COURTS.—TRIAL OF BISHOPS.—
THE GENERAL CONVENTION.—VOTE BY ORDERS.—OPENING AND CLOSE
OF THE SESSION.—DIGEST OF THE CANONS.—SATISFACTORY PROGRESS
OF THE CHURCH.

 " HEN, in the course of Divine Provi-
dence," says the Preface to the Ameri-
can Prayer-book, " these States became
independent with respect to civil government, their ecclesiastical independence was necessarily included." Nor was this all.
The Church was left free to act without legislative
control on the part of the State Governments or
of Congress. Like all Christian denominations it
had a right to expect protection of its property,
and this it has generally received. But it did not
seek or desire the interference or consent of legislatures, presidents, or governors, in the enactment
of canons or the establishment of rules of discipline.
Indeed, it was perfectly clear that a close connection

with governments composed of persons generally alien to the Church, would have been an incalculable injury rather than an advantage. The Church in America had suffered great prejudice from the opinion that the royal supremacy was one of its essentials, rather than an accidental circumstance. Henceforth there was to be no ground left for such a misconception. The real danger was that public opinion, backed by democratic institutions, would become more powerful than a royal supremacy which decides controverted points according to law, and would override the authority of bishops and clergy, canons and rubrics alike.

In order to avert this danger, we have seen that it was considered necessary to employ the laity very largely in the general and local management of Church affairs. It was foreseen that they would not yield a ready concurrence in regulations which they had no share in making, and that merely clerical government was out of the question. To explain sufficiently the ecclesiastical arrangements of the American Church, it will be necessary to describe the principal modes of organisation, as they are *Parochial, Diocesan, and General.*

We begin, then, with the parochial organisation, as the basis of the whole. For certain canonical purposes, a parish is declared to be bounded by the limits, as fixed by law, of any village, town, township, borough, city, or the limits of some division thereof, recognised by the bishop.* In some cases, as in Maryland for example,

* Digest of American Canons, p. 31.

M

a geographical demarcation of parishes was effected in the colonial times, and is acknowledged at the present day. In common parlance, however, and in ordinary practice, a "parish" is not regarded as a district, but rather as consisting of the persons in any neighbourhood who are attached to the doctrine, discipline, and worship of the Church. The minister of the congregation may be expected to use his exertions to increase the number of these persons; still, for most practical purposes, those who attend his church, or receive the benefit of his ministrations, constitute his parish. A parish is "organised," in the first instance, in a public meeting, at which the persons present (having been induced to the step by the exhortations of a clergyman, or by their own convictions) declare their adhesion to the principles of the Church, according to a formula prescribed by the diocesan authorities. The regulations respecting organisation vary in the different dioceses; yet, in every case, the incipient parish adopts certain articles, in which it accedes to the constitution, canons, and discipline of the "American Episcopal Church." At this primary meeting, also, the parish takes its name (St. Peter's or St. Paul's, for instance), and appoints, by ballot, eight or ten vestrymen, two churchwardens, and one or more lay delegates, to represent it in the Diocesan Convention or Synod. At the next annual meeting of the Diocesan Convention, these delegates apply for admission as members of that ecclesiastical assembly, and are never refused if the articles of association, on examination, prove to be correct. The clergyman, if in priest's orders, becomes *ex officio* a member of the same Convention.

In many of the northern States, a parish is usually incorporated by the Legislature of the State (on its own application), like a railway company, an institution of learning, or the congregations · of dissenting bodies. After incorporation, it has the power of holding property, and may sue or be sued in the ordinary courts of law. In Virginia and some other States of the South, there is a jealousy of all ecclesiastical corporations, and Church-property can only be held through the medium of trustees. Yet, as a general rule, a parish can gain and keep possession of endowments, and may enforce, if necessary, by legal process, the collection of its rents and of subscribed money.

The next steps, probably, are to elect a clergyman, by the vote of the vestry, and to erect such a church as may be deemed suitable. In the course of time the parish, perhaps, builds a parsonage, which, together with the church, burying-ground, or any other endowment, is its own property as a corporation.

There was nothing in the constitution of the United States to prevent any particular State from possessing an established religion, and consequently the Revolution did not necessarily affect any of the laws which the several Assemblies had passed in favour of the Church. In Virginia, for instance, although the Legislature soon stopped the annual payments of tobacco to the clergy, the glebes, parsonages, and churches remained intact as late as 1802. In that year it was declared by the Assembly that the property held by the Church before the Revolution was vested in the State at large. Wherever there was a clergyman actually in charge of a parish, the congregation was suffered to retain the use of the church. But, since few clergymen remained, it happened in very many instances that church, churchyard, glebe, parsonage, and communion plate were all sold, ostensibly for the benefit of the public, but really at little more than nominal prices. Some of the churches were bought by the Anabaptists and turned into conventicles, some few became academies, some were eventually recovered by the Church, but many went into a state of dilapidation and ruin in which they continue to the present day.

In Maryland, although the tobacco payment was lost, the glebes and other property were secured by the Legislature to the Church, " with a sense of justice," says Judge Hoffman, " most commendable in those days." I have already mentioned the noble endowment held by the vestry of Trinity Church, New York, originating in a gift of Queen Anne, and now amounting in value to more than a million and a half of pounds sterling. The lands in Vermont, given by Wentworth, the colonial governor, as " glebes " to the Church of England, and as " rights " to the Society for Propagating the Gospel, were applied by the State to the support of education. As late as 1819 an action was brought against the State of Vermont, under authority of the above Society, for the recovery of the " rights," and finally, in 1823, after long litigation, was decided by

the Supreme Court of the United States in favour of
the claimants. At present the "rights" made over by
the Society to the Church in Vermont, and amounting
to half of the original number, produce not far from one
thousand pounds per annum.* The "glebes," on the
other hand, were lost for ever, the title being defective.

There are other endowments in different parts of
America, provided by donors before and since the Revolution; but, as a general rule, the parish is obliged to
depend on its own exertions for every expenditure connected with the erection and repairs of the church and
parsonage, the maintenance of the clergyman and his
assistants, the salary of the organist, and the general
cost of Divine worship. In a few cases these expenses are provided from a weekly offertory, and still
oftener from annual subscriptions, but in the great majority of cases from pew-rents. The sums raised by the
people in large places are often exceedingly liberal, and
frequently, in country villages, altogether the reverse.
Many new churches in America have been erected of
the best materials, and in good ecclesiastical style, at an
expense of ten or twenty thousand pounds, while others
are plain and cheap wooden structures, costing a few
hundreds. The price of a pew may be in the first instance a hundred and fifty pounds, besides an annual
assessment by the vestry of ten or twenty pounds in
addition. On the other hand, there may be merely a
rent of twenty or thirty shillings. The stipend of a

* See the article "Church Lands in Vermont" in the Church
Review for January, 1852.

clergyman in large cities may be well and punctually paid to the amount of a thousand or twelve hundred pounds a year, while in the country, or in new congregations, it may be as low as two or three hundred dollars, and even that by no means certain.

In the absence of any better source of revenue, the system of pew-rents has injured the Church in America by its inevitable tendency to keep poor people, strangers and emigrants, at a distance. Persons of this kind beyond the Atlantic are exceedingly sensitive, and many of them will on no account accept a free seat in a church or meeting-house where the sale or letting of pews is the general rule. Rather than bear the expense of a good seat, or what they would consider the shame of a free or cheap one, they prefer to stay at home and to live in practical heathenism. Happily, in America, the poor are a much smaller class than with us. There are also a few churches open to all without cost, and supported, as I have stated, by the offertory, or by individual benefactors. It may be added that, as in England, aversion to the pew-system is increasing, and that daily service with frequent Communions is becoming more and more common.

The position of the clergyman in regard to his people implies a greater degree of dependence than a sound Church theory seems to warrant. This dependence existed even in Virginia and Maryland long before the Revolution. But the constant expansion of the Church renders it, at present, easy to obtain a new parochial charge, and it is seldom that a really faithful and well-qualified clergyman has just reason to complain. Besides, the clergy are, in almost every case, native Americans, and are accustomed to see perpetual changes in all offices in the gift of the people. Hence, in their pastoral relations, they are prepared for a degree of uncertainty which to a quiet English rector would appear intolerable.

On Easter Monday in every year, the pewholders meet for the election of a vestry and of delegates to the Diocesan Convention. The number of delegates sent by each parish varies in the different dioceses. In Virginia and Maryland, for instance, each parish sends as many lay deputies as it has clergy. In Connecticut, each parish is entitled to *one* delegate, and, if it consist of more than fifty families, to *two*. In some dioceses it is required by the diocesan canons that a lay delegate shall be a *communicant;* but in others it is deemed the wiser course to leave this point to the discretion of the parishes electing. So, also, in some dioceses, every lay delegate has a separate vote in the Convention, while, in others, the lay delegates sent from each parish (however numerous) have but one vote conjointly.

We are now prepared to consider the second organisation, namely, the *diocesan*. A diocese (unlike a parish) is circumscribed by certain fixed geographical limits, and generally consists of all the organised parishes within any single State. As the jurisdiction of an American bishop is considered to extend to persons rather than to places, his strictly correct title is that of " Bishop of the Protestant Episcopal Church in the State or Diocese of ——."

The great increase of the Church in some States has led the ecclesiastical authority to provide for the subdivision of Dioceses. Dioceses too have been sometimes formed by the labours of missionary bishops. But, from the peculiar circumstances of the American Church, a diocesan organisation has often preceded the existence of the episcopate within its limits. Every diocese meets annually in its own Convention for purposes of a local character. The bishop presides, and in a few instances has a qualified veto on the proceedings. But as the weightier matters of the Church are disposed of in the General Convention, where the House of Bishops now exercises an unqualified veto, the want of that power in the Diocesan Conventions, strange as it may seem, is less to be regretted. Every clergyman in charge of a parish is *ex officio* (as I have already stated) a member of the Convention of the diocese in which he officiates. In most dioceses, chaplains in the army and navy, and clerical professors in colleges and incorporated seminaries, are also admitted to seats and votes. Besides the clergy, the Convention embraces (as before stated) the lay delegates from the parishes.

The proceedings of the Convention are commenced in church by solemn religious services, including the Holy Communion and a sermon preached by some clergyman nominated by the bishop. The bishop then calls the Convention to order, a list of the clergy entitled to seats is read, and the lay delegates produce the evidence of their election to a committee appointed for the purpose by the bishop. After this, every clergyman presents to the bishop a written report of the state of his parish, with an account of the number of communicants and Sunday scholars, the amount of contributions for Church purposes, and other useful statistics.*

The bishop then delivers his annual address, in which he refers to the deaths among the clergy during the last year, gives an account of his episcopal acts within the same space of time, and often bestows praise on those clergymen or laymen who have exerted themselves to good purpose. He states his plans for future improvement, and suggests the adoption of such regulations as may appear to him desirable. He mentions particularly the number of Ordinations, Confirmations, and Consecrations performed by him since the last meeting, and often succeeds in quickening the zeal of the assembled representatives of his diocese.

After the bishop's address usually follow the applications of new parishes to be admitted into union with the Convention. Then the Convention elects by ballot a kind of chapter called the Standing Committee, generally composed of clergy and laity, and possessing very peculiar and important powers. The Convention elects, in the same way, four clergymen and four laymen as its representatives in the General Convention. It also appoints trustees for any colleges or academies

---

* See the Appendix.

under its jurisdiction, as well as its quota of trustees
for the General Theological Seminary of the Church,
established at New York.

The next and last business, perhaps, is the enactment
of new Diocesan Canons, or the revision of old ones.
Considerable latitude is allowed to the subject-matter
of these local canons; but in no case may they conflict
with the supreme canons of the General Convention, or
with the Rubrics of the Prayer-book, or the Articles of
the Church. Thus, for instance, they prescribe the
mode of admitting parishes into union with the diocese,
the qualifications requisite for membership in the
Diocesan Convention, the method of providing for con-
tingent expenses, the keeping of parish registers, and
the promotion of Church principles within the bounds
of the diocese. A really good and influential bishop,
possessing the respect and affection of his flock, will
usually, in the course of time, secure (without direct
interference) the establishment of a sound and useful
code of diocesan regulations.

Although elections in the Diocesan Convention are
usually by ballot, the voting on ordinary matters is *vivâ
voce*, the bishop putting the question and declaring
whether the *ayes* or *noes* preponderate. The clergy and
laity usually vote together in one body; but at any
time, when a few members require it, they may separate
into two bodies, when a majority of both is requisite
before any resolution or canon can pass. By this
ingenious piece of ecclesiastical mechanism, it is so
arranged that neither the clergy nor the laity can justly

complain of the undue interference of either party, in doctrinal questions or otherwise.

I have alluded to the Standing Committee as a kind of Diocesan Chapter. In Maryland and Connecticut it consists wholly of priests, *seven* in the former and *five* in the latter. But, generally speaking, the members of it consist of equal numbers of priests and laymen, and if any of the latter are not communicants the responsibility rests with the Diocesan Assembly electing them. The Standing Committee is a council of advice to the bishop. During a vacancy of the Episcopate, it superintends candidates for orders by its clerical members, grants letters dimissory and testimonials to the characters of clergymen removing, and invites the bishop of some neighbouring diocese to perform episcopal acts. It discharges, in a measure, the duties of the Diocesan Convention during its recess, but possesses no authority to legislate on Church matters. Nor can any person be ordained a deacon or priest without testimonials from the Standing Committee of the diocese to which he belongs.

An American bishop is addressed simply as " Right Reverend Sir " or " Bishop," the usual English title of honour having always been carefully avoided. His power appears checked on every side, not only by prevailing democracy, but by the constitution and canons of the Church itself. Yet, as his appointment is derived from the free choice of the clergy and laity of his diocese, he often gains as much in personal influence as he may appear to have lost in titles of honour and in direct authority. The American bishops are free from certain traditional associations with patronage, social eminence and abounding wealth, which, in England, may have tended sometimes to obscure the real religious dignity of the episcopal office. Their position also is one which they hold for life, while the offices of the State are usually tenable but for a few years. Hence they may in the course of time gather around them much of that loyal veneration which in other countries attaches itself to the civil rulers, but which the American Republic has seen fit to dispense with. An American bishop must necessarily be a considerable traveller, as an average diocese, including those in the west, does not materially differ from all England in dimensions. The number of bishops in the United States is now *forty-three*, the want of endowments being seldom permitted to delay the election of new prelates as they may be required.

The support of the bishop in the different dioceses is derived from various sources. In some, for example, the people have voluntarily raised large sums, which, being invested on good security, produce a competent income. A sum exceeding eighty-four thousand dollars has been contributed in New York, which realises about a thousand pounds a year. A house was also purchased and furnished for the bishop, who was thus enabled to devote himself wholly to his episcopal work. In Western New York an endowment of fifty thousand dollars gives the bishop above 600*l.* a year. In Connecticut the capital of the Episcopal Fund amounted in 1859 to twenty-seven thousand dollars, producing, with some augmentations, 700*l.* per annum. In Pennsylvania the endowment is about the same in amount as in Western New York. In Maryland, a similar fund, increased by parochial contributions, produces nearly 1200*l.* per annum. In South Carolina the bishop's endowment is sixty-eight thousand dollars, yielding him nearly 900*l.* per annum. In some dioceses, the parishes assess themselves in their annual Convention for the support of their bishop. In the newer dioceses the bishop sometimes derives his maintenance from a parish of which he has been appointed rector, consequently accepting a double charge and responsibility. In others, again, which may be regarded as missionary ground, the bishop receives a fixed stipend from missionary contributions raised under the authority of the General Convention.

A diocese becomes vacant, in most cases, only by the death of the bishop, as the Church does not sanction translations. When a vacancy occurs, instead of a *congé d'élire,* the Standing Committee summons a *special* Diocesan Convention, which is duly constituted in the usual way. The clergy and laity then separate into two distinct Houses, and a majority of both orders, voting by ballot, is necessary to an election. In most of the dioceses, the clergy nominate the person whom they prefer, and the laity have the power of either rejecting or affirming the nomination. After the election (which usually affords an opportunity for a trial of strength to Church parties), notice is sent to all the Standing Committees in the American Church, a majority of which must confirm the election before the second step of it is complete ; and, thirdly, a majority of all the bishops must approve of the person chosen. After this, the Presiding Bishop (who is always the eldest by consecration) nominates two other bishops to assist him in consecrating the bishop-elect, and appoints the time and place for the performance of the sacred rite. But if the bishop be elected during the year previous to a meeting of the General Convention, the Standing Committees and the Bishops are not separately consulted, the consent of the chief council of the Church being deemed a sufficient confirmation of the election.

When a bishop is unable to perform his episcopal duties by reason of old age or permanent infirmity, an assistant bishop may be elected, with the right of succession. Missionary bishops for foreign countries or States and Territories not organised as dioceses, are elected by the General Convention, on the nomination of the House of Bishops.

Although the senior bishop has duties which in some measure correspond with those of a Primate, there are as yet no archbishops, deans, archdeacons, or rural deans, and the increase of ecclesiastical titles beyond those of bishop, priest, and deacon, is generally deprecated.

The department of the judiciary in the American Church is still in an imperfect condition, though some improvements have recently been effected. Trials of priests and deacons for heresy or immorality are conducted by courts of clergymen, constituted by the bishops of each diocese, according to their respective diocesan canons. No appeal from these courts can be carried to any superior body; the Conventions, both general and diocesan, being simply *legislative* assemblies, and in no respect courts of appeal.

All the religious bodies or denominations in the United States possess the right to try and to depose their ministers or members, provided they adhere in the trial to their own acknowledged canons or regulations. If the accused consider himself aggrieved, he may apply to the civil courts, which will institute proceedings to ascertain whether these canons or regulations have been strictly followed in the trial, but will not undertake to review the evidence. If it appear that the rules of the denomination have been followed, the accused has no alternative but to submit. In 1853, Bishop Wainwright, of New York, was withheld, by an injunction of the Supreme Court of New York, from pronouncing sentence of deposition on a clergyman convicted by an ecclesiastical court of immorality. The Bishop, in defending himself, was put to an expense of nearly a thousand pounds; but the sentence was eventually pronounced, and the guilty person deposed. The laity afterwards subscribed and repaid the Bishop his expenses.

For the trial of bishops, the general canons of the American Church have made very elaborate provision. None but a bishop may pronounce sentence of admonition, suspension, or degradation on any clergyman, whether bishop, priest, or deacon. The trial of lay communicants is conducted according to the respective diocesan canons. The offences for which they may be subjected to discipline are specified in the rubric, which is the same with that in the English Prayer-book.

As the confederated States in the American Union are represented by Congress, so the different dioceses united in the Church are represented by the General Convention. This body meets once in three years, on the first Wednesday in October, at some place determined at the previous session. Special meetings may also be held when required by the exigencies of the Church. The General Convention is composed of two Houses, the consent of both of which is necessary to the passing of any act or canon. The Upper House consists of all the bishops, excepting those engaged in foreign missions. It meets with closed doors (reporters not being admitted), probably with the object of defending itself as much as possible against passing and external influences. The senior bishop presides, while a clergyman appointed for the purpose acts as secretary. The number of bishops now entitled to seats in this truly venerable body is *thirty-eight*.

The Lower House consists of the clerical and lay deputies, four of each from every diocese, and, if full, would now contain *a hundred and thirty-six* clergymen and as many laymen. It elects some able clergyman as its chairman or prolocutor. The debates are open to the public, and parliamentary forms are strictly observed.

Among the lay members (who, by a late provision, must always be communicants) are found persons distinguished as lawyers, judges, governors, and members of Congress or the State Legislatures. Thus some of the best talents of the country are enlisted in the work of Church Legislation, and the practical knowledge of the laity gives point and efficiency to the zeal of the clergy. When the deputies from any diocese require it, the Lower House may practically subdivide itself into a House of Laity and a House of Clergy, when the consent of both is requisite to every act or resolution. The Constitution of the Church declares that " in all questions, when required by the clerical and lay representatives from any diocese, each order shall have one vote ; and the majority of suffrages by dioceses shall be conclusive in each order, provided such majority comprehend a majority of the dioceses represented in that order. The concurrence of both orders shall be necessary to constitute a vote of the Convention." By this provision, not only are the clergy and laity protected from mutual aggression, but dioceses which may happen to be feebly represented are saved from being overborne by those which may have sent their full number of deputies.

At the opening of the General Convention, both Houses unite in public worship in some large church which supplies in its galleries accommodation for the ladies and the numerous spectators who delight in such meetings. The opening sermon is usually preached by one of the bishops. The Holy Communion is celebrated, and sometimes a thousand or fifteen hundred communi-

N

cants partake of the sacred feast.   The bishops in their
robes, and generally with the additional dignity of grey
hairs, appear to great advantage on these occasions.
Divine Service having closed, the business of the Convention begins in the church itself.   The bishops retire to
the vestry or schoolroom, and organise the Upper House.
The Lower House elects a Chairman and Secretary, and
the roll is called by dioceses, as in our own Convocation of
Canterbury.   The session usually continues during several weeks, at the close of which the bishops address a
pastoral letter to the whole Church, both Houses unite
in chanting the *Gloria in excelsis,* and the proceedings terminate with a solemn benediction from the
senior bishop.

The General Convention enacts, modifies, or repeals
canons of a *general* character as distinguished from
the *local* diocesan canons.   These general canons,
having been enacted as circumstances required, are
practicable, intelligible, and suited to the necessities of
the times.   They certainly present a striking contrast
to the English canons, which have remained unchanged
since the age of the Stuarts, and consequently are· far
from creditable to our Church and nation.

There are twenty canons on the "Ministry, Doctrine,
and Worship." *   Under this title the lately published
Digest of the Canons includes the regulations concerning
the three orders of the ministry, candidates for Orders,
provisions and qualifications for ordination ; the duties of

* Digest of the Canons. Pudney and Russell, New York, 1860.

bishops, priests, and deacons; the mode of securing an accurate view of the state of the Church—of publishing authorised editions of the Bible and Prayer-book—of the celebration of Sundays, parochial instruction, and the use of the Liturgy.

Twelve canons refer to discipline, and regulate citations, trials of clerical offenders, the dissolution of pastoral connections, sentences, the discipline of the laity, and other similar matters.

The six following canons refer to the organised bodies and officers of the Church. These include the General Convention, the Standing Committees, the Trustees of the Missionary Bishops' Fund and of the General Theological Seminary, congregations and parishes at home and abroad, and the organisation of new dioceses.

Under the fourth and last head are arranged three provisions respecting the repeal, amendment, and enactment of new canons, and of the time of these canons taking effect.

In 1817, the attention of the Convention was called to the existence of numerous corruptions of the authorised version of Scripture, arising from the want of any supervision over the printers and publishers of the Bible in the United States. After some discussion of the subject, the English edition of Eyre and Strahan was recommended in 1823, as the standard of the American Church until she might put forth an edition of her own.

The General Convention manages the Missions of the Church at home and abroad by means of a Board of Missions triennially elected. This Convention has also power to alter the Rubrics as well as the Services in the Prayer-book after three years' discussion in the Diocesan Conventions. It legislates on points touching relations between different dioceses, intercourse with foreign churches, and the advancement of the Gospel in heathen countries.

The English reader must endeavour to dissociate this statement of *powers* from all idea of State authority. Although the canons have not yet commanded that conscientious and loving obedience which might be wished, they have yet been found, on the whole, adequate to the direction and limitation of the energies of the Church. American Churchmen are quite satisfied that at all events they would not gain additional force from any State enactments which under present circumstances might be conceived as possible.

Whatever objections may be raised to the Constitution of the American Church, and especially to the part taken by the laity, it is certain that a healthful progress has been visible, during the seventy years of its existence, in the action of the General Convention. It is conceded by the bishops and by others accustomed to watch the course of events, that the laity have proved themselves at least as conservative as the clergy, and that if they have ever hindered important legislation, the hindrance has been a wholesome check on premature or ill-considered movements. Influenced by the combined piety and wisdom of the clergy and laity, and with a House of Bishops possessing a right of negative on the proceedings of the inferior orders, the American Church has shown no tendency to go back, or to diminish aught from the Faith. It is true that much remains to be supplied by the exertions of Churchmen. The Consecration of Burial-grounds, forgotten during the absence of bishops, is still generally a desideratum. The " voluntary system " admits of improvement, so that the clergyman may be less directly dependent on the favour of a particular congregation. The leaven of Puritanism, derived from surrounding influences, is susceptible of further wholesome correction. The remaining timidity, inherited from the evil times when the Church was thankful for a bare existence, needs to be wholly swept away. Good regulations on Marriage and Divorce are yet to be established and obeyed. For the future we have reason to entertain sanguine hopes, since we believe that while the numerical increase of the American Church has been almost unprecedented, sound religious and ecclesiastical principles have constantly " grown with her growth, and strengthened with her strength." *

* Church Journal, January, 1859.

CHAP. VIII.

THE POLITICAL UNION.

CONTINUED ADVANCE OF THE COUNTRY.—EXTENSION OF TERRITORY.
—THE SUCCESSIVE PRESIDENTS. — PRINCIPAL EVENTS DURING EACH
PRESIDENT'S INCUMBENCY.—DANGERS OF THE NEW REPUBLIC.—WANT
OF A DEFINITE RELIGION.—DEFECTS IN EDUCATION.—DECAY OF AUTHO-
RITY.—EMIGRATION.—UNIVERSAL SUFFRAGE.—DIVISION OF THE SPOILS.
—POPULAR ORATORY.—LICENTIOUSNESS OF THE PRESS.—SLAVERY.—
PROGRESS OF THE UNITED STATES NOTWITHSTANDING THE DANGERS
OF THE UNION.—GROWTH OF ABOLITIONISM.—ELECTION OF PRESIDENT
LINCOLN.—DISSOLUTION OF THE UNION.

AVING considered the ecclesiastical organi-
sation, we must now briefly trace the his-
tory of the political union, the gradual
development of the principles upon which
it was constructed, and the general progress of the
States by which it was constituted.

After the establishment of Independence, the population continued to increase much in the same ratio as
before the Revolution.   There was the same rich soil,
there was the same productive climate, there was the
same facility for obtaining all the necessaries and many
of the comforts of existence.   Marriages were still con-
tracted early in life, large families were raised up and
easily maintained, and emigrants continued to arrive

from Europe. The great West began to be occupied, and towns and cities arose in situations which had been known only as the haunt of wild animals and savage men. Vermont and Kentucky, formerly portions of New Hampshire and Virginia, were admitted into the Union as free and slave States respectively in 1791; and in 1796 Tennessee was in like manner separated from North Carolina, and advanced to the same dignity. Ohio followed in 1802, and, slavery being excluded from her soil, her population advanced in thirty years from *seventy thousand* to half a million. In 1803 the remaining French territory west of the Mississippi, now including Louisiana, Arkansas, Missouri, and Iowa, was purchased from France for the sum of fifteen millions of dollars. About the same time a treaty was made with the Kaskaskia and Delaware Indians, who transferred to the United States the fertile district now constituting the States of Indiana and Illinois. In 1817 and the four following years, Mississippi, Illinois, Alabama, Maine (formerly a part of Massachusetts), and Missouri came into the growing confederacy. The question of the admission of Missouri caused great excitement in Congress, and throughout the country.* The existence of slavery had given rise to conflicting interests between the North and South. The Northern members of Congress were generally in favour of the exclusion of slavery from the new State, while those of the South were determined that it should be permitted;

* M. Murray, p. 392.

N 4

each section being desirous of possessing the balance of power in the federal government. The North yielded, and Missouri was added in 1821 to the slaveholding States, with a compromise (repealed in 1854) establishing elsewhere the parallel of 36° 30′ as the boundary between the slave and free States west of the Mississippi. In 1820 the territory of Alabama was admitted into the Union as a slave State. In 1821 East and West Florida were purchased from Spain at a cost of five millions of dollars. Arkansas and Florida, both slave countries, were placed about the same time under a territorial government, the President and Congress exercising jurisdiction within their boundaries, until the growth of population entitled them to the rank of States, in 1836 and 1845 respectively. The Mexican province of Texas, having been settled in a great measure by Americans from the South, about this time revolted from Mexico, and adopted a constitution establishing slavery in the place of freedom. Being largely aided with men and means from the slaveholding communities, Texas was enabled to maintain its claim to independence, which was promptly recognised by the United States, England, and France. The Southern States, desiring to increase their political power, proposed the annexation of Texas as a slaveholding State, and, notwithstanding the protest of Mexico and the resistance of the Northern States of the Union, the measure was finally accomplished in 1845. Soon afterwards war was proclaimed against Mexico, although the measure received strong opposition from New England and from the friends of humanity and justice in general. The consequence was the annexation of California and New Mexico, a territory covering an area of eight hundred and fifty thousand square miles, being more than one-half of the entire Mexican dominions. California, being almost immediately enriched and peopled in consequence of the opportune discovery of gold, was admitted into the Union as a free State. Oregon and Washington, on the Pacific, were settled and became territories. Utah, colonised by the Mormons *, and Nebraska, between Missouri and the Rocky Mountains, soon occupied a similar position in the Republic. Wisconsin, Iowa, and Minnesota, in the North-West, rapidly increased in population, and became respectively free States, and eventually Kansas, further south, was added to the confederation on terms prohibiting slavery. At the present time the number of States is thirty-four in place of the old thirteen. The area of the whole covers a space of about three millions of square miles, which is more than twenty-five times the extent of Great Britain and Ireland.

During this rapid extension of territory there have been sixteen Presidents, of whom Washington, Jefferson, Madison, Monroe, and Jackson, being re-elected, held office during eight years each. John Adams succeeded Washington in 1797, and his son, John Quincy Adams,

* For the history of the Mormons, see the Author's "Prophet of the Nineteenth Century" (Rivingtons), and "America and the American Church" (Mozleys).

was inaugurated in 1825, coming between Monroe and Jackson. Jackson was succeeded, in 1837, by Van Buren, who was followed by Harrison in 1841. After a short month in office Harrison died, and was succeeded by Tyler, the Vice-President, according to the arrangements of the constitution. Polk was inaugurated in 1845, and Taylor in 1849. The latter was removed by death in 1850, and was succeeded by the Vice-President, Fillmore. Pierce became President in 1853, Buchanan in 1857, and Abraham Lincoln took the oath of office in the present eventful year, 1861.

The death of Washington took place unexpectedly in the winter of 1799. The character of the first American President belongs rather to the old colonial days than to those of the Republic. In that character may be seen a type of human excellence to which it is difficult, on the whole, to find a parallel. Washington seems to have arisen " to teach all ages, and especially those which are inclined to worship violence, the greatness of moderation, and civil duty." *   " He grew up on the soil of America; he was nurtured at her bosom. She loved and trusted him in his youth; she honoured and revered him in his age; and though she did not wait for death to canonise his name, his precious memory, with each succeeding year, has sunk more deeply into the hearts of his countrymen." † Yet it must not be forgotten that, ranking as he did with the old

* Smith's Lecture before the University of Oxford, 1860.
† Oration of the Hon. Edward Everett, 1860.

"Federalist" party, Washington was far from being democratic in his political principles, or sanguine as to the working of republican institutions. He was by no means averse to certain respectable and time-honoured observances which, though now associated in the American mind with the pomp of monarchy, involve principles which cannot be neglected with impunity.

Besides the great enlargements of territory already mentioned, the following events may be specified as having occurred during the times of the respective Presidents. Under the Presidency of Washington the public credit was restored, and a national bank was established, though violently opposed as aristocratic in its tendency and contrary to republicanism. A dangerous insurrection in Pennsylvania, occasioned by a tax on spirits, was suppressed. The Indians in Ohio were subdued, and a treaty of peace effected. In 1793, the exports of the United States had risen to nineteen and a half millions of dollars, while the imports were twenty millions. About the same time, by the invention of the cotton-gin, the cotton of the Southern States, which previously had scarcely sufficed for domestic consumption, became a staple production, and the value of negroes was in consequence greatly enhanced.

While John Adams was President, the city of Washington became the capital of the United States, and Congress assembled there for the first time in November, 1800. There had been difficulties with the revolutionary government of France, amounting, in fact, to a state of war, but peace was concluded about the date of the opening of the new "Capitol." At the next election the federalists lost ground, and, the republican party coming into power, Jefferson, the infidel, was raised to the Presidency. He was a complete democrat, although, at the same time, a man of wealth and a considerable slave-owner. From this time the idea of the sovereignty of the people prevailed, and those who were formerly considered the chosen rulers of the nation were regarded merely as public servants.

During Jefferson's eight years of power, the western country was explored as far as the Pacific by an expedition sent out by the government, under Lewis and Clarke. A war of several years' duration, and of doubtful advantage, was carried on against the petty state of Tripoli. Aaron Burr, the late Vice-President, after killing an eminent person in a duel, was accused of conspiring to erect the south-western portion of the Union into a separate government, and to invade Mexico, then a Spanish province. He was acquitted for want of sufficient evidence, but never altogether acquitted in the minds of the people. In the following year, 1807, Robert Fulton constructed his first steamboat, and a great impulse was consequently given to the progress of the country. The rivers and lakes of the West became highways, by which population and commerce were diffused over the immense districts now laid open to the enterprising settler. About the same time American manufactures received great encouragement from events connected with the war then raging between the British government and Napoleon.

Great Britain had prohibited neutrals from trading with France or her allies, excepting on condition of paying her a tribute. On the other hand, Napoleon's "Milan Decree" declared that every neutral vessel submitting to pay this tribute should be confiscated. As the British government also insisted on the right of impressing seamen on board American ships, it became difficult to carry on foreign commerce with advantage, and the people turned their attention to the manufacture of those goods which previously had been imported from England. Henceforth New England became the chief seat of American manufactures. The coal and iron of Pennsylvania gained new value, and, as already mentioned, Pittsburgh became eventually the Birmingham of the West.

Early in the Presidency of Madison all intercourse was prohibited with England and France in consequence of their hostile edicts. The latter nation revoked her decrees; but as England maintained her position, war was declared against us by America in 1812, while we were fully occupied by our European contest. Hostilities were carried on by sea and land during two years and a half with various success. Michigan was taken by the British, and retaken by the Americans. Canada was invaded by the Americans, who, after burning York (now Toronto) and other places, were driven from the province. On the other hand, the British attacked the city of Washington, drove away the President and other officers of government, and burnt the Capitol, the President's house, and

all the public buildings, except the Post-office. At sea
the Americans had considerable success, and during
the early part of the war their privateers, built for rapid
sailing, captured some hundreds of British merchant-
ships. In an engagement on Lake Erie, the British
squadron surrendered, and a similar reverse was afterwards experienced on Lake Champlain. After the
downfall of Napoleon our government was able to send
additional ships and troops to America. The coast of
Maine afforded an easy conquest, and various islands
on the New England coast submitted to our naval com-
manders. The people of New England had been constantly opposed to the war, by which their commerce
lost far more than their manufactures gained. In
December, 1814, a convention of the delegates assembled at Hartford, in Connecticut, and took the subject
of their grievances into consideration. But further
proceedings were rendered unnecessary by the conclusion of peace, the treaty being signed at Ghent on the
24th of the month just named. On the 8th of January,
1815, fifteen days after the signature of the treaty, the
battle of New Orleans took place, in which the Americans, under General Jackson, gained the victory. Had
the present system of steamers and telegraphs then
existed, the speedy arrival of the intelligence of peace
would probably have prevented the conflict, and the
loss of nearly two thousand lives.

A short war with Algiers, and the institution of a
United States bank, with a charter for twenty years,
were among the last events of Mr. Madison's Presi-

'dency.   Under Mr. Adams, the second President of the name, the Creek and Kansas Indians ceded their lands in Georgia and Missouri, and in 1828 a bill passed Congress for the protection of American manufactures, by charging a duty on the importation of such articles as could be made at home.   The tariff was agreed to by a small majority, the Southern States (which had no manufactures) considering it detrimental to their interests.   In 1826 a remarkable coincidence occurred in the death on the same day, and that day the *fourth of July,* of the two Ex-Presidents, Jefferson and Adams.

During the Presidency of Jackson, the Bank of the United States was obliged to close its operations, the President refusing to sanction a renewal of the charter. In 1832 the State of South Carolina determined to resist the tariff, and threatened to dissolve the Union in the event of its being enforced.   The President, on the other hand, took prompt and decisive measures to collect the revenue and prevent rebellion, and Congress overcame opposition to the tariff by a bill providing for a gradual reduction of the obnoxious duties.   In 1835 difficulties arose with France, but through the mediation of England a war was averted.   Hostilities were, however, commenced against the Seminole Indians in Florida, who had harboured fugitive slaves, and had been accused of other acts of depredation on the property of the white inhabitants.   The war continued during seven years, and cost above forty millions of dollars.   Many of the enemy were killed or captured, and the remainder were, for the most part, transported to the western territories.

Some of the principal events subsequent to Jackson's Presidency have been already mentioned, such as the acquisition of Texas and the war with Mexico, followed by a great increase of the slaveholding power. The South appears to have generally governed the country, and the principal statesmen were for the most part advocates of Southern interests. Of the first five Presidents, all were Virginians, with the exception of John Adams. But the Northern and North-Western States were now preponderating in wealth, population, and intelligence, and it was evident that the time was approaching when the free States would obtain a decisive and permanent superiority.

. The American Union was a grand idea, but the practical working of it belongs to a class of experiments which sometimes require ages for their completion. It had, undoubtedly, one great disadvantage in its very commencement. The divisions of the people, growing out of the circumstances of their early settlement, and the neglect and misfortunes of the mother-country, prevented any national recognition of a definite Christianity. Something was done, indeed, for which we have reason to be thankful. National fasts and thanksgivings were appointed by the Federal and State authorities, the Christian era was acknowledged, Sunday was observed as a day of rest, and chaplains of various "denominations" were appointed for the army and navy, and for Congress itself. The Presidents also, in their Messages, usually made some proper allusion to Divine Providence. But the general education of the American people has suffered greatly from these unhappy divisions, and more of late than formerly. Republican institutions, depending as they do upon the will of the majority, require the support of a virtuous and intelligent community. A solid Christian education is the only source of public virtue on which men can safely rely. The great Washington said in his farewell address on retiring from the Presidency, " Let us with caution indulge the supposition that morality can be maintained without religion. Whatever may be conceded to the influence of refined education on minds of peculiar structure, reason and experience both forbid us to expect that national morality can prevail in exclusion of religious principles." But it is impossible that religious principles of any practical value can be inculcated in the absence of a definite form of religion, or where different systems are assumed to be equally true or equally false. Now, although the free States have generally made ample provision for schools of secular learning, any particular system of religious teaching would be regarded as *sectarian*, and would not be tolerated. The mention of judgment to come would offend the believers in universal salvation, the doctrine of a personal God would irritate the Pantheists, and allusions to infant baptism, or forms of prayer, would exasperate the Baptists and Independents. Nothing favourable to either Sacrament could safely be inculcated in the neighbourhood of Quakers; the English version of the Bible would not be tolerated by Roman Catholics, and Scriptures of any version would hurt the feelings of those who deny all revelation whatever, and whose "conscience," like that of others, must be respected in a land where all are equal. Hence the public schools have been compelled to exclude not only all catechisms, creeds, and explanations of revealed truth, but eventually even the Bible itself. Thus we find a state of things existing in the midst of Protestantism not unlike that which is laid to the charge of the most bigoted Popery. Denominational Sunday-schools cannot effectively counteract the godless teaching of the rest of the week, and the bulk of the population consequently grows up, if not in absolute unbelief, at least without the blessing of a true, definite, and hereditary religion. The tone of public conscience necessarily becomes relaxed, and the respect to law proportionately weakened. The solemn oath in courts of justice loses its awful sanctions, and responsibility to God is forgotten. "This divorce of religion from education," says a New York paper*, "was unknown to our fathers." It is to be feared there is too much truth in the words of Bishop Otey, of Tennessee †: "In a *vast majority* of instances, the young who are just rising into manhood are *totally ignorant* of the nature and extent of their obligations as moral and accountable beings. They can give shrewd and intelligent answers to all questions concerning traffic and trade and the value of

---

* Church Journal.
† Primary Charge to the Clergy of the Diocese of Tennessee.

various kinds of property; but as to the nature and extent of those obligations by which man is bound to 'do justly, love mercy, and walk humbly with God,' they have been taught nothing, they know nothing, and oftentimes care nothing. The example of their parents has led them to regard money as ' the chief good,' and in its acquisition all advantages are to be taken which the law will allow, or which artful evasions of the law will enable them to compass. The social affections are swept away in this struggle for gain, there is no place for their exercise, and the kindly offices of charity and benevolence are unknown. The children of the country are thus in a measure trained up with feelings almost hostile to their species. The idea they have of public liberty is that they may do as they please, regardless of the comfort and even the rights of others. Reverence for age and character is unfelt, sympathy for suffering and distress is destroyed, and respect for law and authority despised as meanness. Effrontery is taken for manliness, rudeness for gentility, and impudence for easiness of manners. Is it any wonder that, under this hardening process, future heroes in crime are formed, and that we hear and read of deeds of daring villany and desperate wickedness?"

Another source of danger arose from the decay of authority consequent on the Revolution. The very principle of obedience seemed to have been subverted, and while men believed themselves to be simply getting rid of King George, they were, in fact, overthrowing the power which should of right belong to every magistrate, parent, pastor, master, teacher, and officer. Bishop Potter, of Pennsylvania, in his charge of 1849, says: " May we not tremble for the future of our land, when we see how the bands of parental authority and domestic affection are relaxed, and how much insolent contempt is expressed for the wisdom of the past?" Bishop Hopkins, of Vermont, said in 1854, though admitting that the picture might be overdrawn * : " It is well known that the wives of our age have no notion of submitting to their husbands, and that sons and daughters are accustomed to throw off the yoke of their parents, and to do precisely as they please, while the reverence for magistrates, ministers, and teachers, which marked the early days of the Republic, is generally exploded as obsolete. Democracy has extended from the public rights of the citizen to the private relations of the family and the school. The sacred authority of the master and the father is merged in deference to the will of the majority at home. And the political privileges which the constitution intended to be exercised by intelligent and virtuous men, are practically assumed in every other department by fools and children." In fact, rebellion came to be regarded as something good in itself, and the doctrine of the sovereignty of the people laid the foundation of a new form of tyranny, and tended " to annul the greatest step in the progress of humanity, by placing will, though it be the will of

* Address delivered before the Convocation of Trinity College, Hartford, Connecticut.

the many, above reason and the law." * The people virtually made and unmade laws at their pleasure, until they ceased to respect them; and, in some States, even the judges were elected for short periods by the votes of a majority. It is not, therefore, marvellous that the sovereign mob should sometimes take the law into their own hands, and, without the formalities of a regular trial, should perpetrate the barbarous acts known as "Lynch-law," acts unknown even in the most recently settled communities of British America. Under the operation of universal suffrage, "the direct and immediate agency of the whole people in the conduct and administration of the government became," in the words of an American writer, " a preponderating and crushing element in the system, the operation of which reduces to nothing all the well-adjusted theoretical distinctions between the departments of the Federal government, by the ease with which it overbalances them all." †

To this we must add another danger arising from the great and increasing emigration from Germany, Ireland, England, and other European countries, amounting sometimes to nearly half a million in a year. Along with some honest and well-meaning persons, there has been a constant influx of the depraved and lawless, who, casting off all the restraints of home, are soon admitted to the suffrage in America, and courted and flattered, for the sake of their votes, by the aspirants to political power.

It is quite certain that universal suffrage, however it

* Smith's "Lecture before the University of Oxford," p. 19.
† Church Review, 1859, p. 535.

may work in a population of agricultural proprietors, is practically an enormous evil in cities such as New York. Americans tell * us that in this great metropolis, cabmen, butchers, policemen, and men without property, morals, or education, the very dregs of the populace, elect persons of their own party to offices of power and trust, and divide among them immense sums of money levied on the wealthy. Throughout the country generally, we are informed on similar authority † that " the possession of great talents, dignified habits, and polished manners, renders a man an object of suspicion, as an aristocrat, to the great bulk of the electors. Such men, accordingly, are often prevented from serving their country, and spend their lives in comparative retirement." " Bribery," says Bishop Hopkins, " is practised in all our elections, and the spoils of office are expected as a matter of course by the victorious party."

This division of the spoils, which began long since the days of Washington, takes place at every presidential election. The effect of this election is to convulse the whole country once in four years, to expend a vast amount of time, money, and exertion to very little purpose, and to encourage the formation of factions, which, although generally devoid of any important meaning, pursue one another with a violence and a malignity inconceivable to a foreigner.

It is taken for granted that the new President will eject multitudes of persons from office, and supply

* Western World Revisited, p. 49.   † Ibid. p. 250.

their vacant places with those who have promoted his own advancement. " There are, for example, nearly twenty thousand postmasters in the United States, of whom all receiving a salary of a thousand dollars per annum are appointed by the President, and the remainder by his nominee, the Postmaster-General. These persons are removed from their situations on the accession of a new party, and make way for an army of new and probably inexperienced postmasters, to the manifest detriment of the public service." * Although, under this system, party leaders are of course idolised by their followers, comparatively few great statesmen are produced, and the fathers of the Revolution, trained in the old colonial period, have never been surpassed. The mass of the people necessarily become partisans, and the American character and manners receive injury from the undue predominance assigned to a kind of politics by no means elevated in its aims or ennobling in its tendency.

Many evil effects have also arisen from the peculiar kind of oratory which has generally found favour with the people. On the 4th of July, for instance, the anniversary of the Declaration of Independence, custom requires an oration in every town, village, and neighbourhood throughout the United States. In these orations, the Declaration is read, the causes which led to the Revolution are recounted, the events of the old quarrel are raked up, and the whole blame of the contest is laid

---

* Western World Revisited, p. 266.

upon despotic and tyrannical England. The orator,
perhaps, takes occasion to assert that England, although
smaller in extent than Virginia, envies bitterly the prosperity of the United States, and constantly endeavours to
arrest their progress, slander their statesmen, and misre-
present their institutions.   Kings, princes, nobles, and
priests are held up to public execration.   The history of
the times is told in a manner adapted to flatter the self-
love of the audience, and the people are encouraged to
regard themselves as the most free, the most brave, the
most wise, the most religious, and the most intelligent
of mankind. " We may well mourn," says Bishop
Potter, of Pennsylvania, " that there is sometimes
among us so much impatience of the restraints of law,
and always such overweening national self-esteem,
combined with a tone of detraction so ungenerous and
undistinguishing in respect to the institutions and
condition of other lands." *

As a general rule, the press only too faithfully follows the tone of the popular oratory. The Bishop of
Tennessee said in his charge in 1837 : " The press,
generally under the influence of party organisation and
subservient to party purpose, has become the chief instrument in promoting licentiousness." " The newspapers of the day disgorge upon society crimination
and vituperation in every quarter of the country." Dr.
Cleveland Coxe, of Baltimore, writing in 1860, tells us †
that the American press " suggests cause for anxiety

---

* Charge, 1849.
† The Church and the Press, p. 7.

and alarm. It already battens upon popular vice and passion. It is made a tremendous agent of corruption. By night and day, by the untiring energy of steam, and as it were with the very flame of Tophet, it sends forth elements of pollution, the most corrosive." Bishop Hopkins says : "The press has its full share in the general deterioration. Party-spirit there finds its convenient organ to scatter poison throughout the land. There is the ready instrument to manufacture a spurious reputation for one candidate, or to vilify the worthy fame of another. There is the beguiling sophistry which lifts the freebooter to the rank of a revolutionary hero. There is the daily trumpeter of every nauseous deed of individual villany. There is the retailer of every jest which may provoke a laugh at the expense of religion. There is the willing adjunct of infidelity, profanity, rebellion, false morality, and every form of assault, direct and indirect, upon the principles of law and order."

To the above-mentioned dangerous influences must be added the great evil of slavery. Having been introduced early in the colonial period, slavery had become so deeply rooted in the habits of the Southern States, that, although Washington and others looked forward to its eventual abolition, it was considered impossible to eradicate it at the Revolution, and an express provision for its protection was introduced into the Constitution. Indeed, had any measure hostile to it been entertained by the Revolutionary Congress, the union of the States against England would have been out of the question. We have seen the rapid spread of this institution over the new South-Western States, and the energy with which its promoters favoured every scheme which tended to its diffusion. Slavery could not exist together with general intelligence, and while, in the North, secular education flourished, the South regarded the ignorance of the labourer as necessary to the permanence of society. As England originally introduced slavery, so England has shared largely in the maintenance of it to the present day. But for the invention of the cotton-gin, it is possible that at this time there might not be a slave in America. The demands of modern commerce are imperative; our manufactories must be supplied with the raw material; and nearly two-thirds of the American cotton are received by England. The Southern "Institution" has thus become an important part of the great system which has its centre in Manchester.

Already it had been predicted that the combined effects of slavery and of opposite commercial interests would ultimately break up the Union. The anticipations of such a calamity might be quoted to any extent. De Tocqueville, in his profound work on American democracy, said, "If ever America undergoes great revolutions, they will be brought about by the presence of the black race on the soil of the United States; that is to say, they will owe their origin, not to the equality, but to the inequality of conditions."* An article published twenty years ago in a Presbyterian Review contains the following remarkable language: — "The

* American translation, 1840, p. 278.

opinion that slaveholding is itself a crime must operate to produce the disunion of the States, and the division of all ecclesiastical societies in this country. Just so far as this opinion operates, it will lead those who entertain it to submit to any sacrifices to carry it out and give it effect. We shall become two nations in feeling, which must soon render us two nations in fact." Five years earlier, Mr. Robert Wickliffe, a Kentuckian, in an oration before the University of the State, said: — "That there is danger to this Union, and that there are men who seek its ruin and would rejoice in its downfall, are facts too true and too alarming not to be perceived. But how long will such men continue to distract their unhappy country? How long will they continue to make the downfall of the Union the only means of their own elevation? Is there nothing noble, nothing useful, in this Union, that men will thus labour to bring about its destruction? Let the North cease to meddle with the domestic concerns of the South ; let the South bear a more tolerant and benignant spirit towards the North, and all will be well."

Notwithstanding, however, the dangers which beset the Republic in the want of definite religion, the decay of authority, the growth of political corruption, the licentiousness of speech and of the press, and the existence of slavery, the progress of events was in other points of view decidedly hopeful and encouraging. So many were the sources of wealth and the elements of material prosperity, that the political constitution must have been bad indeed which could have greatly interfered with their development. Besides, whatever evil effects an overpowering democracy may have exerted on some departments of the General Government, a check more or less effectual was found in the State legislatures, which, since the year 1800, had been constantly rising in comparative importance. " The limitation of the granted powers of Congress, the reservation of the rights of the several States, and the organisation of the Senate as their representative, give to the smallest States equal weight with the largest in one branch of the national legislature, and impose a very effectual check on the power of a numerical majority." *   Thus a number of smaller democracies, each having its reserved rights, were supposed to be a balance against the single great democracy, which otherwise might have tyrannised over the continent. In some of these commonwealths the respect paid to religion and law has always been much greater than in others, and a higher tone of morals and manners is a necessary result. In America generally " the last thirty years stand pre-eminent for immense improvements in the arts. The earth is traversed with a speed which exceeds the most extravagant anticipation. Intelligence is transmitted on the wings of electricity, and men converse together with ease across the continent. The number of travellers is multiplied more than a thousandfold. Inventions have sprung up in every other department, as if some new and unaccountable energy was urging

* Everett's Oration, 1860.

the human mind to its ultimate earthly developments. Nothing is too vast to be undertaken, nothing too strange to be believed." * To the same purpose Mr. Everett, late American Minister in England, speaks in an oration delivered at Boston on the 4th of July, 1860 : — "Merely to fill up the wilderness with a population provided with the ordinary institutions and carrying on the customary pursuits of civilised life, though surely no mean achievement, was not the whole of the work allotted to the United States. The mechanical arts have not only been cultivated, but they have been cultivated with unusual aptitude. Agriculture, manufactures, commerce, navigation, whether by sails or steam, and the art of printing in all its forms and in all its applications, have been pursued with surprising skill. I believe that in the cities of Boston, New York, and Philadelphia, more money, in proportion to the populations, is raised by taxation for the support of common schools than in any other cities in the world. There are more seminaries in the United States where a decent academical education can be obtained, — more, I still mean, in proportion to the population,—than in any other country except Germany. The fine arts have reached a high degree of excellence. The taste for music is rapidly spreading in town and country; and every year witnesses productions from the pencil and chisel of American sculptors and painters which would adorn any gallery in the world. Our astronomers, mathematicians, naturalists,

* Address before Trinity College, 1854.

chemists, engineers, jurists, publicists, historians, poets, novelists, and lexicographers, have placed themselves on a level with their contemporaries abroad. In no part of Christendom is religion more generously supported, while the American missionary operations have won the admiration of the civilised world. Our charitable asylums, houses of industry, institutions for the education of deaf mutes and the blind, for the care of the pauper and the discipline and reformation of the criminal, are nowhere surpassed. In a word, there is no branch of the mechanical or fine arts, no department of science, no form of polite literature, no description of social improvement, in which, due allowance being made for the means and resources at command, the progress of the United States has not been satisfactory, and in some respects astonishing."

But while men were thus congratulating themselves on the improvement of the country, and while the Census of 1860 was proclaiming the advance of the population to nearly thirty-two millions, a worm was at the root of the luxuriant and widely spreading "gourd" of the American Union. Dissension between North and South approached a point at which all reasonable hope of adjustment would cease. With the view of carrying into effect the provisions of the Constitution, Congress had enacted a "Fugitive Slave Law," making it the duty of the officers of the several States to seize fugitive slaves and return them to their owners. The Northern States, considering this law an encroachment on their rights, had passed "Personal Liberty Laws," denying the assistance of these officers. The celebrated "Dred Scott" * decision, pronounced by the Chief Justice of the United States, had shown that a negro descended from slave ancestors could not become entitled to the rights of a citizen of the United States, even in the Western country north of the parallel of 36° 30′; and that slaves were not made free by their owners taking them to reside permanently in free States. By the "Nebraska Bill," overthrowing the Missouri Compromise, the people of the Territories had acquired a right derisively called "Squatter Sovereignty." Being left to decide the question of slavery for themselves, emigrants from the North and South had hastened to settle the point, and Kansas in particular had become the scene of fearful violence, and even bloodshed. On the one hand, without any particular love for the negro, who was still viewed with a feeling akin to disgust, many in the North, in speaking or writing of the South, revived the bitter and denunciatory temper and language of the Puritans. Philanthropy towards the slave was less evident in this party than misanthropy towards the slave-owner. The abolitionists, to use the words of the well-known

---

* Dred Scott, a negro slave, had been taken by his master to a place west of the Mississippi, and north of latitude 36° 30′, and consequently on free soil. Here he married and had two daughters, one born north and one south of that line. By the Missouri Compromise, slavery was prohibited on the north of 36° 30′. Dred Scott was however taken by his master into the slave State of Missouri, and there sold with his family. Having brought an action before the Circuit Court of the United States to recover his freedom, he was defeated on two grounds: first, that he had no right to sue, not being a citizen; secondly, that the Missouri Compromise was unconstitutional, and therefore void.

Dr. Channing, "fell into the common error of enthusiasts, that of exaggerating their object, of feeling as if no evil existed but that which they opposed, and as if no guilt could be compared with that of countenancing and upholding it. The tone of their newspapers has often been fierce, bitter, and abusive. They have sent forth their orators, some of them transported with fiery zeal, to sound the alarm against slavery through the land, to gather together young and old, pupils from schools, females hardly arrived at the years of discretion, the ignorant, the excitable, the impetuous, and to organise these into associations for the battle against oppression. Very unhappily, they preached their doctrine to the coloured people, and collected them into societies. To this mixed and excitable multitude, minute, heart-rending descriptions of slavery were given in piercing tones of passion; and slaveholders were held up as monsters of cruelty and crime. The abolitionist, indeed, proposed to convert slaveholders; and for this end he approached them with vituperation, and exhausted on them the vocabulary of abuse." Some were not content with hard words, but proceeded to action. Inflamed by private wrongs endured in Kansas, as well as by the furious speeches of ultra-abolitionists, John Brown and a party of mistaken men invaded Virginia in 1859, with the expectation of exciting the negroes to insurrection. The objects of their sympathy gave them no encouragement; they were captured after causing some bloodshed and much alarm, and Brown, with the other leaders of the party, perished

on the gallows. This line of conduct on the part of individuals was preceded and followed by action on the part
of States. "Legislative bodies enacted and re-enacted
statutes which declared that if a Southern man, under
the shield of the Constitution, and with the decision of the
Supreme Court of the country in his hand, should come
within their jurisdiction, and set up a claim to a fugitive slave, he should be punished with a fine of two
thousand dollars and fifteen years' imprisonment."* On
the other hand, there were many in the South who now
put forth the most exaggerated statements on the other
side of the question. Formerly slavery was generally
admitted to be an evil, — necessary, indeed, but yet an
evil. It was now declared to be the corner-stone of the
American Constitution, a civilising moral institution,
necessary to the welfare of the negro, and deserving of
being preached and propagated like Christianity itself.
Governor Wise, of Virginia, breathed forth rage and
defiance against the North, and indeed against all men
who presumed to question the absolute perfection of
the system of slavery. "To suppress slavery," exclaimed
an orator at Charleston, "would be to make American
civilisation retrograde two centuries." † A rigorous
censorship now stopped at the frontier of the South the
books and newspapers of the North, and persons sus-
pected of holding anti-slavery principles were expelled,
sometimes with violence, from Southern territory.

---

* Sermon preached at Brooklyn in 1860 by H. Van Dyke.

† Clarigny on the Election of Mr. Lincoln, translated by Sir
Willoughby Jones.

Tyranny over white men was clearly invf 'lved in the slavery of the black. But abolitionism was now embraced by a sufficient number to hold the balancee of power between contending parties in many districts an~d States. Aspirants for the Presidency seized upon it as a weapon for gratifying their ambition or avenging their disappointments. In the halls of Congress were heard the outpourings both of Northern and Southern violence.* The House of Representatives, and even the Senate Chamber, were more than ever disgraced by fierce passion and violent denunciation.

The Presidential election of 1861 approached, and it was evident that the tide which had long flowed towards the South was setting in the opposite direction. Douglas was the favourite candidate of the "Democrats" and slave-owners, while Abraham Lincoln, a man of humble origin and imperfect education, was selected as candidate by a Northern Convention of "Republicans" held at Chicago. The Constitution had designed that the difficult and dangerous business of the Presidential election should be conducted by Electoral Colleges, chosen in each State, and composed of men selected from the body of the people on account of their experience, judgment, and integrity. Under the actual working system, these Colleges have never been anything but cumbrous and superfluous instruments for signifying to the Central Government the choice of the President already made by the people in their primary assemblies.† Accordingly,

* Clarigny.   † Church Review, 1859, p. 536.

although the existing President did not vacate his office until the 4th of March, 1861, and the choice of his successor was not announced by the electoral body until the 13th of February (Ash-Wednesday), it was known early in December, 1860, that Abraham Lincoln was the chosen President of the United States.

This event was followed by immediate action on the part of the Southern States. Preparations had already been made for a movement, in which hatred for abolitionism and contempt for the negro bore leading parts, though commercial considerations were not without their influence. South Carolina, through a Convention promptly summoned, put forth a declaration of independence, which appeared like a parody of the original of 1776. In this document, after recounting the wrongs inflicted upon the South in regard to slave property, and the insults heaped upon it by the North, the members of the Convention pronounced the severance of their connection with the Union, and in defence of their new position pledged, according to the old formula, "their lives, their fortunes, and their sacred honour." The great independence of the several commonwealths rendered secession a very simple process, and in the course of the winter six other States followed the example of South Carolina. They soon arranged the basis of a new confederacy, designed to be, in some respects, an improvement upon the older one. There were no abolitionists to disturb their harmony, and they proceeded with remarkable coolness and sagacity to prepare their new constitution, and to lay down the general principles of their policy. Already the Northern States had become alarmed at the progress of events, and had repealed many of their " personal liberty" laws, considering that the question of slavery was of little moment compared with the pre- servation of the Union. At the same time there was a strong disposition to coerce the rebels; but a difficulty presented itself at the very outset. From the dread of executive power, the President's authority had been made too weak for decisive action, while to Mr. Lincoln's predecessor it appeared that by the Constitution no means existed of preventing the rebellion of entire States, or of obliging those which had seceded to return to the Union. The interregnum always taking place between the virtual election of a new President and his inauguration enabled the seceders to prosecute their de- signs without interference on the part of the government at Washington. Mr. Lincoln, on his accession to power, found a rival President in Mr. Jefferson Davis, elected for six years, a Southern army already organised and nearly equal to his own, and a new confederacy sur- rounded with the ordinary attributes of government and emblems of nationality.

Thus, on account of wrongs in which the civilised world could feel but little sympathy, the adventurous and spirited South commenced a new political existence. Thus, after a duration of eighty-four years, the lapse of but one long life, the Union so thoughtfully adjusted by the veterans of the Revolution seemed to meet its long-predicted and perhaps inevitable dissolution.

CHAP. IX.

DR. COKE'S APPLICATION FOR THE REUNION OF THE METHODISTS.—
PROPOSAL OF THE BISHOPS.—A MISSIONARY BISHOP DESIRED.—
BISHOP CHASE.—A MISSIONARY SOCIETY FOUNDED.—PROGRESS OF THE
OLDER DIOCESES, AND OF THE CHURCH AT LARGE.—ESTIMATE OF THE
EXPENSES OF DIVINE WORSHIP, ETC.—ENGLISH EMIGRATION.—GENERAL
CONVENTION AT RICHMOND IN 1859.—SERMON BY DR. VINTON.

HILE the American Union was thus advancing on its eventful career, the Church rose from its ashes and attained a degree of influence and prosperity which appeared fully to justify the course adopted by Bishop White and the General Convention of 1789. It had a Liturgy, so revised that many dissenting objections had lost their point. Its constitution had been arranged in harmony with that of the Republic, and, above all, it had its long-desired bishops, who, with their limited authority, could not be suspected of designs against the liberties of the people.

One of the first important events after the completion of this organisation was an application for reunion on the part of Dr. Coke, one of the superintendents or bishops appointed by John Wesley. In a letter to

Bishop White*, dated at Richmond, Virginia, April 24th, 1791, Dr. Coke wrote: "I am not sure but I went farther in the separation of our Church in America than Mr. Wesley, from whom I had received my commission, did intend. He did indeed solemnly invest me, as far as he had a right so to do, with episcopal authority, but did not intend, I think, that an entire separation should take place. He, being pressed by our friends on this side of the water for ministers to administer the sacraments to them (there being very few clergy of the Church of England then in the States), went farther, I am sure, than he would have gone if he had foreseen some events which followed. And this I am certain of, that he is now sorry for the separation. But what can be done for a reunion, which I much wish for, and to accomplish which Mr. Wesley, I have no doubt, would use his influence to the utmost?" The writer then proposed that all the Methodist ministers should receive Episcopal ordination, continuing, however, under the government of Wesley's superintendents and their successors. He foresaw difficulties on account of the ignorance of the learned languages on the part of the Methodists, as well as from the expected opposition of his colleague, Mr. Asbury. Still he hoped that Bishop White would consider the subject, and proposed an interview with him. He afterwards wrote in a similar strain to Bishop Seabury.

Bishop White, in reply, expressed his readiness to

* Bishop White's Memoirs, p. 425.

converse with Dr. Coke, and said that it was "rather to
be expected that those who agreed in fundamentals
should make mutual sacrifices for a union, than that
any Church should divide into two bodies, without a
difference being alleged to exist in any leading point.
For the preventing of this," he added, " the measures
you may propose cannot fail of success, unless there be
on one side, or on both, a most lamentable deficiency of
Christian temper." Dr. Coke received the news of
Wesley's death in the short interval between the dates
of the two letters, and immediately left his residence at
Baltimore, on his way to England. As it was necessary
for him to go through Philadelphia, he visited Bishop
White, and had several interviews with him. Nothing
passed that gave any ground of expectation of a reunion on the principle of consolidation, or on any other
principle than that of the Methodists continuing a distinct and self-governed body. On the one hand, Coke
proposed that Asbury and himself should be consecrated
as bishops, and that the Church should allow the
Methodist preachers to minister to her congregations.
On the other hand, it was by no means clear that the
clergy would have a corresponding access to the congregations of the Methodists. In consequence, however, of what took place, Bishop Madison, in the
General Convention of 1792, obtained the consent of
the other bishops to the following proposal: "The
Protestant Episcopal Church in the United States of
America, ever bearing in mind the sacred obligation
which attends all the followers of Christ to avoid

divisions among themselves, and anxious to promote that union for which our Lord and Saviour so earnestly prayed, do hereby declare to the Christian world that, uninfluenced by any other considerations than those of duty as Christians, and an earnest desire for the prosperity of pure Christianity and the furtherance of our holy religion, they are ready and willing to unite and form one body with any religious society which shall be influenced by the same catholic spirit. And, in order that this Christian end may be the more easily effected, they further declare that all things in which the great essentials of Christianity or the characteristic principles of their Church are not concerned, they are willing to leave to future discussion; being ready to alter or modify those points which, in the opinion of the Protestant Episcopal Church, are subject to human alteration. And it is hereby recommended to the State Conventions to adopt such measures or propose such conferences with Christians of other denominations as to themselves may be thought most prudent, and report accordingly to the ensuing General Convention."

The public mind was in no respect prepared for this well-intended scheme. The desolating effects of disunion were not yet sufficiently understood by the sectarian bodies, and in the Lower House of the Convention the proposal of the Bishops was considered as tending to produce distrust of the Church system without the least prospect of embracing any other religious body. Accordingly the document was withdrawn, and this measure in favour of Christian union came to nothing.

Early in the present century the greater part of the clergy ordained in the colonial period had passed away, and their places had been supplied by men trained up under the new circumstances of the country. The infidelity which had been fashionable in the last generation was passing away like the shadow of a dark cloud, and persons of powerful intellect and strong religious character came over from the sectarian ranks, and were added to the ministry of the Church, and even to its episcopate. In 1811 there were eight bishops and two hundred and thirty-two clergymen; and about the same time Dr. Bowden, of New York, was calling attention by his writings to the historical arguments in favour of episcopacy.

The vast regions beyond the Alleghany mountains were now rapidly increasing in population. Dissenters of every variety had pre-occupied the ground, and only two or three clergymen were to be found in the whole of Western America. The appointment of a missionary bishop was strongly urged by one of these gentlemen, the Rev. Joseph Doddridge, a relation of the eminent nonconformist of the same name. But the weakness of the Church prevented immediate action on this important point, and a great opportunity was lost.

The condition of the diocese of Virginia was as discouraging as can well be conceived. Bishop Madison, though a good scholar, was far from active, and "had a low estimate of the spiritual power inherent in the office which he held." * His Diocesan Convention at

* Bishop of Oxford.

length ceased to assemble, and the country abounded with the mouldering ruins of the houses of God. But the Bishop died in 1812, and the first sign of life within the diocese was the meeting of a Convention to elect his successor. In a State which formerly had more than a hundred clergy of its own, thirteen clergymen and twelve laymen were all that could be assembled. Failing in their first attempt at an election, they met again in even smaller numbers in 1814; but on this occasion they selected as their bishop an earnest-minded and holy man, Dr. Richard Moore, of New York. After receiving consecration at Philadelphia, Bishop Moore entered on his work with vigour, and in a very short time the Church began to revive. Ten new churches were soon building by voluntary contributions, and eight of those in ruins were reported as being under repair. An Episcopal fund was commenced in order that the bishop's attention might not be detained from his higher duties by the charge of a parish. Although the clergy were poor, their ranks were being recruited from the best and oldest families in Virginia.

After the resignation of Bishop Provoost, in 1800, Dr. Benjamin Moore was consecrated for New York, and during the ten years of his episcopate there was a gradual improvement in the state of the diocese. His successor, Bishop Hobart, was a man of remarkable vigour and determination of character, and at his death, in 1830, the diocese was rapidly increasing in numbers and in hearty appreciation of Church principles. Through his exertions, the General Theological Seminary of the

Church was established at New York, under the control of trustees appointed in the several dioceses. A fund also was commenced for the education of young men of piety desirous of entering into holy orders. From the time when the Church thus took into her own hands the education of the clergy, the number of her ministers rapidly increased. In 1814, they were little more than two hundred and forty; but in forty-seven years this number increased to about two thousand four hundred, being a tenfold multiplication. In the same space of time the population of the United States advanced from about eight millions to nearly thirty-two millions, being a fourfold multiplication. As there is reason to think that the progress of the Church has been to some extent proportionate with that of the clergy, it may be safely inferred, that, notwithstanding all the known and admitted difficulties of an imperfect voluntary system, the Church has increased even more rapidly than the nation.*

Nearly contemporaneously with Bishop Hobart, the meek and amiable Griswold entered on the charge of the Eastern diocese, then including all the New England States excepting Connecticut. In 1815 Dr. Croes became the first Bishop of New Jersey. In 1819 the intrepid Philander Chase was consecrated Bishop of Ohio. He was a native of New Hampshire and a descendant of Captain Aquila Chase, a Puritan from Cornwall, who settled in America in 1640. The family records state that this

* See Appendix.

Aquila was on one occasion brought to trial because, on his reaching home on Sunday morning after a long voyage, his wife gathered and dressed her first dish of green peas to welcome him. In vain he pleaded the danger of scurvy, and the necessities of health : the utmost favour he received was to escape the infliction of "forty stripes save one" by paying a heavy fine. Philander Chase was the fifth in descent from Aquila, and of the same religious persuasion. He first became acquainted with the Prayer-book in his nineteenth year, while a member of Dartmouth College, in New Hampshire. He tells us, in his "Reminiscences," that "amidst the manifold divisions, not to say schisms and heresies," to which the Puritan system had led, "the Prayer-book seemed a light, mercifully designed by Providence to conduct himself and his friends into the paths of peace and order." He became an earnest Churchman, and his convictions were shared by his parents and other near relatives. Instead of repairing their meeting-house, in which the father and grandfather of young Chase had officiated as Congregational deacons, the people determined to pull it down, and erect an Episcopal church in its place. Philander was ordained deacon by Bishop Provoost in 1798, and priest in the following year. After doing good service as a missionary in the western parts of New York, and afterwards as the first clergyman of the church at New Orleans, he became rector of Christ Church at Hartford, in Connecticut. Hence he removed to Ohio in 1817, and, after exerting himself as a missionary during two years, became the first bishop west of the mountains. Having appealed for aid to the friends of religion in England, as well as in America, he succeeded in establishing Kenyon College, which has assisted greatly in supplying the western country with a native ministry.

In 1818, a Missionary Association was formed in Pennsylvania, which planted a few churches in the western part of that State and in Ohio. A few years afterwards, this Society, under the auspices of the General Convention, became known as the "Domestic and Foreign Missionary Society of the Protestant Episcopal Church." In 1835, its income, at first very small, had considerably increased, and it maintained clergymen not only in the Western States, but in China, Africa, and at Athens. It was now determined that the whole Church should be regarded as a Missionary Association, and that the General Convention should appoint a Board of Missions, having two Committees, domestic and foreign. It was also decided that missionary bishops should be provided for the States and Territories destitute of episcopal supervision, and ultimately for the stations in heathen lands occupied by the American Church. Under this provision, Dr. Kemper was consecrated as Missionary Bishop for the North-West, and, three years afterwards, Dr. Polk (a near relative of the President of the same name) for the South-West. Bishop Chase, meeting with painful difficulties in Ohio, resigned his charge of that diocese, and was elected Bishop of Illinois, where he founded another College under the name of Jubilee. Dr. Ravenscroft, the first Bishop of North Carolina, was consecrated in 1823, and Kentucky, in like manner, received Dr. Smith as its bishop in 1832. In the same year the Church in Vermont had become sufficiently strong to separate from the Eastern diocese, and Dr. Hopkins, whose Address has been quoted, was elected and consecrated its bishop. Four years afterwards, Dr. Otey, also mentioned in a former chapter, was consecrated for Tennessee.

During these events, the Church in Virginia continued to recover her lost ground under the venerable Bishop Moore and his assistant, Bishop Meade, consecrated in 1829. A Seminary was founded within her limits at Alexandria, which began to send forth clergymen in 1823, and which during nearly forty years has supplied a considerable number of pastors to the Southern and Western dioceses, as well as missionaries to foreign countries. There was now a great rekindling of personal devotion, and an ardent zeal generally pervaded the younger clergy. The two Virginian bishops worked happily together, and when the aged Bishop Moore was gathered to his rest in 1842, he was succeeded by his coadjutor, who in his turn found an assistant in Bishop Johns.

In 1859, the number of the Virginian clergy was 113, and of the parishes and churches 174, with 7519 communicants, and perhaps 38,000 or 40,000 regular worshippers, out of a population of 1,421,661.

In Maryland the recovery has been still more striking. Dr. Claggett, the first bishop, was succeeded by his assistant, Dr. Kemp, a Scottish Episcopalian. After Bishop Kemp's sudden decease party-spirit ran so high, and the mode of election was, in that diocese, so defective, that several years elapsed before a successor could be appointed. In 1830, a compromise was effected and Dr. Stone was raised to the episcopate. At his decease the old animosities burst forth, and, after another interregnum, the present learned and able prelate, Dr. Whittingham, was consecrated in 1840. Although the population of Maryland is little more than a third of that of Virginia, the number of its clergy, in 1859, was a hundred and fifty-nine, with ten thousand five hundred and eighty communicants, and about fifty thousand worshippers. It has a Diocesan College, that of St. James, which, in 1859, numbered a hundred and sixteen students. In this State, the Diocesan Convention enjoys the remarkable privilege of being a body corporate under the laws of the State.* The glebes remain in possession of the ancient parishes, and in some cases include as much as three hundred acres. The entire Church property is estimated at about a million of dollars over and above the value of the churches themselves. The pew-rents, for the whole diocese, produce about fifty thousand dollars, or ten thousand pounds per annum, besides a larger sum in voluntary contributions. The churches are a hundred and seventy-three in number, containing forty-five thousand sittings. The stipends of the clergy amount to eighty thousand dollars,

* Journal of General Convention for 1859.

or sixteen thousand pounds per annum, averaging about a hundred pounds a year each. The other expenses of public worship come to about the same amount.

The diocese of New York was divided in 1839, and has since continued under two bishops. In the entire State there were, in 1859, four hundred and seventy clergymen, with thirty-five thousand three hundred and twenty-five communicants, a larger number by far than in any other State of the Union. But the population was at the same time rather more than three millions. In the city of New York alone, exclusive of the suburbs, there are now about sixty Episcopal churches.

In Connecticut, once noted for the " Blue Laws," the growth of the Church has always been satisfactory. Bishop Seabury died in 1796, and was succeeded by Bishop Jarvis, who gave place at his decease to the present venerable senior bishop, Dr. Brownell, who has presided over the diocese during forty-two years, and has been assisted since 1851 by a valuable coadjutor in Bishop Williams. The population of Connecticut is but a quarter of s! that of Virginia, yet the Church has a hundred and thisirty-three clergymen, and eleven thousand five hundred amnd seventy-five communicants. Trinity College, at Hartford, has long continued to raise up a supply of clergy, and now a divinity school at Middletown, on the Connecticut River, named after Bishop Berkeley, is advancing the same good work.

Rhode Island, formerly considered by the Puritans the " sink of New England," has a bishop (Dr. Clark) and thirty clergymen, with three thousand one hundred and forty-two communicants out of a population under a hundred and fifty thousand, little more than a third of Connecticut. In Massachusetts, from whence the two Browns were ignominiously expelled for reading the Common Prayer, Dr. Eastburn is bishop, with seventy-seven clergy and seven thousand seven hundred and eighty communicants. New Jersey, with a population rather exceeding half a million, has Dr. Odenheimer as bishop (the successor of the England-loving Bishop Doane), and a hundred and three clergymen, with five thousand communicants. In Pennsylvania, Bishop White continued happily to preside over the Church until he had seen the abundant fruit of his early labours, and of his wise and conciliatory conduct in the General Conventions of the preceding century. It was the good fortune of the writer of this work to form his acquaintance at his own home in 1829, and to hear from his own lips an account of his consecration at Lambeth, and of his presentation to King George and Queen Charlotte. He died on the 17th of July, 1836, in the eighty-ninth year of his age, the sixty-sixth of his ministry, and the fiftieth of his episcopate. He was succeeded by Dr. Onderdonk, his assistant, who gave place to Bishop Potter, who in turn received an assistant in Bishop Bowman. The old Quaker colony now has two bishops, a hundred and ninety-three clergymen, and above fourteen thousand communicants, in a population of more than two millions and a quarter. Philadelphia, with a population of perhaps half a million, has about forty Episcopal churches, many of which (like those of

New York) have been constructed at a great expense, and are capable of accommodating large congregations.

The reader is now informed as to the outward condition, two years since, of the more flourishing dioceses of the American Church. There is great progress elsewhere; but in the new Southern and Western States Church-work is comparatively new, and consequently less in advance. Thus, Ohio, with two bishops, Drs. M‘Ilvaine and Bedell, has but eighty-four clergymen, with less than six thousand communicants out of a population nearly equal to that of Pennsylvania. In Wisconsin, too, notwithstanding the labours of the indefatigable Bishop Kemper, and of the Theological School at Nashotah, the clergy, in 1859, were only forty-six, with about two thousand five hundred communicants out of a population of five hundred and fifty thousand.

It is satisfactory, however, to know that in all the States and Territories there is now episcopal superintendence, together with at least the framework of diocesan arrangements. It would be needless in this place to say more than that, in addition to those mentioned above, bishops and clergy are provided for Maine, New Hampshire, Delaware, North and South Carolina, Georgia, Florida, Alabama, Mississippi, Louisiana, Texas, Indiana, Missouri, Kansas, Michigan, Iowa, Minnesota, California, and Oregon. Bishops are also placed over the Missions in China and Western Africa.*

* See Appendix.

The receipts of the Board of Missions, in its two departments, domestic and foreign, are now about thirty thousand pounds per annum, besides considerable sums raised for an American " Church Missionary Society," under the management of some of the " Evangelical " party. Most of the dioceses have also their separate missionary funds for the advancement of the Church within their own limits. The entire annual contributions for missionary and charitable purposes connected with the Church, were reported, in 1859, as amounting to five hundred and forty thousand dollars, or a hundred and eight thousand pounds. The stipends of the clergy, at a hundred pounds each, amount to about two hundred and forty thousand pounds, and other expenses of divine worship may be nearly the same. To these items must be added the cost of building perhaps seventy new churches in every year, which, at eight thousand dollars each, would be equal to a hundred and twelve thousand pounds. It appears then that American Churchmen pay voluntarily, for the support and diffusion of their religion, not less than seven hundred thousand pounds per annum. By the " Journal of the General Convention," it appears also that, in 1859, the number of communicants in the entire Church, was a hundred and thirty-nine thousand six hundred and eleven. According to the proportion which obtains in Maryland, this would give six hundred and sixty thousand as the number of actual Church-people at that time in the United States. But to this estimate must be added multitudes of persons attached to the Church, and under its influence in various degrees, who yet can hardly be considered as its members. A large number of Church people are also scattered over the country, singly or in small quantities, unconnected with any congregation, and therefore not reported to the Convention. Altogether we may perhaps safely conclude that not far from two millions of Americans, and those usually of a superior class, are more or less connected with Protestant Episcopacy.

It may be thought that the advance of the American Church is due in some considerable measure to emigration from England. Unhappily this is not the case. Although, sometimes, forty or fifty thousand persons from this country (exclusive of Ireland) have removed to the United States in a single year, few of the number attach themselves to the Church in America. The best of our emigrants prefer a residence in the colonies. A very large proportion of those Englishmen who choose the United States as their country are usually indifferent or opposed to all religion. Some are ordinary dissenters, some are dupes of the Mormon imposture, and those who were Churchmen in England often think that in parting from their native country they also part from the Church.* They generally make no attempt to obtain introductions to

---

* See the papers of the Emigrants' Aid Society (published by Rivington), of which the writer is a Secretary. The design of this Society is to introduce our poor emigrants to the American clergy, and to assist in supplying them with ministers and in erecting their first humble churches in the new settlements.

the American clergy; they settle without regard to the proximity of a church, and are lost by thousands in the wildernesses of the West. Those who remain faithful to their spiritual mother are certainly not a tenth, perhaps not a twentieth, part of the whole. The American Episcopal Church, unlike the Church of Rome, expects little from emigration, and gains chiefly by natural increase, and by the numerous accessions which she is constantly receiving from dissenting bodies and the world at large. A deputation from the Society for Propagating the Gospel, of which the writer was a member, proceeded to America in 1853, to confer with the General Convention on the advancement of missions by the joint efforts of the parent and daughter Churches. After much discussion it was finally agreed that our emigrants afforded a wide field for the exertion of Christian philanthropy, and that a system of introductions, if properly carried out, would supply an effectual means of keeping our poor people within the fold of the Church after their removal beyond the Atlantic.

The General Convention of 1859 was held at Richmond, in Virginia, when the union and good feeling between Churchmen of the North and of the South was an occasion of mutual rejoicing. The Presbyterian and Methodist " denominations " in America had been rent asunder by the slavery question; but the Church remained undivided, and by her tone of moderation was considered to have acted as a bulwark against the double fanaticism which threatened to tear the country in pieces. Even the invasion and capture of John

Brown, which happened during the session, failed to disturb the equanimity and brotherly affection of the assembled bishops, clergy, and laity. But in the very next year the Union was apparently, at least, broken up, and in seven of the dioceses the Church ceased to pray for the President and Congress, as it had formerly ceased to pray for the King and Parliament. With bitter grief, Churchmen found themselves torn asunder, and to many it seemed but too probable that no General Convention would again assemble, to represent the wishes and to direct the action of North and South alike.

The following portion of a sermon preached by Dr. A. Vinton, of Trinity Church, Philadelphia, will serve to show the feelings of many Churchmen at this serious crisis, and at the same time will afford a specimen of American pulpit oratory : —

" A Divine and Almighty hand is stretched out continually to shed down blessing and glory upon the upright and virtuous State, to chasten its waywardness with a calamitous rod, or else to sweep it away, as with a sharp scythe of vengeance, on account of its iniquities. It may laud itself in its arrogance, and forget the God that sitteth above. But He laugheth it to scorn; and, although, in His Almighty patience of endurance, He may lengthen the tether of its privilege, and extend the term of its probation, yet there is an overhanging doom to fall upon its guiltiness, when its guilt grows inveterate. A mightier nation, whom God sends, shall tread upon its heels in the pursuit of vengeance, or its own dangerous elements shall internally combine, and the judicial madness of the people shall explode the political fabric, and confusion shall overthrow the State, and dragons shall be in her palaces. This is the theology of history, forgotten, so far as I know, by all historians but one, and the forgetfulness of which has made all history profane, in a bad sense. This is the piety of politics, scorned by almost all politicians, whose scorning is the most fearful omen that overhangs our civil destiny. I call upon you to acknowledge to-day, my friends, with heartfelt adoration, that Jehovah reigneth over the nation.

" For if ever we had need to acknowledge it, it is now. This day of civic thanksgiving threatens to be among those latter days which shall leave our grand political fabric among the things that have been, when our thanks must be given for civil blessings perished and lost. We cannot think of it without a shudder, and that shudder is made up of patriotism, fellowship, and pride, all violated and broken. God has permitted, on this American land, a sublime and fearful experiment of self-government. It is a sublime thing for thirty millions of people to undertake the work of controlling themselves by their own sense of right and duty, with no power above them but that of their own laws, sworn to no allegiance but that of truth and justice, mutually conceived and universally acknowledged, and with no king but conscience.

" In such a government, man approaches his sublime ideal, guided not by power, but by principle. Every energy may be put forth to the utmost, with none other than a moral check, and liberty may run on, step by step with reason, until the whole humanity is developed in the dignity of its godlikeness. This is the theory of our government, sublime if successful, but awful in its failure. If passion, pride, envy, avarice, injustice, dishonesty, possess the people's hearts, then comes the crash and havock of a great force out of gear—the wretchedness of conscience perverted with passion, and the hopelessness of liberty run mad into licentiousness.

"Thus far, we have thanked God for the nation, great, united, and free. We have sung a jubilate which has echoed over the seas till half the world has heard it. And more than half the world has sent its tribute of glad emigrants to swell our glory and strength, till it appeared as if God was forming a grand amalgam of the nations, gathering all the specimen tribes of men into one, to make of that one the controlling power of the world, until, by its influence, it should constrain all other nations into one great brotherhood like itself.

"So plainly had all this been wrought and aided by Providence, that our love for this great Union took a sacred tinge, and our patriotism was piety. In the days past, so holy seemed the bond of fraternity, that no Christian prayer was uttered with more assurance of acceptance than the prayer that God would preserve the Union; and the same pious breath that uttered the supplication, was thought to be not less pious when it imprecated a palsy on the arm that should strike a blow, a scorching to the tongue that should utter a scoff or scorn, and a blighting of the mind that should conceive a plot against the brotherhood of States. But all this is past and gone.

" Thirty years ago began, in some parts of the land, the cold-blooded calculation of the value of the Union. The generation whose young intellect was first stimulated by that problem has grown up into the conviction that the Union is worthless. And now, within that conviction, stiff and hard as cast iron, there boils an enthusiasm of passion which threatens at any moment to explode the whole fabric, and turn the Republic into a shapeless mass of fragments. Shall it be thus? Shall the wheels of time be rolled back to the period of our severance and vassalage? What, then, becomes of all the past—the glorious past? To whom, then, belongs the glory of our national independence—the fruit of the mingled blood of North and South? Whose, then, is Washington? Whose the heritage of fame, world-honoured, but now split into parcels? Who would dare to boast of Revolutionary pedigree? What tongue would not falter to claim an ancestry whose nobility was earned by strife and blood, for the very Union which that tongue scoffs at and repudiates? Whose ears would not tingle at the name of a patriot grandsire shaming the posterity who trample his martyr-blood in the dust of his broken Republic? Who shall give us another 4th of July? What becomes of the grand lesson which we have been teaching to the world of popular sovereignty, and the dignity of freedom? How will absolutism laugh, and abjectism clank its chains with severer woe? Austria in glee. Hungary.

in tears.   Young Italy with the dew of its birth yet fresh
upon it, will not its exulting life turn pale and sickly
again with despondency?   What becomes of the American name, potential in all lands?   Who will know
America? What, is America broken to pieces? Brethren,
it requires the sternest stuff that religious faith was ever
made of, to stand beneath this burden of sad reflections
and fears, and look up to heaven, and calmly say, ‘The
Lord reigneth; let the earth rejoice.’   Yet the one
must be said, and the other must be done, and if
we rightly recognise the truth of God’s dominion, we
shall be ready to do the duty of rejoicing and praise,
whatever may befall.   If the Lord reigneth, then has
He not suffered this sorrowful fear to fall upon us for
our sins against him?   Our great experiment of freedom
could only succeed by being based upon the moral
virtue of the people and their clear intelligence.   Are
these conditions to be found with us?   I will not
answer in detail, for you can answer as well as I; but
when official corruption becomes so prevalent as to
reach the highest stations in the land, when bribery and
intemperance, and quarrels, infest and poison our legislation, when, with our growing prosperity, our pride,
self-will, covetousness, selfishness, and passions, swell
and effloresce into all sorts of immorality, must we not
fear to know that the Lord reigneth?   Do we not de-
serve a day of rebuke and chastening?   Ought not our
towering crest to be brought low?

“ When the national conscience is drugged and
stupefied, does it not need a wound to awaken it?

Because God has not abdicated His dominion, may it not be that He is teaching us to be still, and know that He is God? And yet, because He reigneth, may we not learn a lesson of duty that shall yet save the Republic? If any one part of the nation has invaded the rights of another part by offensive and unbrotherly legislation, may there not be time to repent, and amend, and retract the offence, doing right first, and then asking the reward of right-doing?

" And because the Lord reigneth, we may pray that He would so rule the wills of his people, that whatever is done, shall be done deliberately, rationally, peaceably, and with His approval; and then, though the nation be divided, we may still rejoice. If His Divine wisdom shall order the separation of the brotherhood, then shall we not be forsaken, though we be alone. And even if, like all other democracies, we should be destined to be riven asunder, and disintegrated from sea to sea (for the spirit of schism is procreative), even if States be resolved into towns, and communities divided into classes, and classes broken into factions, and factions beaten into pieces of individuality, to carry out the independence and self-will of us Americans, then — why, even then rejoice that the Lord reigneth; for if there be no reigning Lord God Omnipotent, to sway the unruly wills of men, and turn their hearts like rivers of water, alas for us and our children, and alas for man! Resort to Him, then, in the thick-coming evils, and show how devoutly grateful you are for His sovereignty, by making use of it for the nation's weal. In the cordial remembrance of our civil blessings to-day, recount, along our nation's history, the steps of a divinity which has thus far shaped our ends, and let His past mercies be the argument to fill our mouths when we plead for the conservation of the people's rights and the nation's life."

CHAP. X.

THE CHURCH AND OTHER SOCIETIES.

HE General Convention held in New York in 1853 (at which the English deputation was present) was marked by many signs of awakened zeal. Among these may be reckoned a Memorial, much in the spirit of Bishop Madison's proposal in 1792, signed by several distinguished clergymen, and presented to the Bishops.* This memorial suggested the general question, whether the posture of the Church was all that could be wished, in view of the distracted and divided state of American Christianity, the new forms of unbelief, the progress of Romanism, and "the utter ignorance of the Gospel among a large portion of

* The Memorial Papers, edited by Bishop Potter, of Pennsylvania, and published at Philadelphia by Butler and Co., 1857.

the lower classes of the population." The memorialists inquired whether the usefulness of the Church might not be enlarged by relaxing somewhat the strict rule of the liturgical services, and by conferring Holy Orders on conditions somewhat less stringent than before. That this memorial expressed a widely prevalent feeling, may be concluded from the fact that it was referred by a large majority in the Upper House to a Commission of five Bishops, with instructions to consider the subject, and to report to the next Convention.

A circular with questions, inviting communications, was accordingly addressed by the Bishops to many persons of influence at home and abroad, both within and without the pale of the Church. The principal answers received fill a considerable volume. Some of them were valuable, and the proposals of Presbyterian, Congregationalist, Baptist, German Reformed, and Methodist divines, added considerably to the interest attached to the correspondence.

A Presbyterian wrote, " The Episcopal Church can do much to conciliate and harmonise Protestant Christendom; but every movement in that direction will relatively tend to increase her influence and numbers, and to diminish ours."

A Congregationalist suggested the need of a ministry of limited literary acquirements, in addition to a well-educated clergy. He proposed also the ordination of a diaconate, ineligible to the higher orders of the ministry.

A Baptist observed that, through the operation of

societies for helping young men to prepare for ordination, the ministry had become in a great measure elee-
mosynary. " Able men keep out of it, and it is the
resort of moderate men, who, thus brought up, bow
before wealth, and are destitute of all moral courage."
He proposed that the masses should be aroused, and
every man taught to be a propagandist of Christianity.
He admired the responses in the Church services, and
wished the principle extended to congregational singing.
He would have several deacons in every Church, labouring among the poor.

A German Reformed minister, after mentioning that
his own community was rapidly approximating to a
Liturgy like our own, expressed his hope that the
Episcopal Church, without giving up any of the advantages of her time-honoured form of government and
worship, would relax the exclusive rigour of this form,
and allow the clergy freedom to adapt the Church to
the great mass of the people, " instead of being confined
almost, as is now too much the case, to a particular class
of society."

A Methodist minister wrote, " I have always regarded
the Church of England as the central framework and
life of Protestantism in Great Britain and her dependencies ; and I have regarded the Protestant Episcopal
Church in America as containing the same elements of
durability and life. And yet I believe that neither in
England nor in the United States has the Church fully
accomplished her great mission to the masses of the
people. Why has she failed, when she has the essential

elements of durability and life in her organisation, in her teaching, and in her worship ? The answer is, She is hindered by external restraints. She is not at liberty to approach the masses of the people in her public service, in the places and under the circumstances in which they actually exist, and to speak and minister to them as their varied conditions require." He proceeded to remark that, "by her excellent government and order, and by her scriptural and beautiful liturgy, the Church is admirably calculated to cherish and edify those whose hearts have been drawn to her." But the difficulty is to draw them. In order to do this, he would suggest a greater freedom and earnestness in preaching, and in other services adapted to the varying wants of the people. He anticipated, however, a great difficulty in the way of the Church becoming, as proposed by the memorialists, "a central bond of union among Christians." This difficulty he found in "the growing impression that the Protestant Episcopal Church is gradually settling down into the conclusion that the ministries of other Churches are invalid, and that the Sacraments ought not to be received at their hands." To remove this obstacle, he thought that, while preferring and holding as of best authority and most efficient her own ordination and orders of the ministry, she ought to accept and respect the validity of the ministries in the other Protestant Churches.

In regard to this last proposal, it may be well to remark that an acknowledgment of dissenting orders would be an act for which, in the absence of direct proof of their validity, the Church would be wholly incompetent. The ordination of the different dissenting bodies rests also on various grounds, and it would be impossible to acknowledge it in one instance without denying it by consequence in others. We have seen that the Methodist ordination is wholly derived from Wesley, who was himself only in priest's orders. Presbyterianism, under its different names, rests upon a foundation essentially the same. But if Presbyterian or Methodist ordination is declared to be regular and right, it follows necessarily that Congregational or Baptist ordination is irregular and wrong. The Congregationalists (or Independents) reject the idea of any succession in the ministry, whether through Bishops or through Presbyters. They regard the lay congregation as having full power to confer the ministerial commission, and to ordain its own pastors. This system is not more ancient than the beginning of the seventeenth century. The Baptists sprang from the Congregationalists, and originated in 1639 with Roger Williams, the founder of Rhode Island, previously a minister of the Church of England. Mr. Ezekiel Holliman, a layman, immersed Mr. Williams, and, in turn, Mr. Williams immersed Mr. Holliman. The Baptist ordination has the same authority with that of the Congregationalists, and no more. The Quaker goes further than even the Baptist, and rests the proof of his authority to minister, not on any ordination, but on his own simple assertion of an inward movement of the Holy Spirit. Is the American Church to acknowledge the Methodist and Presbyterian, and to reject the

Baptist, the Puritan, and the Quaker, or is she at once to go the length of acknowledging the Quaker, and thereby declaring that all ordination, whether Episcopal, Presbyterian, Congregational, or Baptist, is alike a baseless assumption? This would be to pour contempt not only on her own fathers, who so earnestly sought the Episcopate from England, but upon the ordination still regarded as sacred by eleven-twelfths of Christendom.

The five Bishops forming the Commission, after duly weighing the numerous suggestions received by them, drew up a valuable document in the shape of a Report. In this they recommended the cultivation of extempore preaching, and maintained the necessity of more force and directness in sermons, and more special adaptation to the varying circumstances of the people. They proposed that, in adjusting the length of the public services, more regard should be had to the physical ability of ministers and people, especially during the debilitating heats of summer. Different employments, they wrote, should be found in the Church for persons of different qualities of mind and body. Those who are cordial, frank, and fond of moving from place to place, might be employed as evangelists, while those who have powers of organising and swaying bodies of men should be called to rule. Thus the Church would be saved the shame of having "ministers who yet do not minister, rectors who cannot govern, and pastors who do not feed the flock." Positive and regular instruction of their children was recommended to parents, catechising to the clergy, and severe mental discipline to candidates for Orders. Ministers were exhorted to read the Liturgy more devotionally, and to bring their people to love sacred music and to join heartily in public worship. Attention was called to the wasted energy and unemployed power of the women of the Church, and the Bishops declared that "the Sisters of Charity in the Romish communion are worth, perhaps, more to their cause than the combined wealth of their hierarchy, the learning of their priesthood, and the self-sacrificing zeal of their missionaries."

In regard to Christians of other denominations, the Bishops recommended Churchmen, "in view of the momentous interests involved in the final disposition of this question, to strive to keep the unity of the Spirit in the bond of peace." They exhorted them to do justice to the merits of other systems, to repress a spirit of self-laudation, and to infuse into the divine services "more of the ancient and historical element on one side, and of the popular and practical on the other." They advised also a more cordial manner towards the ministers of other religious bodies, a lessening of canonical impediments in the way of their regular ordination, and, above all, an increase of the attractive power of the Church by more abundant self-denial, charity, and devotion.

Having thus been led to the subject of American Dissent (for such it remains in fact, though an Establishment is wanting), the reader will naturally expect further information on this important point. The American Census of 1850 contains a considerable mass of interesting religious statistics, and continues to be our best authority since present troubles have delayed the publication of the abstract of the Census for 1860. Of course, allowance must be made for the increase of the people in the meanwhile from twenty-three to more than thirty-one millions.

In America * we find the sectarian principle developed to a greater extent than in any other country in the world. Americans are accustomed to this state of things, and often glory in it as an illustration of their freedom. But it is quite evident that the original plan of Christianity allowed no place for separate, unconnected, and opposing systems, each following its own rule, and judging of truth under the bias of local and sectional prejudices. The idea which we gather from Scripture is, that mankind should form a society of disciples, taught by men commissioned from above, to observe and do all things whatsoever Christ has commanded. When this idea has been generally lost sight of, our holy religion loses, in a great measure, its character as a bond of peace and harmony. Meanwhile, any system of belief which has once come into existence, advances with a life of its own, perhaps as little dependent on the conclusions of sound argument as the trees of the forest or the weeds of the garden. Indeed, some bodies, called religious, are little more than organised forms of ignorance, imposture, or malignity.

---

* A portion of the following account of American sects was originally written by the author for the "Churchman's Magazine" in 1854.

The American mind has not given birth to many new sectarian elements, for it has generally been content, in schism as well as in politics, to build on the foundations already laid. But, in the United States, the sects which in Europe are more or less separated by geographical or social distinctions, are seen growing side by side in the same districts, the same towns and villages, and often under the same domestic roof. All, of course, believe themselves to be guided by their own judgment; but consequences follow like those which might be expected in a field sown with different varieties of seed. A number of hybrid species are produced; and though much good grain is ripened, the crop is not, on the whole, of the most satisfactory description.

It may be questioned whether the American revolutionary veterans would approve of the present state of American politics. It is quite certain that the Swiss and German Reformers, if permitted to revisit the earth, would be sorely perplexed by the divisions and subdivisions of American Protestantism. Yet, by glancing further south, at Mexico, a country colonised by the devoted servants of the Papacy, and from which private judgment on religion has been diligently excluded, they might view with more complacency the effect of their own work. They would feel that if an Ultra-Protestantism has produced bitter fruits in one direction, unreformed Romanism has failed at least as conspicuously in another.

The entire population of the United States in 1850 amounted to more than 23,000,000. Of these

15,000,000 were of Anglo-Saxon origin; three millions
and a half of African; and the remaining five or
six millions of Irish, French, and German descent.
The entire accession to the population, by means of
emigration, since the year 1790, had been only 3,000,000;
and of that number not more than half were living.
The 15,000,000 Anglo-Saxons constituted the bone
and sinew of the country.

It would therefore be reasonable to expect that
English forms of religion should preponderate over
others. This, accordingly, we find to be true in fact.
There were within the limits of the States, in 1850,
not less than 36,011 places of worship, able to accom-
modate 13,849,896 people. Of these more than one-
third (viz. 12,467) were Methodist meeting-houses,
capable of holding *four millions and a quarter.* Next
to these in number were 8791 Baptist places of worship,
built for *three millions* of people. Then followed 4584
Presbyterian houses, for *two millions.* The Lutherans,
with accommodation for half a million of people,
occupied 1203 places of prayer and preaching. After
these came 1112 churches and cathedrals, accommodating 620,950 Roman Catholics. Next to these on the
list of the Census are the persons called *Christians,*
acknowledging the Atonement in words, but denying
the Trinity, and in other respects Baptists. This sect
had 812 meeting-houses with sittings for 300,000.
The 280,000 Quakers counted 714 places of meeting.
The Universalists, with 494 congregations, preached
the doctrine that the wicked should *not* be cast into

hell. The Unitarians "proper" were estimated at 140,000, with 243 meeting-houses. There remained 2495 places of meeting, divided among the Moravians, German Reformed and Dutch Reformed, and other sects far inferior to them, such as Jews, Mormons, Swedenborgians, Tunkers, and Shakers. Bishop Burgess, of Maine, in his Charge for 1853, gives us to understand that the above enumeration of sittings conveys an exaggerated idea of the number of persons attending divine worship. He says, " Few would venture to compute the collective number of men who on the Lord's Day are found in all places of worship, and compare it with the census of the country."

In 1850, our own Church occupied in American religion a position similar to that of our own earth in the solar system, being, with its 1500 churches and 700,000 sittings, inferior in magnitude to some bodies and superior to others. It stood between the Presbyterians and the Lutherans, and, like our earth, was subject to influences emanating from its more powerful neighbours. It may, however, be said with truth, that the American Church is far more important in reality than she could be made to appear by the enumerations of a census. Most of the sects which figure so largely on paper have already undergone the catastrophe once supposed to have happened to a planet. They have split into fragments, many of them considerably smaller than the body with which it is our own happiness to be connected. The Methodists, apparently so vast a " denomination," are divided into three or four sects, some of which reject the Wesleyan Episcopacy. Even those who call themselves members of the " Methodist Episcopal Church " are divided into two distinct organisations, North and South, which separated on the question of the sinfulness of maintaining negro slavery. The Baptists, again, are divided into a multitude of minor sects, the very enumeration of which would be painfully tedious. We may mention among others the Seventh-day Baptists, who keep their Sabbath on Saturday, the Campbellite Baptists (from whom many of the peculiarities of Mormonism were derived), the Free-will Baptists, the Ironside Baptists (fatalists like the Mohammedans), and the Six-Principle Baptists. The Presbyterians again, besides the division between North and South, have their old and new school party (each with its separate General Assembly), Cumberland Presbyterians, Associate Presbyterians, Reformed Presbyterians, Associate-Reformed Presbyterians, and perhaps others.

Considering the great influx of Irish and German emigrants, it appears remarkable that, in 1850, the Roman Catholic worshippers should have been estimated as low as 620,950. But, in the first place, vast numbers of that " denomination " are engaged as workmen on railways, as domestic servants in remote places, and in other situations where they cannot readily be collected into congregations. And, secondly, multitudes of the Irish and Germans, after landing in America, bid farewell to the priest, and attach themselves to some

Protestant body, or become vicious and profligate infidels.

The researches made during the Census showed that the average cost of each of the 36,000 places of worship existing in 1850, was about 500*l.*, and the average sittings in each 384. The estimated value of the whole amounted to about 18,000,000*l.* sterling. In regard to architectural cost, the Church appears to great advantage, considering the disproportion of numbers. While the Methodist meeting-houses were valued at about 3,000,000*l.*, and the Presbyterian at something less, the Episcopal churches stood third on the list, and were estimated at 11,250,000 dollars, or 2,250,000*l.* Romish churches and cathedrals are valued at 1,800,000*l.*; Congregational meeting-houses at 1,600,000*l.*; Dutch Reformed at 600,000*l.*; and Unitarian at 400,000*l.* The most costly houses of worship were those of the wealthy and fashionable Unitarians, the average of each being nearly 2700*l.* Next are the Dutch, formerly the established order in "New Amsterdam" and its dependencies. The average cost of a Dutch Reformed place of worship is 2600*l.* The Jewish Synagogues follow, each of which appears to be worth 2400*l.* A Romish place of worship costs 1600*l.* One of our own churches in America is erected at an average expenditure of 1580*l.* Presbyterian, Methodist, and Baptist meeting-houses are decidedly cheaper, and the cheapest of all are those of the German "Tunkers," each of which is set down at an average of 177*l.*

The religious "accommodation" varies in different parts of the country. In 1850 the most abundant was found in Florida, Indiana, Delaware, and Ohio, in which States there was a place of worship of some kind for every 510 of the entire population. The worst districts in this particular, at the above date, were Texas, Iowa, Louisiana, and California ; the Californian churches and meeting-houses being in the ratio of *one* to every 7000 of the inhabitants. The average accommodation throughout the whole United States was *one* place of worship for every 646 of the entire population. About 600,000*l.* were annually expended on the erection of new edifices of this description ; while the yearly remuneration of the 28,000 or 30,000 ministers, of all denominations, was little less than 2,000,000*l.*, or rather under 70*l.* each. If living were in general as expensive as in England, this would be starvation indeed. Nothing is more common in America than the existence of half a dozen or a dozen poor ministers, each with his frail and small meeting-house, in some village which, if united, could decently support one well-educated rector, with an assistant, and maintain one good and substantial church, with manifest advantage to the comfort and harmony of all.

The enumeration of the Census gives a vast preponderance to the professedly Trinitarian denominations of Methodists, Baptists, Presbyterians, Congregationalists, Episcopalians, Lutherans, and Roman Catholics. It will be noticed that out of 14,000,000 sittings in the various places of worship, more than

12,000,000 are provided by those who, if only they adhere to their original principles, maintain great and fundamental truths of Christianity. It is also satisfactory to observe that the worst and most mischievous sects appear to possess little vitality in themselves, or to have been mercifully kept in check by an unseen hand. Those which rose up in England with the greatest amount of energy and self-dependence, have been generally the most successful in enlisting proselytes beyond the Atlantic. We have much comfort in believing that among the Trinitarian bodies, notwithstanding their divisions, the Scriptures are held in considerable veneration, and that, although sectarian traditions too often nullify many portions of Holy Writ, there are multitudes of individuals, beyond the limits of our own Church, who live under the influence of Divine Truth, and " walk with God." Far from denying the salvability of such individuals, we regard them with admiration, and thankfully behold in them the character of true saints. Doubtless many American Christians who have enjoyed no religious advantages beyond the Bible and the rudest sectarian preaching, will, in the day of judgment, condemn those who, with all the advantages of apostolical ordinances and well-defined doctrine, have proved comparatively barren and unfruitful. Yet we cannot close our eyes to the danger of those who are committed to the teaching of bodies which have no well-grounded claim to the character of true Churches of Christ. Most of the American sects have shown a decided want of stability, and in too many cases the general tendency has been towards deterioration. For example, a very large proportion (one half, it is said) of the Puritan congregations have departed from their old orthodox doctrines. In these congregations, which are bound by no common creed or confession, the truths of our Lord's Divinity and Atonement have often been more and more omitted in the public ministrations until finally they have come to be openly denied. The children of religious men are thus gradually betrayed into Socinianism, and the grandchildren, perhaps, become Deists or Pantheists. The Presbyterians of the "new school" are said to lean towards the denial of original sin, and of the "Eternal Sonship" of Christ. The Methodists are in danger of an extravagant pietism, accompanied by a contempt of doctrinal truth. Among the Baptist sects every kind of heresy is active. One believes in a Sabellian Deity, another denies the mercy of God to children, while a third holds Christian education to be a sinful attempt to interfere with the divine predestination.

Dr. Chapman, a vigorous and striking American writer, truly said * : — " In these United States, there are hundreds of preachers who cannot even read the Bible they undertake to expound. The qualifications of others are limited to vociferation and riot, excitement and passion, incredible tales and incoherent exclamations. Sermons have degenerated into a disconnected series of anecdotes, and pastoral visits into convenient

* Sermons, p. 349.

vehicles for the retail of gossip. For the form of sound words, we have jargon. For the excellency of sound doctrine, multitudes are destined to listen to the vagaries and the cant of empiricism."

" Revivalism " has been a very common feature of American dissent, and seems to accord with the American habit of thinking and acting in masses rather than as individuals. The effects which followed Mr. Whitfield's preaching among the Puritans in New England are described as follows, and may be taken as a sample of revivals in general, when uncontrolled by better influences.

" Whitfield found the flame of piety," says the Bishop of Oxford, "already burning low amongst the Independent congregations; for in the institutions of no separatists from the Church has the gift of enduring spiritual vitality been found. He boldly charged them with having left the ' platform ' of their ancient doctrines, and reviled them in his sermons under the unwelcome titles of ' hirelings and dumb dogs, half beasts and half devils.' He endeavoured to revive the ancient spirit by a series of violent excitements. . . Fanaticism in its maddest forms triumphed for a while; introducing new divisions in its train, and leading many into the open profession of Antinomian tenets." " A number of vagrant preachers arose," says a contemporary writer, "and by their boisterous behaviour and vehement crying, ' Come to Christ,' many were *struck*, as the phrase is, and made the most terrible and affecting noise, that was heard a mile from the place. . . . Many, after the amazing horror and distress that seized them, received *comfort* (as they term it), and five or six of the young men are continually going about, especially in the night, converting, as they call it, their fellow-men. Their meetings are held almost every night, and the most astonishing effects attend them; screechings, faint-ings, convulsions, visions, apparent death for twenty or thirty hours, actual possessions of evil spirits, as they own themselves. This spirit in all is remarkably bitter against the Church of England."

To this we may add that since the re-appearance of necromancy, under the name of "spiritualism," more dangerous by far than the old witchcraft of Massachu-setts, many persons, otherwise intelligent, have learned to "seek unto them that have familiar spirits," under the belief that they may thus obtain better revelations than those contained in the Bible.*

The mixture of sects produces in some minds a deplorable latitudinarianism, and an indifference to the distinction between truth and error. The more the sects are blended together the greater becomes this form of evil. Society cannot but be sensible of the misery of division, and naturally endeavours to recon-struct itself on some wide and general basis. Hence many good people readily engage in mixed religious and benevolent associations, the leading principle of which is the exclusion of all denominational peculiari-ties. The consequence is, of course, most prejudicial to

---

* See a Lecture by the Rev. Dr. Randall, delivered in Pitt's Street Chapel, Boston, 1858.

those bodies which hold the greatest number of definite truths, and on Church-people in particular the necessary effect of such associations is a slight esteem for Sacraments, Orders, Liturgies, and old religious forms in general. Great numbers again, after carelessly asking Pilate's question, "What is truth?" reject inspiration, and stand aloof from all religious organisations whatsoever. Indeed, from the early prevalence of division, absolute indifference to religious distinctions became a principle of the political institutions of the country, and political considerations are ever uppermost in the ordinary American mind.

Bishop Burgess says in the Charge quoted above: — "The sentiment that children should be left to form their religious opinions in riper years, attests the utter want of personal confidence in the truths of revelation. Every young man accordingly finds himself surrounded by a clashing variety of assertions. He has no ability to judge in some controversies; of others he becomes impatient. He sees nothing which is not denied by some party, and he is invited by each to join its standards. Three courses of conduct are open to him. He may disbelieve entirely; or he may believe with some one body of those who profess themselves Christians; or he may postpone all decision, and be governed, in the partial support which he gives to one body or another, by education or circumstances, or some half-formed impression. The first of these three courses is taken by few; but the third is the choice of the majority. The miserable sense of uncertainty remains; and those who might be the strength and glory of the Church of Christ live for this world, and die without distinct belief or personal hope."

Yet, after all, there is a movement among the more respectable sects which, in the long run, must tend, we may hope, to improvements. The recent introduction of Liturgies into public worship by several of these bodies is one of the most significant marks of an inclination to return to primitive usage. The "denominations" which in former days inveighed most strongly against an educated ministry, have now more colleges than the Church itself possesses. Once it was considered a sin to have instrumental music in the sanctuary, while there is now scarcely a place of worship in the cities and towns which has not an organ. Clerical vestments are coming into use, and crosses are sometimes erected even on the spires of Puritan meeting-houses. The old style of meeting-house, with its two rows of square windows, is generally abandoned, and edifices having all the outward appearance of "Gothic" churches are becoming more and more common.

Another more important sign of progress in a right direction has already been noticed. The American Episcopal clergy have been supplied in a very large proportion from the ranks of the dissenting bodies.* The late Bishop Griswold stated in 1841 that of two hundred and eighty-five clergymen ordained by him, two hundred and seven came into the ministry from the

---

* Dr. Randall's Lecture, quoted above.

ᵖsurrounding "denominations." Of the eighteen hundred clergymen in the Episcopal Church a few years since, it was estimated that about twelve hundred had been gathered in from the Presbyterians, Congregationalists, Methodists, Baptists, Roman Catholics, Unitarians, and other external sources. Considering how much benefit the Church has derived from the energy and ability of many of these recruits, we are led the more earnestly to desire a general union of Christ's flock on the basis of sound ecclesiastical principles. How great a blessing it would be to America and to Christendom, if, instead of wasting their strength and temper in mutual rivalry, the believers in One Redeemer were to become truly " members of one another," and assist in advancing by their joint prayers and efforts the kingdom of God upon earth. Unbelief would then be deprived of one of its most plentiful sources of supply, religion would be a visible effectual bond of union, and the Gospel would be propagated with vigour and effect throughout the globe.

The American Episcopal Church unquestionably affords a centre of unity which can be found in no other body calling itself Protestant. A practical proof of this is supplied by the fact that the members of other communities, whether Presbyterian, Methodist, Quaker, or Roman Catholic, are usually ready to admit that the Church stands second only in their regard to the sect to which they respectively belong. " Where," says Bishop Hopkins, " is the Church which deserves so well to be called the Church of the Bible—the

s

Church of the Apostles — the Church of God? What other Christian community can prove to the same extent its harmony with the early age of primitive purity and devotion? What other can bid defiance to every assault of heresy and schism? Look at Protestant Germany, torn into fragments under the baneful influence of neology, and rationalism, and pantheism. Look at the pulpit of Calvin, filled by such Socinian teachers as Calvin himself would have committed to the stake. Look at the constantly multiplying divisions of all the sects in Protestant Christendom, and they tell the same melancholy tale of incapacity to hold fast the " faith once delivered to the saints." Is there any *centre of unity* to be found amongst these? Alas, no! There is but one Church which presents the aspect of steadfast, immovable, Scriptural and Apostolic constancy, which these distracted times require; and that is the privileged Church of our happy communion. Notwithstanding our personal demerits, the broad facts of the case remain indisputably certain. The wise providence of the Almighty has stamped upon the Church those great marks of Scriptural truth, of apostolical ministry, of primitive worship, of firm stability, and of steady advancement, which can be found nowhere else in the whole length and breadth of Christendom. And I assert them in the strongest confidence of deep sincerity, because they seem to manifest the true function of the Church, as the only centre of unity to the jarring, unsettled, and storm-tossed divisions of our Protestant brethren."

CHAP. XI.

THE CHURCH AND SLAVERY.

AMERICAN SLAVERY AN INHERITANCE. — ITS GRADUAL ABOLITION ARRESTED. — EVIL EFFECTS OF SLAVERY ON THE WHITE POPULATION. — RELATIVE POSITION OF THE AFRICAN AND AMERICAN NEGRO.— REAL EVILS OF INVOLUNTARY SERVITUDE. — SCRIPTURAL ARGUMENTS USED IN THE SOUTH IN SUPPORT OF IT. — POSITION OF THE AMERICAN CHURCH IN REFERENCE TO SLAVERY.—OPINIONS OF ENGLISH DIVINES. — EFFORTS OF THE CHURCH IN·SOUTH CAROLINA.— THE BISHOPS AND THEIR SLAVES.— ABOLITIONISM ALLIED WITH INFIDELITY. — CHARACTER OF SOUTHERN RELIGION.— SECONDARY SLAVERY OF THE FREE NEGRO. —ACTUAL DEMERITS OF SLAVERY.—DUTY OF THE CHURCH.

E have already seen how the United States, inheriting from us their blood, their laws, their religion, and their schism, inherited also our English system of colonial slavery, and our original English opinions in regard to that system. Slavery continued, in fact, exactly as we left it, with such modifications only as circumstances rendered necessary or expedient. Like other systems, it had acquired a life of its own; and customs, laws, morals, and religious doctrines, had accommodated themselves to it, according to their respective degrees of pliability. At

the Revolution, as we have observed, the union of the different colonies or States was essential to their success. But this union was practicable only on the condition that the local institutions of the several States should be left untouched. Accordingly the new Constitution, recognising slavery, provided that the whole power of the government should be employed, if necessary, to defend it in case of aggression,· and to prevent the escape of fugitives. Thus the bonds of black men were riveted that a high theory of political freedom for white men might be established. Not only was slavery perpetuated, but even the slave-trade, through the influence of Northern shipowners, was continued down to the year 1808.

At the same time, the framers of the Constitution, aware of the inconsistency of slavery with the principles avowed in the Declaration of Independence, carefully avoided the word "slave," and introduced the circumlocution of "person held to labour." Even the word "servitude" was struck out, and "service" substituted instead, as expressing rather the obligations of free persons than the condition of slaves.* Madison said, "It is wrong to admit into the Constitution the idea that there can be property in men."

The leaders of the Revolution seem to have believed that the principles of liberty were so dear to the people that they would not long deny to others what they claimed for themselves. Southern men were foremost

* Speech of Mr. Sumner in the Senate of the United States, June 4, 1860.

in speaking of slavery as an evil, and though some palliated it, and desired that its extinction might be gradual, none considered it as a permanent institution of the country. Washington wrote in 1786 :—"I never mean, unless some particular circumstances should compel me to it, to possess another slave by purchase, it being among my *first wishes* to see some plan adopted by which slavery in this country may be abolished by law." * By his last will, all Washington's slaves were made free. Similar sentiments to those of Washington were openly expressed by Jefferson, Madison, Monroe, Franklin, Adams, and many others.

For half a century after the Revolution, English and American slavery existed side by side in the West Indian Islands and on the neighbouring continent. But justice and religion began to raise their voice against the system, and, under certain circumstances, the voice was heard. Wherever the profits of slavery were the least, people most readily opened their eyes to its evils, and adopted measures for its abolition. In the northern New England States, where the climate and soil render slave-labour comparatively unprofitable, emancipation was complete before the commencement of the present century. New York, Rhode Island, and Connecticut soon followed their example. Proceeding further south, we find that in Pennsylvania and New Jersey abolition was delayed much longer. In Pennsylvania, according to Mr. Hall, there were nearly four

* Helper, p. 193.

s 3

thousand slaves in 1790, and *six* remained as late as
1850. In New Jersey there were more than eleven
thousand in 1790, and the last State Act for the abolition of slavery was passed as recently as 1846. The
work of emancipation by England did not commence
until America had made considerable progress in the
same direction. If the whole of our southern counties
had been adapted by soil and climate to slave-labour, it
is possible that to this hour philanthropy would have
struggled in vain for the introduction of a more
righteous system. Nor is it likely that the colonial
legislatures of the West Indies would have themselves
ventured upon the experiment of abolition. But our
slave colonies were weak, and the population of England
was strong; the will of the feeble consequently suc-
cumbed to the determination of the powerful, and at
a cost of twenty millions the negroes of the West Indies
were advanced to the dignity of freemen. In America
the case was very different. Abolition, having proceeded as far south as the boundaries of Maryland and
Virginia, was arrested in its course by its competition
with a powerful slaveholding interest. Here it approached the region of rice, cotton, and sugar, in which
the compulsory servitude of men of African race was
considered necessary to the development of the resources
of the soil. Here the profits of slavery constantly augmented with the manufacturing prosperity of Manchester. The slave States, instead of occupying the
position of weak and distant colonies, possessed the advantage of being integral portions of the American

Union, and were abundantly represented in the National Congress. Each State had its own legislature; its institutions were protected by the Constitution, and the question of servitude was beyond the jurisdiction of the Federal authorities. If these States desired to emancipate their slaves on the English plan of compensation to owners, whence should the amount be obtained? Not twenty, but five hundred, millions of money * must be raised by the slave-owners to be paid to themselves. Hence it is a fact by no means surprising, however deplorable, that slavery, although extinct in Barbados and Jamaica, maintains a vigorous existence in the broad expanses of the Southern States.

That slavery is a great evil to the white population requires but little proof. President Jefferson, in his "Notes on Virginia," says:—"There must doubtless be an unhappy influence on the manners of our people produced by the existence of slavery among us. The whole commerce between master and slave is a perpetual exercise of the most boisterous passions—the most unremitting despotism on the one part, and degrading submission on the other. Our children see this and learn to imitate it; for man is an imitative animal . . . The man must be a prodigy who can retain his manners and morals undepraved by such circumstances."

President Monroe, in a speech to the Virginian Con-

* In 1850 the entire value of the slaves in the United States was estimated at 1,280,000,000 dollars, or 256,000,000*l.* It is now reckoned at more than double this amount.

vention, spoke of slavery in words which at the present time would be regarded as seditious:—"We have found that this evil has preyed upon the very vitals of the Union, and has been prejudicial to all the States in which it has existed."

In 1837, the Governor of Kentucky, himself a slave-owner, said in his Message to the Legislature of the State:—"We long to see the day when the law will assert its majesty, and stop the wanton destruction of life which almost daily occurs within the jurisdiction of this commonwealth. *Men slaughter each other with almost perfect impunity.*" In the same year another slave-owning governor in Alabama made a similar official declaration:—"We hear of homicides in different parts of the State continually, and yet have few convictions, and still fewer executions. Why do we hear of stabbings and shootings almost daily in some part or other of our State?"

A few words in President Buchanan's Message of December, 1860, afford a sufficiently painful view of the alarms which beset Southern society. "Many a matron throughout the South retires at night in dread of what may befall herself or her children before the morning." The liberty of the "free-born republican" is curtailed by this institution to a degree hardly conceivable to a British subject. He may chastise his slaves at his discretion, but may not educate them, and may not emancipate them except on conditions which in many instances would render emancipation a doubtful advantage. The press, the post-office, and the pulpit, are under fetters, and nothing can be printed, preached, or circulated, which the mass of the people regard as dangerous. Innumerable instances might be quoted to show the fearful tyranny of public opinion in the South. A white person, for example, was publicly flogged in the market-place for being in possession of abolitionist newspapers. A professor in a Southern university, who expressed opinions favourable to liberty, was peremptorily dismissed from his post, ignominiously subjected to the indignities of a mob, and then savagely driven beyond the borders of his native State.* From the South this species of tyranny has extended to those parts of the North which are connected with slavery by the ties of a common interest. Thus, in Illinois, a mob murdered a Presbyterian minister for printing a publication hostile to African servitude. In Boston an abolitionist who pleaded for the negro's rights was dragged through the streets with a halter about his neck.† The violent conduct and ferocious language of Southern members of Congress would alone be sufficient to prove that, even in the higher grades of society, slavery tends to barbarism.

The whole tribe of overseers, slave-dealers, and slave-hunters, are placed in a position which, to say the least, is eminently unfavourable to the formation of a just, merciful, or Christian character. The moral and physical energies of the young are not wholesomely developed, and labour is regarded as something mean and

* Helper, p. 306.   † Speech of Mr. Sumner.

despicable.   Whether in a commercial or a mechanical, a financial or a literary point of view, the slave States are far behind those of the North.   We are told on apparently good authority * that the annual *hay* crop of the free States is worth considerably more than all the cotton, rice, tobacco, hay, hemp, and sugar annually produced in the wide domains of slavery.

As to the effect of slavery on the negro, it should be recollected that however low may be the condition of the black American, it is a considerable improvement on the state of his forefathers in Africa.   Of the hundred and fifty millions supposed to inhabit † that unhappy continent, three-fourths have been slaves from time immemorial, the slaves, too, of heathen and Mohammedan masters, treated like herds of cattle and constantly liable to be sold to foreign countries.   True, their slavery has been in many respects far from severe, and has not been aggravated by difference of colour.   But it has been accompanied with fearful barbarities, with the terrors of witchcraft, and with all the abominations of the worst forms of heathenism.   The negro in America is not to be regarded, nor does he regard himself, as lowered beneath a former level.   The hopes of Christianity are accessible to him, and he is capable of feeling the motives of the Gospel.   His bodily comforts are generally sufficiently provided for, and, if we were to judge him by appearances, we might say that he was one of the most light-hearted and cheerful

* Helper's Impending Crisis.
† Quarterly Review, April, 1861.

ˋof mortals. If an outdoor labourer, he is often allowed
an allotment of land, on which, after the regular hours
of labour, he may work on his own account, like many
of our English peasantry. If a domestic servant, he
may expect, on the whole, to be well treated, in return
for which he will probably show faithful attachment to
his master's family.

Irresponsible power is, of course, a dangerous possession, and the man must be more than mortal who is
not in danger of abusing such an endowment. Considering all that has been written on the subject by
credible witnesses, it is unnecessary to adduce proofs
that negroes are often treated in a manner which
evinces a want of common sense and humanity. In
America, slavery has always worn a character more
severe, in some respects, than ancient servitude. In
the countries mentioned in Scripture, compulsory servitude was usually the result of successful war, and the
captive was not only of the same colour with his master,
but was often his superior in birth and education.
Hence slavery was not associated with entire degradation. The slave was often treated as a son or a brother,
he might be admitted into his master's family by
marriage, and was sometimes advanced to the highest
offices of the State. But the negro was brought to
America, and to our colonies in general, solely with a
view to commercial profit, and mainly with that view
has he continued to be employed to the present day.
Hence his owner regards him, by a traditionary estimate, according to his material worth, and is constantly

under the temptation of forgetting that the slave, equally with himself, is a *man*. Let not those who are placed under this temptation be regarded as necessarily more blind or unfeeling than others. It is not so easy as it may seem to rise above the general standard of public opinion, and to become superior to the established mode of considering the great social questions of our age and country.

The evils of slavery are not to be estimated principally by the bodily sufferings which grow out of the system. Its crying iniquity is that it tends to perpetuate a mental and moral degradation incompatible with the interests of humanity. It makes ignorance a necessity, it too frequently denies to the negro the sacred ties and purifying influences of marriage and family, and it utterly disarranges the natural relations between parents and their offspring. The negro, like his master, is generally the creature of surrounding circumstances, and seldom rises above the standard of morals resulting from his position. It might indeed have been anticipated that he would be prone to sensuality and licentiousness, vain, trifling, and dishonest, skilful in the arts of deceit and subterfuge, cowardly, cruel, revengeful, and superstitious. These ordinary vices of slavery have indeed grown up abundantly in the South, though happier influences, especially those of religion, have often been interposed with success to check their luxuriant growth.

In the South, the believers in Holy Scripture defend the principle of slavery by considerations like the fol-

lowing, abridged from a work by a respectable Presbyterian minister of Georgia, the Rev. J. C. Stiles.*

"Not one word of censure is pronounced in the Bible
upon slavery, though the relation of master and servant
is brought up frequently, and discussed abundantly, in
both Testaments.

"In the covenant with Abraham, in the Ten Commandments, and in the Gospel, slavery is contemplated
as an existing state of society, and though regulations
are laid down in regard to it, nothing is expressed
against its legality. He whom God selected as the
father of the faithful was a great slave-owner. He whom
God pronounced the best man on earth, the pattern of
human patience, was the proprietor of many slaves. He
whom our Lord declared to have greater faith than any
in Israel was made known to Him only through his
ownership of a slave, and described himself as a man
under authority, saying to his slave, 'Do this, and he
doeth it.' The only slave reported by the New Testament as a fugitive from his master's service, was restored to his owner by an Apostle."

"In Leviticus (xxv.) God directed the Jews, at a time
when they were not slaveholders, concerning the manner
in which they should afterwards form the relation of
master and servant. It is argued that God could not
direct His creature in the formation of a relation sinful
in itself. So, in the slave-laws of Moses, the Jews are
directed what to do when they should become owners

* Modern Reform Examined, p. 21.

of slaves. ' Ye shall buy bondmen.' ' They shall be your possession.' ' He is his money.' ' Ye shall take them as an inheritance for your children after you.' ' They shall be your bondmen for ever.' There is a recognition in both Testaments of the owner's claim to control, correction, service, honour, and love, and an explicit statement of the duties of masters to their slaves, and of slaves to their masters."

The question is often asked whether the American Church is not peculiarly implicated in the evils of slavery. To this it must be replied that the word "Church," as used in American books, includes every sect which chooses to be considered Christian. When, therefore, the writer of a lately popular fiction accused the "Church" of participating in the guilt of slavery, she must be understood as accusing Presbyterians, Methodists, Baptists, Independents, and Unitarians equally with that class of Christians who, according to the more correct use of language, are known in England as "the Church." Probably churchmen do not own a sixth part of the number of the slaves belonging to Baptist proprietors.* The entire

---

* The following extract from the "Montgomery Mail," a newspaper printed at the present capital of the Southern Confederacy, shows the feelings of a slaveholding Baptist towards a Baptist abolitionist : —

"Last Saturday we devoted to the flames a large number of copies of Spurgeon's Sermons, which a Baptist friend presented for the purpose. We trust that the works of the greasy cockney vociferator may receive the same treatment throughout the South. And if the pharisaical author should ever show himself in these parts, we trust that a stout cord may speedily find its way around his eloquent throat. He has

population of the slaveholding States, by the Census of 1860, was about 12,210,000, including 3,952,801 slaves. Among this great population, the Church numbers about fifty thousand communicants, and less than half a million of worshippers, with fifteen bishops, and perhaps seven hundred clergymen. It is very plain, therefore, that in the South, as well as in the North, the Church is greatly overshadowed by other religious bodies.

Still, however, it may be said that fifteen bishops and seven hundred clergymen might exert a considerable influence by lifting up a united voice against surrounding evils. How then does the American Church habitually treat the subject of slavery?

It must be replied that, like the Mother Church in England, and like other branches of the Catholic Church, the American Church has never by any public act denied the lawfulness of slavery in the abstract. On the other hand, her general belief on the subject may be expressed in the words of many of our English divines.

Archbishop Manners Sutton* says, " Christianity hath left all temporal governments as it found them, without impeachment of any form or description whatever." So Paley says: " Christianity can only operate as an *alterative.* By the mild diffusion of its light and influence, the minds of men are insensibly prepared to perceive and correct the enormities which folly or

---

proved himself a dirty, low-bred slanderer, and ought to be treated accordingly."

* Quoted in the " Christian Remembrancer " for October, 1832.

wickedness or accident has introduced into their public establishments."

The Bishop of Lincoln, in a sermon preached before the Society for Propagating the Gospel in 1768, spoke as follows : — " Though the dealing in men seems a very unnatural kind of traffic, and any treatment of them contrary to the allowed and unalterable rights of humanity cannot plainly be justified, yet I know not that we are warranted by any precept delivered in the Gospel, or by any example recorded in the Apostolic writings, to say that this practice is expressly forbidden there ; for the founder of our religion did not make or propose to make any change in the different constitutions of government, or in the personal condition and privileges of private men."

The bishops and clergy in the South are probably not inferior in Christian character to any clergy in Christendom. In becoming ministers of religion they have sacrificed the worldly advantages which America presents so freely to the enterprising in other lines of life. Some respect, therefore, is due to their opinion in regard to the proper course of the Christian ministry in a slaveholding country. I believe it may be stated, without hesitation, that they consider themselves bound to avoid all direct attacks upon the principle of slavery, and to confine themselves to the general inculcation of Christian truth and duty. The services of the Church, the Sacraments and other holy ordinances, with the stated preaching of the Gospel, cannot be without their effect in rendering masters kind and gentle, and in supplying hope and consolation to the slave. There is reason to believe that Church-people in the South have done much to convey Christian instruction to the negroes, and to mitigate evils which cannot altogether be avoided.

The following account of a single diocese may, perhaps, be regarded as a sample of some others.* South Carolina is the leading State of the pro-slavery region. The blacks there are rather more numerous than the whites, and abolitionist doctrines are generally held in utter abhorrence. In the year 1857, in that diocese, with considerably less than a hundred white congregations, there were already forty-five churches and chapels built on plantations for the slaves, and about a hundred and fifty organised congregations in which the Gospel was preached to them by the clergy. The number of persons *confirmed* among them was nearly three times as great as among the whites. The bishop visits these black congregations as regularly as the others, and takes especial pleasure in the work. And in regard to the subject of marriage among the slaves, the Diocesan Convention, composed largely of slaveholders, appointed a committee on the subject which reported as follows, in 1859 : —

" Resolved : That the relation of husband and wife is of divine institution, and the duties which appertain to it are of universal obligation, and bind with the same force the master and the slave.

" Resolved : That the injunction of our Saviour for-

* See New York Church Journal, 1861, p. 53.

T

bidding man to separate those whom God has joined together, is obligatory upon the conscience of every Christian master, and prohibits the separation of those who have been united in marriage.

" Resolved: That the power over the slave which is conferred upon the master by the law of the land, should be exercised by every Christian in conformity with the law of God; and, therefore, every Christian master should so regulate the sale or disposal of a married slave as not to infringe the divine injunction forbidding the separation of man and wife."

In this connection it may be stated that in the year 1860, though, as I have stated, the white population is little less than the black, there were in South Carolina twice as many marriages celebrated by the clergy of the Church among the slaves as among the whites; and every care is taken by conscientious Christian men that such marriages shall be considered sacred. Besides the bishops and clergy, thousands of communicants are labouring among the slaves, not indeed teaching them to read, but giving them oral instructions in Holy Scripture, in the liturgy, in the catechism, in psalms and hymns, in chanting, and in a decent mode of congregational worship.*

* The following is one of the parochial reports delivered to the Diocesan Convention of South Carolina in 1857 : —

"ALL SAINTS, WACCAMAW.

The Rev. Alexander Glennie, Rector.   The Rev. Lucien C. Lance, Assistant Minister.   The Rev. Henry L. Phillips, Missionary.

Baptisms : adults, 1 white, 38 coloured; children, 3 white, 99 coloured; total, 141. Marriages : 2 white, 8 coloured; total, 10.

All these labours would speedily be brought to a close if the bishops and clergy were to commence an attack upon slavery as a political institution. They would encounter a persecution incomparably more severe than that which fell upon the loyalist clergy at the Revolution, and at the same time the slaves would be deprived of those who at present are among their best friends.

The Bishop of Louisiana assured the writer, in 1853, that while engaged on an episcopal tour he had visited the country on Red River, the scene of the fictitious sufferings of " Uncle Tom," where he had found the temporal and spiritual welfare of negroes an object of solicitude with the proprietors. He had confirmed thirty black persons near the situation assigned to Legree's estate. He was himself the owner of four hundred slaves, whom he endeavoured to bring up as Church people. He baptized the children, and taught them the catechism. All, without exception, attended

Burials: 2 white, 4 coloured; total, 6. Communicants, last reported : 47 white, 173 coloured; total, 220. Admitted: 2 white, 38 coloured : total, 40. Removed: 5 white, 1 coloured; total, 6. Withdrew: 7 coloured; died, 1 white, 8 coloured; total, 9. Present number: 43 white, 195 coloured; total, 238. Congregations, Non-communicants: 30 white; children under 14, 35 white; families, 26 white; families belonging also to other congregations of P. E. Church: 4 white. Children catechised on 20 days, 10 white; on 307 days, 495 coloured; total, 505. Confirmed by the bishop, 78 coloured. Public worship, parish church, 27 Sundays, 11 other days; Southern Church, 21 Sundays, 2 other days; Summerset's, 11 Sundays; for negroes on 15 plantations, and at Summerset's, 300 times; whole number of times, 372. Contributions: Communion alms, 114 dols. 35 c.; Missions : diocesan, 55 dols.; domestic, 234 dols. 39 c. ; foreign, 290 dols.; other purposes, 405 dols. ; total, 1098 dols. 74 c." = £219.

the Church, and the chanting and singing were credit-
ably performed by them.   Ninety of the whole number
were communicants, marriages were celebrated according
to the ritual, and the state of morals was not unsatis-
factory.   Emancipation in Louisiana was rendered by
law all but impracticable, and the Bishop's slaves would
have regarded it as a fearful calamity, expatriation being
one of its necessary conditions.

The present Bishop of the diocese of Virginia emancipated his slaves on condition of their removal to the
free colony of Liberia in Western Africa, thereby sacri-
ficing property to the amount of some thousands, and
rendering himself comparatively a poor man in an
unendowed church.   A clergyman in Virginia, known
to the writer, at one time possessed a handsome property in the shape of black men and women.   From a
sense of Christian duty he emancipated them all, doing
to them as he considered that he would wish others to
do to himself if he were in the same circumstances.
For some time he continued poor and dependent on
the contributions of a country parish.   At the same
time his emancipated negroes became wretched vagabonds, and often came to him for relief as common
beggars.   Ultimately, by marriage, he again acquired a
considerable slave property, but profiting by experience
he granted no second emancipation, and confined himself to the promotion of the temporal and spiritual
welfare of his people, and to a provision by will designed to secure their comfort in the event of his
decease.   It is a fact worthy of notice that one of the

most earnest and eloquent opponents of abolition in the South is a clergyman of the Church of England (once a member of the University of Oxford), who as rector of a parish in Jamaica witnessed the results of emancipation in that once prosperous island.

Dr. Palmer, an eminent Presbyterian minister of New Orleans, preached a sermon in November last, from which the following is an extract : —

" The worst foes of the black race are those who have intermeddled in their behalf. We know better than others that every attribute of their character fits them for servitude. By nature the most affectionate and loyal of all races beneath the sun, they are also the most helpless; and no calamity can befall them greater than the loss of that protection they enjoy under the patriarchal system. Indeed the experiment has been grandly tried of precipitating them upon freedom, which they knew not how to enjoy; and the dismal results are before us in statistics that astonish the world. With the fairest portions of the earth in their possession, and with the advantage of a long discipline as cultivators of the soil, their constitutional indolence has converted the most beautiful island of the sea into a howling waste. It is not too much to say that if the South should, at this moment, surrender every slave, the wisdom of the entire world, united in solemn council, could not solve the question of their disposal. Their transportation to Africa, even if it were feasible, would be the most refined cruelty; they must perish with starvation before they could have time to relapse into their primitive barbarism. Their residence here, in the presence of the vigorous Saxon race, would be but the signal for their rapid extermination before they had time to waste away through listlessness, filth, and vice. Freedom would be their doom; and from it they call upon us, their providential guardians, to be protected."

It has escaped the notice of many opponents of slavery in this country, that American abolitionism is closely connected with utter infidelity. Because the Old and New Testament recognise the existence of slavery, and give rules for the respective conduct of masters and slaves, many of the more fanatical abolitionists have rejected the Scriptures as a revelation from God. I find the following statements in a sermon preached before a highly respectable Presbyterian congregation in the State of New York, in December, 1860 * : — "In this country all the prominent leaders of abolitionism (outside of the ministry) have become avowed infidels † ; and all our notorious abolition

* The Character and Influence of Abolitionism, by the Rev. Henry J. Van Dyke.

† Innumerable proofs of the infidelity of abolitionism might be readily produced. The following, quoted by Mr. Stiles, are a few specimens of the speeches and writings of leading abolitionists : —

"Shame on the nation, and shame on its politics, and shame on its religion, I say, and shame on such a God. I defy Him, I scorn Him; He is not my God." "If the Bible sanctions slavery, and is thus opposed to the self-evident truth that 'all men are created equal, and have an inalienable right to liberty,' the Bible is a self-evident falsehood." "Anti-Slavery will triumph, but only on the ruins of the American Church. Humanity will surely come off victorious over what this nation calls God, and hurl Him for ever from His throne of blood, simply because that God has staked His claim to our worship on the support of slavery."

preachers have renounced the great doctrines of grace as they are taught in the standards of the reformed churches."

On the other hand, we have the following testimony in regard to Southern religion from Mr. Stiles * : — " There is a defect in the religion of the North. The Northern mind is inquiring and inquisitive. Consequently you will find in the North more speculation and abstraction in the pulpit; and more new lights, heresies, and infidelity among the people. The Southern population brought less intelligence and religion with them, and very naturally an inferior appreciation of literary and religious institutions. They settled, too, in a portion of the country where neither the climate nor the soil admitted of an uniformly dense population, and adopted a method of life which threw society apart. Consequently the Southern Church is decidedly inferior to the Northern, not only in religious and auxiliary institutions, but also in general Christian knowledge and efficient Christian training. Yet the people of the South possess one superiority over the North. If they have less investigation, they have more faith. There is yet a confiding simplicity, an unreasoning reverence, in the structure and habits of the Southern mind; a willingness to hear anything from God, which will be found to embody much veneration for the Scriptures and the ministry, and certainly a great freedom from vagaries, heresy, and infidelity." Then follows some

---

* Modern Reform Examined.

curious statistical information, from which it would
appear that in the five years ending with 1854, the
sermons preached by Episcopalians, Presbyterians,
Methodists, and Baptists in the free States amounted
in length to 33,246 years, and in the slave States to
only 24,918 years. Yet the thirty-three thousand years
of preaching in the North had been the means of
bringing only 164,553 persons to bind themselves by a
religious profession, while the twenty-four thousand
years of sermonising in the South had produced the
same happy effect on 214,918. In other words, "a
Christian force in the South one-fourth less, works a
Christian result one-fourth greater than in the North."
"The Southern States," says the same author, "have
been compelled to pass laws forbidding emancipation,
in order to discourage that sympathy of the master
which would otherwise inordinately augment, in the
bosom of Southern society, a shiftless and wretched
population. The border States, Maryland, Virginia,
Kentucky, and Missouri, have seen the day when the
whole population have been brought very near to a proclamation of liberty to all the captives within their
bounds. The South is supposed to have freed nearly
three hundred thousand slaves. If we value them
singly at five hundred dollars, we are authorised to
affirm that the South has substantially surrendered
the sum of one hundred and fifty millions of dollars
(30,000,000*l.*) in testimony of its sympathy with the
freedom of the race." The reader will observe that
this sum (whether rightly estimated or not) is one-

half greater than the whole cost of our West Indian emancipation. Whatever may be the philanthropy of individual slave-owners, the national prejudice of America in regard to African descent must be in some way surmounted before the negro race can be materially advanced in the social scale. Even in the Northern States the free negro enjoys little more than the name of freedom. In some of them he is forbidden to remain, and, if he persevere in doing so, he may be fined, imprisoned, and eventually sold again into slavery. The white people, even though politically they may be abolitionists, loathe fellowship with the blacks and mulattoes, and exclude them from the more elevating and profitable employments. Their colour and descent render them objects of an unreasoning antipathy, and in the large towns and cities they have sometimes become the victims of popular fury.

Amidst the difficulties of the subject, a few points must now be tolerably clear. It is very evident that whatever may have been the intention of the Revolutionary Fathers, negro slavery, with many superadded evils, has in fact found a stronghold in the Constitution of the United States. It has constantly brought into political affairs increased confusion and entanglement, it has led to costly and demoralising wars, and it is now rending the Union to pieces. It is the fruitful parent of Lynch-law and other tyrannies, it is the cause of constant alarm to slave-owners themselves, it has kept the Southern States in a condition of inferiority to the North, it has become the shame and reproach of

America in the eyes of the civilised world. Though, according to the letter of the Old Testament, a certain form of slavery, at a certain age of the world, was evidently permitted, and though our Saviour and His Apostles did not interfere with the existing structure of society, yet the spirit of the Gospel, and the general instincts of Christian nations, seem opposed to a system which necessitates ignorance, breaks up family ties, and leads, by almost inevitable consequence, to injustice, cruelty, and many other abominations.

It does not, however, appear certain that immediate abolition would be a benefit to the negro, and, on the contrary, it might be a terrible calamity to him. It is plain, too, that so long as commerce renders the cultivation of cotton eminently profitable, and so long as the Southern States continue to regard the labour of slaves as necessary to their crops, abolition without compensation is most improbable. Compensation, we have seen, is utterly out of the question. Although, therefore, much may be done by legislatures, associations, and individuals, to mitigate the evils of slavery, the overthrow of the entire system, unless by some fearful catastrophe, is not yet to be expected.

The American Church, under these circumstances, seems manifestly released from the obligation of preaching abolition at all hazards. Yet Christendom has reason to expect from her that in all matters connected with slavery involving questions of right and wrong, she should lift up her voice without fear, trusting that God will increase her influence with men in proportion as she does her duty. We have seen that she has exerted herself to good purpose in South Carolina. Testimony to a similar effect from Virginia and some other States would be a source of joy to all who wish her well. Perhaps some future chronicler of American affairs will record that the Church in the South, represented by her clergy and laity, has determined to put forth a general effort to raise American slavery in all respects to the standard of Holy Scripture. There will be additional cause for gratitude if it should appear that the Church in the North has set herself against the secondary slavery of the free negro, and that she has exerted herself to remove from the minds of her children that antipathy to African lineage which is the source of so much misery and degradation.

CHAP. XII.

CONCLUSION.

OUR EARLY OPPORTUNITIES IN AMERICA. — PARTIAL FAILURE OF THE
DESIGNS OF WASHINGTON. — THE BISHOP OF VERMONT ON THE CON-
SERVATIVE INFLUENCE OF THE CHURCH. — IMPROBABILITY OF A PER-
MANENT RE-UNION OF ALL THE STATES. — ADVANTAGES OF SEPARATION.
— JEFFERSON'S IDEAS OF THE DIVINE JUSTICE.— AMERICAN OPINIONS OF
ENGLAND AND THE CHURCH OF ENGLAND. — REACTION IN FAVOUR OF
THE CHURCH ANTICIPATED. — POSSIBLE ALTERNATIVE.— PROSPECTS OF
AMERICA AND OF THE TRANSATLANTIC CHURCH.

HE preceding chapters have laid before
the reader the gradual progress of the
events which have made the United
States what they are at present. In
becoming possessed of North America,
opportunities were placed in our hands greater than we
have ever enjoyed in any portion of the world, not even
excepting British India. Had we also possessed a
wisdom rather divine than human, had we been united
in our views of religious and political truth, had we
understood precisely when to govern and when to let
things take their natural course, we might have built
up a community which would have been the wonder
and admiration of the universe. From our various

spheres of life, we should have sent forth a homogeneous population to the North and to the South; we should have carefully avoided the causes of religious dissension; we should have refused to allow society to be contaminated at its sources by the admixture of criminals and fugitives; and, above all, we should have been careful to exclude African bondage. Considering the materialising influences of a new country, and the loss of many a holy association when the emigrant removes far away from the church-bells of his native place, we should have made our religion co-extensive with our dominion. The mild and truthful, yet definite system of Christianity which commended itself to our fathers, would have been set up in its integrity from Maine to Georgia, and a sufficient number of well-trained and active pastors would have watched over the people under the superintendence of earnest and devoted bishops. The wishes and feelings of the colonists would have been respected, the Americans would have been treated as our equals, and their love to the mother-country would have met with a hearty return. Innumerable bonds would have maintained the union between England and her colonies, and when a separation of governments became a mutual convenience, the event would have taken place without the rupture of kindly feeling, or detriment to the moral and material interests of either party. The system of the Church of England, amended in its details, and adapted to a more expanded sphere, would be at this time the religion of more than thirty millions of people. The government of America, probably under a monarchy like our own, would be sustained by a population educated in the fear and knowledge of God. The authority of the parent, the master, and the magistrate, would be supported, together with that of the sovereign. The best talent and the highest principle of the nation would always be available for the service of the State, and the double tyranny of slavery and of the mob would be unknown. The present causes of disunion would not exist, and, from the Atlantic to the Pacific, abundant scope would be afforded for the energies of a free, united, and loyal people.

But nations, like individuals, are short-sighted, and our own conduct in reference to America was in some respects far from provident. Accordingly sectional antipathies arose, religious unity ceased to be valued, truth and error were confounded, and the Christian education of the people became more and more enveloped with difficulties. Democracy grew up and flourished by the side of slavery. A revolutionary war gave intensity to evils already existing, and almost extinguished the feeble light which was beginning to shine from the Church. Under these circumstances the public and private character of the Americans was formed. If in that character we perceive any unpleasant features, let us, in all justice, trace them to their origin.

It is evident that the expectations of the founders of the Republic have in many respects failed of accomplishment. Washington would utterly disavow principles which are now openly maintained by leading politicians. It is not impossible that present troubles may lead to a higher appreciation of the conservative wisdom of the first President. Some will go farther and will begin to think that sound philosophy, as well as practical utility, are involved in monarchical principles. Many will learn by experience that although liberty is good, law is better, and that, in the West no less than in the East, government and obedience are necessary to the happiness of nations.

If from the troubled State we turn to contemplate the comparatively peaceful and harmonious Church, we see much which is calculated to excite our thankfulness and our admiration. We cannot but think highly of the perseverance with which, in the old colonial times, Churchmen prayed for an episcopate, and of the devotion with which so many Americans sought ordination in England when peculiar dangers attended such an expedition. The rapid progress of the Church from a state of ruin to comparative prosperity is a fact replete with encouragement. We feel too that American Churchmen are indeed our brethren, and we gladly reciprocate the kind sympathies which they entertain for us. We see in their "Protestant Episcopacy" a system which more than all others is calculated to check that tendency to extremes which spoils so much that is good among our transatlantic kindred. We believe that the time is at hand when Americans will discover in the Church a natural ally of concord and moderation, and a foe to fanaticism and disorder. We agree with the eloquent Bishop of Vermont, who says: —

" I claim an unspeakable value for the influence of

the Church on the union of the nation.   For there is no other religious body which is perfectly free from the perilous hostility between North and South, and which, from the happy structure of her constitution, can never be drawn aside to any political or sectional issue. There is no other so thoroughly trained to reverence the authority of law and order.   There is no other which is so secure from the spirit of dangerous excitement.   There is no other so thoroughly imbued with the love of unity, harmony, and peace."

The union of many States, if not of the whole, may long continue; the States which have now seceded may possibly return for a time to the original union; but a final and permanent separation of the South and North is far within the limits of probability.   If united again, whether by conquest or consent, the same causes of contention will exist as before.   The North will never be silent on the subject of slavery, and a power stronger than law, the will of a multitude which knows no master, will continue to prevent the arrest of negro fugitives.   The evils of separation will however be balanced by certain advantages.   The North will be set free from many entanglements, and will press forward with increased activity in the path of material prosperity.   The South will quickly work out in her own way the difficult problems connected with slavery, unchecked by any political hostility in the Congress of Washington.   It is not utterly impossible that the Southern Legislatures may find it expedient, under their new circumstances, to adopt conciliatory measures towards the blacks, and to commence preparations for changing the slave to a serf, and the serf eventually to a peasant. But if insane views of the excellence and blessedness of the present system should prevail, and especially if aggressions on Mexico, Cuba, and other countries should be undertaken by Southern armies, the moral and economical evils of slavery may soonprove fatal to the society which, by its own profession, isfounded upon it.* Jefferson, though a Deist and a slave-owner, said in his "Notes on Virginia:"—"I tremble for my country when I reflect that God is just; that His justice cannot sleep for ever; that an exchange of situations is among possible events; that it may become probable by supernatural interference. The Almighty has no attribute which can take side with us in such a contest." And again:—"We must wait with patience the workings of an overruling Providence, and hope that it is preparing the deliverance of these our brethren. When the measure of their tears shall be full, when their groans shall have involved heaven itself in darkness, doubtless a God of justice will awaken to their distress. Nothing is more certainly written in the book of Fate than that *this people shall be free.*" †

Our present colonies in Australia, Africa, and America have in many instances been led by circumstances to follow the example of the United States. Religious

* Mr. Stephens, Vice-President of the Southern Confederacy, said, in a speech delivered at Savannah, March 21, 1861:—"The corner-stone of our new government rests upon the great truth that the negro is not equal to the white man, and that slavery is his natural and normal condition."

† Quoted by Helper, pp. 196, 198.

U

divisions have exercised their baneful influence on education, and on the Legislatures; in some cases democracy has become the main principle of political action; and the press only too faithfully copies the American example. But happily as yet their cities and towns have been free from the mischiefs arising from universal suffrage, and long may the colonies be preserved from the peculiar eloquence of the 4th of July, and the innumerable evils resulting from a revolutionary war! Through the exertions of the friends of religion at home, they have been supplied with bishops whose character and labours entitle them to a high rank among the chief pastors of Christendom. In no respect have they justified the terrors formerly felt by American dissenters, who believed that a colonial bishop must necessarily be a spiritual tyrant. On the contrary, by their self-denial, their charity, their active exertions, and often by their administrative skill, they have done much to give the Anglican Episcopate a higher place in general esteem and regard than it previously occupied. With the increase of bishops, the colonial clergy have also been augmented in number and in character, and the sad ecclesiastical history of Virginia is not likely to be repeated.

In regard to the mother-church in England itself, the following words of an American clergyman, a convert from Presbyterianism, may be read with interest and profit* : —

---

* The late Rev. C. C. Colton, late Professor in Trinity College, Hartford, Connecticut, in his "Genius and Mission of the Protestant Episcopal Church," p. 127, &c.

" Under all her disadvantages, and for the very reason of them, the Church of England has acquitted herself in a manner which will enforce respect, if not admiration. Not to speak of the extension of the Church over the colonial portions of the British empire, which has been on a grand scale and with signal success, there has been a revival of a marked vitality and efficiency in her domestic operations. The multiplication of churches has been going on for many years, and is still in progress with increasing demand for church room. There has been a simultaneous growth of the zeal and efficient action of the bishops and clergy. They have, at least in a measure, kept pace with the spirit of the age, as well for internal reform as for the enlargement of the Church. One of the chief objects of the restoration of the power of Convocation is the revival of discipline.

" The British government has been educated in the Church; it has ever been regarded as a part of the Church, and is so by the constitution of the empire. For a long period, especially of late years, there has been manifested by the government an apparent conscientiousness in the discharge of its high duties, as imposed by the constitution, towards the Church. The appointment of bishops and archbishops has apparently been judicious, and all other functions of government in church affairs seem now to be discharged with a view to make the Church most efficient in promoting the cause of religion and Christianity at home and abroad. We are not aware that any impeachment of the fidelity of the British government, in this respect, would fairly lie.   It would seem as if the revival of Christian piety and zeal in the Church of England, of late years, may in no small degree be attributable to this influence of Government, directly and indirectly.   The Church of England has greatly prospered under this régime, and is still going on to prosper.   Never since the Reformation has she done so well.   There is not, perhaps, a church in the world which, during the same or an equal period, has improved so much in her general economy, in spiritual vigour, and in efficiency.   She came out from the Church of Rome, under Henry VIII., as a fragment of that body, with a redeeming leaven of Protestantism in her bosom.   During the subsequent brief interval of Papal power in England, under Mary, the martyr blood of her prelates and laymen was freely poured out for the Protestant faith.   The universities of England have for ages sent forth the most accomplished men of all history, to adorn, instruct, and edify the Church, and to leave a vast body of literature behind them, in the various walks of Christian learning, which can never be excelled, and which will constitute standards of good taste and Christian piety while taste and piety are held precious in the earth.   The zeal of the Church of England for promoting the interests of a true Christianity at home and abroad, and her means of moral power for this object, are constantly being augmented, and she exhibits the front, bearing, and discipline of a Christian host, of no uncertain promise for enacting a prominent part in evangelising the world.

" It will be found in all countries where Christianity has been introduced, that the polities of the Churches planted have, for the most part, been organised and shaped in adaptation to the institutions and genius of the people who are to be acted upon by them, and that they naturally acquire that form. So the polity of the Church of England has grown out of the institutions of the country, and is necessarily adapted to the genius of the people. As the latter has changed, the former in its practical operation has been accommodated to it. Such modifications are slow, but as unavoidable as they are expedient. The Church of England is not the same thing now that she was three centuries or two centuries or even fifty years ago ; and what is pleasant to observe, she has been constantly improving. She has wisely adapted herself to the times in the practical operation of her machinery."

The above extract represents the general opinion of well-informed American Churchmen in regard to the ecclesiastical institutions of England. Their view of our political constitution is for the most part equally favourable, and many of them look with alarm on the attempts which are made, from time to time, to disturb the existing balance of the great powers of the nation. In our fixed attachment to our sovereign they see a principle of order which they desire may never be shaken. As to our elective franchise they regard its further extension as an experiment of the most dangerous character. Understanding as they do the practical working of universal suffrage and vote by ballot, they smile at the simplicity of those Englishmen who consider that our liberties would be increased by our imitation of these institutions of republican America.

If, on the one hand, the condition of the United States affords no encouragement to the expansion of the democratic element in our constitution, it is equally plain that the history of the American Episcopal Church does not warrant us to conclude that many of its peculiarities might advantageously be adopted among ourselves. True it is that the lay element has worked well in the councils of our sister-church; but the reader has seen, on the authority of Bishop White himself, that it was introduced simply as " a substitute for the parliamentary sanction to legislative acts of power." Our laity are represented in the Houses of Parliament, on the throne and in the councils of the sovereign, and so long as the faithful members of the Church are satisfied with this representation, a lay element in church councils seems to be unnecessary. But if ever it should appear that our legislators, as a body, have ceased to regard the real good of the Church, and that, like an American Congress, they no longer acknowledge in religion any difference between truth and error, the arguments which prevailed with the restorers of the American Church will undoubtedly be admitted to have their weight in England. Even now the advantages of lay co-operation are more and more admitted by our clergy, and in several of our dioceses mixed assemblies are regularly held for the discussion of the more secular points of ecclesiastical business.

The free election of the bishops in America, unquestionably, has much to recommend it, and it cannot be doubted that it is well suited to the habits of the people and agreeable to the practice of primitive times. But while our English dioceses continue to embrace so large a number of parishes as they do at present, a popular election by the clergy and laity would lead to numberless inconveniences, and would probably fail to secure the appointment of the most eligible candidate. When the real interests of our dioceses are, on the whole, carefully considered, the present mode of nomination in England, with all its anomalies, has advantages in practice which perhaps too many of us are apt to overlook.

The history of Liturgical Revision in America affords salutary cautions to which the attention of the reader has been already directed. It would be unreasonable to assert that our Prayer-book is not susceptible of improvement, and the time may be approaching when the subject of revision can be discussed with advantage by our revived convocations. Some of the alterations in the American Prayer-book might well be admitted among ourselves, if introduced on sufficient authority, and with a reasonable prospect of removing difficulties from the path of Christian people. Let us hope, however, that, instead of lowering our theory to the level of defective practice, we shall be enabled to raise our practice, where defective, to the height of our truly primitive theory.

In regard to finance, we have seen that the principle of endowments has never been rejected in America, and that, in fact, the Church is protected by law in the possession of considerable endowments, the value and number of which are constantly increasing. We have seen that the "voluntary system" was not adopted from choice, but from the urgent necessities of the case, and that its operation has been in some respects far from satisfactory. The want of a better system has occasioned those heavy charges on pews which have been undoubtedly most prejudicial to the religious interests of the poorer classes. Then it must be recollected that the usefulness of ministers of religion is closely connected with their personal independence. "Among the trials painful to our nature," the late venerable Bishop Griswold (of Massachusetts) enumerates the being "constrained to reprove and rebuke those on whom we depend for our daily bread."* If this trial is painfully felt in America, how much more injurious would be its effects upon the clergy of England! A sense of constant dependence may indeed be a check upon gross irregularities, but it certainly tends to obstruct the development of the higher virtues of the clerical character. At present the endow-

---

* Discourses, p. 1.

'ments of the Church of England are sufficient, in general, to encourage the minister of a parish, with the help of his private means, to maintain an independent position, to speak the truth without fear, and to act as a father to the poor people committed to his charge. Our American visitors are always deeply impressed with this feature of our system, so different from their own. With admiration they perceive that our rectories and vicarages are so many centres from which temporal no less than spiritual good flows forth abundantly among the surrounding population. They recognise in the village pastor, with his schools, his charities, and his general influence, something more than the mere preacher, and to the stability of his position they trace the interest which he evidently feels in the permanent welfare of his flock. An American Presbyterian minister, the late Rev. Mr. Mines, was converted to the Church by what he saw of parish work on a visit to this country.* " I saw," he wrote, " the happiest combination of qualities in those individuals who had been moulded under the lofty and ennobling influences of the Church. I became acquainted with numbers of persons whose simplicity, and fervour, and single-mindedness, introduced me to a religion which I had not supposed to exist on earth. I saw a piety without cant, which I had never seen before; a zeal without noise; a charity without show; a character, in short, so formed by the precepts of the Blessed

* America and the American Church, 2nd edition, chap. xi.

Master, that I could not but feel that here was indeed the Church of God."

It is quite conceivable that through the combined influence of the successors of the Puritans, the Romanists, and those who deny all revelation, a state of things may be produced in England not unlike that which has for some time existed in America. Division may be encouraged by our legislature until all religions come to be regarded as equal, irrespectively of their several tendencies and of the essential difference between truth and error. Religious education in our schools may be denounced and forbidden, the churches may be treated as national property, the clergy may be irritated and discouraged by annoying enactments, and finally Church property may be swept away in England as it was in Virginia. Even in these extreme circumstances, the example of our American brethren teaches us that the Church need not utterly despair. She might again rise on new foundations, and, though despoiled of much that is valuable, might succeed in maintaining an honourable position among the conflicting sects with which in public estimation she would be identified. But, on the other hand, we may reasonably indulge in better anticipations for our country and our Church. We may hope that the destructive career of democracy in a kindred nation will act as a warning to our politicians at home, and that Englishmen will be encouraged to maintain their ancient institutions in their integrity. At the same time we may trust that there will be a general disposition on the part of churchmen to remove any abuses which may still remain in our system, and to clear away all unnecessary obstacles which may impede the return of separatists to our communion.

As to our kinsmen in America, we have no reason to regard their case as by any means hopeless. No doubt they must look forward to political convulsions, extending over many successive years. But our own country has not attained her present position without passing through the ordeal of civil wars and revolutions. It may be necessary that America should undergo a similar course of trial before her politics or her religion can acquire that consistency and permanency which are necessary to a great nation.

The Church in America will lose nothing by the present contest, and probably will gain much. She has taken no part in the fanatical and hot-headed schemes of either party, and when calm reflection shall have succeeded to passion, she will find her reward in a more general appreciation on the part of the people. The General Convention may well admit of subdivision, and as in England we have the Convocations of York and Canterbury, so in America there may be provincial synods of the North and South, and, if necessary, of the East and the West. The diocesan unity will still remain unimpaired, and among the bishops the same good understanding which previously existed will unquestionably continue. Even though the political union should utterly perish, the union of the Church will still remain. She will be a bond of peace not only for Americans, but for the children of our Reformation wherever dispersed throughout the world.

APPENDIX.

INCREASE OF THE CLERGY COMPARED WITH THE INCREASE OF THE POPULATION.

BY THE REV. DR. CHAPIN, OF GLASTONBURY, CONNECTICUT.

A.D.	Population of United States.	Time required for doubling in the same ratio.	Clergy.	Time required for doubling in the same ratio.
1790	3,929,328		190	
1800	5,309,758	28·4	210	95·0
1810	7,239,903	27·5	218	262·0
1820	9,638,166	31·0	331	19·5
1830	12,858,670	29·9	534	16·3
1840	17,063,353	30·5	1026	10·8
1850	23,263,498	27·5	1632	16·9
1860	31,429,891	28·4	2250	26·4

From the above table it appears that since 1810 the increase of the clergy has been far more rapid than that of the people.

DIOCESES.	BISHOPS.	Lay Readers.	Candidates for Orders.	Clergy Canonically resident.			
				Bishops.	Presbyters.	Deacons.	Total.
Maine	George Burgess, D.D.		3	1	17	1	19
New Hampshire	Carlton Chase, D.D.			1	14		15
Vermont	John H. Hopkins, D.D.	16	3	1	25	2	28
Massachusetts	Manton Eastburn, D.D.		9	1	77	2	83
Rhode Island	Thomas M. Clark, D.D.	7	7	1	26	4	31
Connecticut	{T. C. Brownell, D.D. } {J. Williams, D.D. }		23	2	118	11	131
New York	Horatio Potter, D.D.		55	2			352
W. New York	Wm. H. De Lancey, D.D.		19	1	126	11	138
New Jersey	W. H. Odenheimer, D.D.		11	1	87	15	103
Pennsylvania	{Alonzo Potter, D.D. } {Samuel Bowman, D.D.}		26	2	168	25	193
Delaware	Alfred Lee, D.D.	1	1	1	14	4	19
Maryland	W. R. Whittingham, D.D.	27	18	1	148	11	159
Virginia	{Wm. Meade, D.D.} {John Johns, D.D. }		18	2			113
North Carolina	Thomas C. Atkinson, D.D.	30	11	1	34	12	47
South Carolina	Thomas F. Davis, D.D.		10	1	68	6	75
Georgia	Stephen Elliott, D.D.		4	1	25		26
Florida	Francis H. Rutledge, D.D.	6	1	1	7		8
Alabama	N. H. Cobbs, D.D.		8	1	24	5	30
Mississippi	Wm. M. Green, D.D.	1	2	1	29	2	32
Louisiana	Leonidas Polk, D.D.		2	1	33	2	36
Texas	Alexander Gregg, D.D.	2	2	1	12		13
Tennessee	Jas. H. Otey, D.D.		6	1	24	2	27
Kentucky	Benj. B. Smith, D.D.	5	6	1			32
Ohio	{C. P. Mc Ilvaine, D.D. } {G. T. Bedell, D.D. }		15	2	77	5	84
Indiana	Geo. Upfold, D.D.		3	1	24	4	29
Illinois	H. J. Whitehouse, D.D.	12	5	1	58	2	61
Missouri	Cicero S. Hawks, D.D.	4	5	1	25	2	28
Kansas			1		10	1	11
Michigan	Saml. A. Mc Coskry, D.D.	10	3	1	44	4	49
Wisconsin	Jackson Kemper, D.D.		9	1	44	1	46
Iowa	Henry W. Lee, D.D.			1			32
Minnesota	Henry B. Whipple, D.D.		2	1	19	2	22
California	Wm. I. Kip, D.D.		3	1	10	2	13
		121	291	37	1387	156	2065

Convention for 1859.

Church Edifices.				Confirmations.	Baptisms.			Marriages.	Burials.	Communicants.	Sunday Schools.	
Consecrated (new).	Whole number.	Sittings.	Parsonages.		Infants.	Adults.	Total.				Teachers.	Scholars.
3	17	6,700		555	769	273	1,042	180	412	1,442	192	1,508
1	14		2	232	286	92	378	71	141	726	59	482
1	31	4,000	5	569	413	243	656	176	327	1,998		1,351
3				2,163	3,711	559	4,270	1,185	2,181	7,780		5,721
5	30	11,600	6	899	893	420	1,313	425	772	3,142	352	2,665
7	113			2,924	3,261	963	4,224	1,195	2,892	11,575	1,229	7,577
17				8,760	15,061	2,275	17,334	4,516	7,127	24,491	2,150	24,268
5	130		55	2,063	4,038	1,209	5,247	1,295	2,222	10,834	1,221	8,773
5				1,756	2,864	625	3,489	558	1,486	5,000	504	4,410
21	172		44	4,834	8,803	1,554	10,357	2,302	4,467	14,106	2,059	19,753
4	27	7,200	4	335	824	119	943	191	409	992	277	2,181
13	172	45,000		3,076	7,054	541	7,695	1,717	2,835	10,580		
13	174		50	2,165	3,029	568	3,597	1,100	2,019	7,487	892	5,597
6	67		18	1,015	1,680	351	2,031	253	652	5,036		1,294
12	75		17	1,942	3,657	1,088	4,745	667	1,404	5,672	274	2,243
1	25		9	482	857	216	1,073	227	544	1,998	159	1,526
1	10		4	183	376	58	434	72	171	630	80	600
5				581	1,107	230	1,337	254	337	1,673	143	930
4	21		8	528	1,080	378	1,458	322	508	1,400	82	568
5				737	2,693	291	2,984	751	543	1,667	141	1,455
	11		1	70	384	37	421	110	91	700	90	643
2	21		3	458	886	202	1,088	170	312	1,300		755
1	29	7,050	3	715	1,070	256	1,326	182	513	1,936	301	2,354
6	76			1,143	1,907	433	2,340	781	1,237	5,680	807	5,731
2	24			389	622	132	754	187	346	1,192	158	1,036
12			13	1,231	1,939	368	2,307	651	812	3,000	516	2,903
6	16	6,870	6	573	745	153	898	221	360	1,393	153	916
3	4			50	50		50			160		
9	40	12,300	5	1,016	1,066	369	1,435	561	666	2,701	342	2,557
6	48	11,100		1,039	1,804	390	2,194	412	625	2,500	300	2,000
6	22	5,000		425	497	116	613	124	222	1,488	280	1,198
10	18			216	296	84	380	64	101	597	48	474
3	8	2,400	1	288	731	78	809	305	287	733	110	859
198	1395		254	43,401	74,555	14,282	89,289	21,225	37,021	159,611	14,019	115,912

No. II.—COMPARATIVE VIEW OF THE CHURCH STATISTICS OF 1856 AND 1859. (From the Same.)

DIOCESES.	Candidates for Orders 1856	1859	Clergy 1856	1859	Deacons ordained 1856	1859	Confirmed 1856	1859	Baptisms Infants 1856	1859	Baptisms Adults 1856	1859	Communicants 1856	1859	Gain Net gain	Gain per ct.	Total Contributions 1856	1859
Maine	4	3	18	19	6	3	273	555	386	769	134	273	996	1,442	446	45	$11,398 72	$16,520 59
New Hampshire	1		14	15		1	132	232	165	286	40	92	581	726	145	25	5,039 61	4,453 46
Vermont	2	3	20	28	1	6	239	569	293	413	96	243	1,929	1,998	69	3	12,116 00	21,727 92
Massachusetts	9	9	77	83	9	7	960	2,163	2,504	3,711	296	559	6,027	7,780	1,753	29	114,263 87	49,755 00
Rhode Island	2	7	32	31	7	7	488	899	675	933	205	420	2,736	3,142	406	15	30,000 00	38,257 15
Connecticut	27	23	122	131	26	28	1,938	2,924	2,721	3,261	697	963	10,389	11,575	1,186	11	104,224 71	264,964 47
New York	38	55	309	332	49	42	5,778	8,769	12,398	15,061	1,407	2,273	22,549	24,491	1,942	9	649,411 92	1,066,588 14
W. New York	14	19	120	138	10	13	2,294	2,063	3,268	4,038	870	1,209	9,226	10,834	1,608	17	42,621 00	231,818 91
New Jersey	14	11	80	103	9	13	1,411	1,756	2,304	2,864	399	625	4,352	5,000	668	15		134,331 88
Pennsylvania	28	26	161	193	21	39	3,242	4,834	8,002	8,303	1,016	1,554	12,816	14,106	1,290	10	394,125 28	426,921 22
Delaware	3	1	19	19	3	7	279	335	468	824	69	119	813	992	179	22	38,032 24	78,005 87
Maryland	16	18	147	159	11	16	2,511	3,076	6,043	7,154	621	601	9,596	10,580	984	10	197,000 00	393,395 00
Virginia	12	18	111	113	20	25	1,400	2,165	2,371	3,029	482	588	6,527	7,487	960	15	135,877 89	192,221 89
North Carolina	7	11	45	47	10	9	804	1,015	1,918	1,680	370	351	2,475	3,036	561	22	63,751 53	86,775 68
South Carolina	8	10	70	75	9	8	1,853	1,942	2,976	3,657	891	1,088	5,993	5,672			68,223 00	115,573 00
Georgia	8	4	22	26	2	8	577	482		857		216	1,736	1,998	262	15	36,890 43	59,513 28
Florida		1	7	8	2		210	183		376		58	515	630	115	22	11,688 98	abt. 20,000 00
Alabama	4	8	28	30	6	5	547	531	1,206	1,107	275	230	1,461	1,673	212	14	34,612 99	21,700 10
Mississippi	4	2	31	32	4	4	491	623	1,112	1,080	409	373	1,037	1,400	363	35	35,123 00	83,941 75
Louisiana	3	2	32	36	1	4	559	737		2,693		291	1,421	1,667	246	17	45,000 00	49,305 37
Texas			13	13	3	2	105	70	238	384	49	37	500	700			12,721 00	44,230 00
Tennessee	4	6	21	27	3	4	291	458	564	836	119	202	862	1,300	438	51	21,782 00	66,022 16
Kentucky	2	6	31	32	16	14	513	715	900	1,070	192	256	1,465	1,936	471	32	52,519 23	96,809 43
Ohio	5	15	86	84	4	5	1,212	1,143	1,492	1,907	268	433	4,992	5,680	688	13	132,860 00	160,923 18
Indiana	5	3	24	29	8	5	364	389	520	622	136	132	1,058	1,192	131	13	18,104 35	46,652 58
Illinois	9	5	49	61	8	4	733	1,231	1,272	1,939	226	368	2,393	3,000	607	25	7,470 23	39,789 00
Missouri	3	3	23	28	8	1	320	573	572	745	71	153	1,098	1,395	297	27	63,612 41	75,340 50
Michigan	2	3	40	46	1	6	404	1,016	914	1,006	196	369	1,962	2,701	739	37	18,378 65	16,446 89
Wisconsin	12	9	46	46	1	10	465	1,039		1,801		394	1,172	2,500	1,328	113	34,290 23	
Iowa	3		20	32		5	132	425		407		116	500	1,488	988	198	21,768 98	9,863 00
California		8	10	13	4	4	116	298	350	731	22	78	363	733	370	97		37,983 86
Kansas		1		11		1		30		60				160	160			
Minnesota		2		22				216		296		84		597	597			23,519 18

No. III.—TABULAR VIEW.

Increase in Fifteen Years.

	In 1844.	In 1859.
Total number of Clergy reported	1,096	2,065
Candidates for Orders	203	291
Deacons ordained	191	301
Churches consecrated	143	198
Communicants . . . . . . :	72,099	139,611
Parishes reported: in 1853, in 22 Dioceses, 1150 .		2,120
Dioceses	24	33

Summary and Comparative Views of Chief Items.

1841.

Clergy in 25 Dioceses 1,052

Baptisms { Adults, in 14 Dioceses . 4,729
Infants, in 14 Dioceses . 22,496 } . . . 34,465
Not specified, in 9 Dioceses . 7,240

Communicants added in 9 Dioceses. 3,678
Total of Communicants in 25 Dioceses 55,427
Marriages in 17 Dioceses 8,604
Burials in 14 Dioceses 14,961
Sunday-school Teachers in 10 Dioceses 3,974
Sunday-school Pupils in 11 Dioceses 32,265
Clergy deceased in 11 Dioceses 28

1844.

Clergy in 24 Dioceses (number in 3 Dioceses not reported) . 1,096

Baptisms { Adults, in 19 Dioceses . . 7,807
Infants, in 19 Dioceses . . 30,254 } . . 39,119
Not specified, in 3 Dioceses . 1,058

Communicants added in 12 Dioceses 12,490
Total of Communicants in 26 Dioceses 72,099
Marriages in 17 Dioceses 8,036

x

Burials in 17 Dioceses 14,330
Sunday-school Teachers in 13 Dioceses 5,037
Sunday-school Pupils in 14 Dioceses 40,012
Clergy deceased in 8 Dioceses 31

1847.

Clergy in 28 Dioceses 1,404

Baptisms {
Adults, in 21 Dioceses . . 4,408
Infants, in 21 Dioceses . . 23,551 } . . . 33,774
Not specified, in 7 Dioceses . 5,815
}

Communicants added in 11 Dioceses 5,125
Total of Communicants in 27 Dioceses 67,550
Marriages, in 19 Dioceses 6,826
Burials in 19 Dioceses 12,814
Sunday-school Teachers in 16 Dioceses 5,279
Sunday-school Pupils in 18 Dioceses 39,437
Clergy deceased in 15 Dioceses 34

1850.

Clergy in 29 Dioceses 1,558

Baptisms {
Adults, in 24 Dioceses . . 5,957
Infants, in 24 Dioceses . . 33,072 } . . . 42,925
Not specified, in 4 Dioceses . 3,896
}

Communicants added in 8 Dioceses 4,987
Total Communicants in 28 Dioceses 79,802
Marriages in 20 Dioceses 3,420
Burials in 20 Dioceses 16,233
Sunday-school Teachers in 17 Dioceses 4,520
Sunday-school Pupils in 19 Dioceses 38,603
Clergy deceased in 16 Dioceses 43

1853.

Clergy in 30 Dioceses 1,651

Baptisms {
Infants, in 24 Dioceses . . 39,565
Adults, in 24 Dioceses . . 6,531 } . . . 48,157
Not specified, in 4 Dioceses . 2,061
}

Communicants added in 11 Dioceses 8,802
Total Communicants in 30 Dioceses 105,136
Marriages in 24 Dioceses 12,974

Funerals in 24 Dioceses 23,558
Sunday-school Teachers in 18 Dioceses 5,531
Sunday-school Scholars in 22 Dioceses 62,376
Clergy deceased in 18 Dioceses 42
Number of Churches in 7 Dioceses 454
Number of Parishes and Congregations in 22 Dioceses . . 1,150
Parsonages added in 5 Dioceses 34
Number of Parsonages in 3 Dioceses 84

1856.

Clergy in 31 Dioceses 1,828
Baptisms { Infants, in 26 Dioceses . . 56,132 }
Adults, in 26 Dioceses . . 9,542 } . . 70,527
Not specified, in 4 Dioceses . 4,853 }
Communicants in 31 Dioceses 119,540
Marriages in 30 Dioceses 21,334
Funerals in 30 Dioceses 36,925
Sunday-school Teachers in 20 Dioceses 9,235
Sunday-school Scholars in 25 Dioceses 82,014
Clergy deceased in 22 Dioceses 58
Number of Churches in 6 Dioceses 335
Number of Parishes in 29 Dioceses 1,825
Number of Parsonages in 7 Dioceses 109

1859.

Clergy in 33 Dioceses 2,065
Baptisms { Infants, in 33 Dioceses . . 74,553 } . . 89,282
Adults, in 33 Dioceses . . 14,729 }
Communicants in 33 Dioceses 139,611
Marriages in 32 Dioceses 21,225
Burials in 32 Dioceses 37,021
Sunday-school Teachers in 27 Dioceses 14,019
Sunday-school Scholars in 31 Dioceses 113,912
Clergy deceased in 22 Dioceses 75
Number of Churches in 27 Dioceses 1,395
Number of Parishes in 33 Dioceses 2,120
Number of Parsonages in 19 Dioceses 254

THE following statement respecting *forty-one* of the Episcopal Churches in the CITY OF NEW YORK (taken from the "Church Journal") will give some idea of the efficiency of the Church in that great metropolis in the year 1860.

Church.	Baptisms.	Confirmations.	Communicants.	Charitable Contributions.
Advent	41	—	115	$1,226
All Angels	54	—	16	197
All Saints	32	—	150	1,254
Atonement	30	31	100	2,250
Calvary	51	55	701	18,206
Christ	18	—	256	6,023
Christ Church Mission Chapel	27	—	50	—
Emmanuel	—	—	—	—
Epiphany	69	22	324	413
Good Shepherd	12	—	30	—
Holy Apostles	165	67	420	3,991
Holy Comforter	19	—	45	—
Holy Evangelists	33	—	137	751
Holy Innocents	46	16	115	3,568
Incarnation	31	27	320	20,886
Incarnation Mission Chapel	44	1	40	—
Intercession	20	—	89	2,249
Nativity	58	12	90	616
Our Saviour	25	—	45	150
St. Andrew's	16	—	109	1,633
St. Ann's for Deaf Mutes	48	30	141	13,755
St. Clement's	32	21	150	1,389
St. Esprit	30	14	220	10
St. George's	154	109	1097	34,767
St. George the Martyr	11	—	77	—
St. James's	22	—	139	1,364
St. John the Baptist	29	17	140	2,022
St. John the Evangelist	87	46	300	5,103
St. Luke's	96	34	275	3,709
St. Mark's	26	25	240	8,111
St. Mark's Mission Chapel	4	8	62	409
St. Michael's	29	7	29	1,255
St. Peter's	162	—	560	12,380
St. Philip's	10	—	—	99
St. Stephen's	26	—	159	—
St. Thomas's	38	26	300	4,011
St. Thomas's Free Chapel	82	21	92	620
St. Timothy's	65	31	106	5,735
Transfiguration	53	43	250	5,986
Trinity	435	245	1253	24,737
Zion	42	32	215	3,073
	2272	940	8957	$ 191,960
Or	.	.	.	£38,392

No reports were received from the following Churches : — Annunciation, Ascension, Grace, Holy Communion, Holy Martyrs', Messiah, Redeemer, Redemption, St. Barnabas, St. Bartholomew's, St. Cornelius', St. Jude's, St. Mary's, St. Matthew's, St. Sauveur's, and St. Simon's — 16.

The parochial report of Trinity Church, New York, to the Diocesan Convention of 1860, furnishes the materials for the following interesting summary : —

Baptisms (adults, 65 ; infants, 362 ; not specified, 8) .	435
Confirmed	245
Communicants, present number	1253
Sunday-school Teachers	209
Sunday scholars	2405

Special contributions of the Vestry of Trinity Church :—

Salary of the Provisional Bishop	$2000
Diocesan Missionary Committee	600
Diocesan Fund	390
General Board of Missions	250
Communion Fund for the Poor	2000
,, ,, ,, ,, ,, at Trinity Church .	600
Christmas and St. Barnabas' Day Celebrations . .	1000
Parish School of St. Paul's Chapel	1000
Lay visitor to Emigrants at Castle Garden . . .	600
Lay visitors at Trinity Church.	450
Lay assistance at St. Paul's Chapel	500
Lay assistance at St. John's Chapel	360
Total .	$9750

Contributions and collections in the several Churches and Chapels of the parish : —

Trinity Church	$2,633
St. Paul's Chapel	5,225
St. John's Chapel	2,252
Trinity Chapel	4,460
Total	$14,570
Contributions of Vestry, as above	9,750
Contributions specially appropriated by the Rector .	416
Total contributions of the Parish . .	$24,736
	£4,947

It will be seen that the communicants at Trinity Church amount to 1253, and at St. George's to 1097. The rector of St. George's gives the statistics of his Sunday-school as follows, for 1860.

	Teachers.	Scholars.
At the Parish Church .	64	1115
Weekly Sewing-school	18	220
	82	1335
Mission English Sunday-school	34	516
„ German „ „	9	140
„ Weekly Sewing-school	18	130
	61	786
Grand total of teachers and scholars .		2264

The charitable contributions of the same parish for 1860 are stated as follows, the amount being equal to nearly 8000*l.*

Bible Society .	$1,721
Foreign Missions	9,078
Domestic Missions .	3,275
Sunday-school offerings for St. George's Mission Chapel	4,224
Contributions from the congregation for Mission Chapel	3,467
Collection for the expenses of Sunday school	575
Anderson's fund for ditto	270
Diocesan Missions and Episcopal Fund	514
Evangelical Knowledge Society	2,367
Seamen's Mission .	264
American Tract Society .	3,000
Alexandria Seminary	450
Kenyon College .	2,882
Education of Young Men for the Ministry	700
Aged and Infirm Clergy .	259
Communion Alms .	2,043
General purposes	2,894
Dorcas Society	786

And some other sums, bringing up the whole to the total amount of $39,769

CENSUS OF THE UNITED STATES.

The following official table, just published, shows the population of he United States and Territories, according to the Seventh Census 1850), and the Eighth Census (1860), respectively: —

States.	Census of 1850.			Census of 1860.		
	Free.	Slave.	Total.	Free.	Slave.	Total.
Alabama . . .	428,779	342,844	771,623	529,164	435,132	964,296
Arkansas . . .	162,797	47,100	209,897	324,323	111,104	435,427
California . . .	92,597	—	92,597	380,015	—	480,015
Connecticut . .	370,792	—	370,792	460,151	—	460,151
Delaware . . .	89,242	2,290	91,532	110,420	1,798	112,218
Florida	48,135	39,310	87,445	78,686	61,753	140,439
Georgia	524,503	381,682	906,185	595,097	462,230	1,057,327
Illinois	851,470	—	851,470	1,711,753	—	1,711,753
Indiana	988,416	—	988,416	1,350,479	—	1,350,479
Iowa	192,214	—	192,214	674,948	—	674,948
Kansas	—	—	—	107,110	—	107,110
Kentucky . . .	771,424	210,981	982,405	930,223	225,490	1,135,713
Louisiana . . .	272,953	244,809	517,762	376,913	332,520	709,433
Maine	583,169	—	583,169	628,276	—	628,276
Maryland . . .	492,666	90,368	583,034	599,846	87,188	687,034
Massachusetts .	994,514	—	994,514	1,231,065	—	1,231,065
Mississippi . .	296,648	309,878	606,526	354,699	436,696	791,395
Missouri . . .	594,622	87,422	682,044	1,058,352	114,965	1,173,317
Michigan . . .	397,654	—	397,654	749,112	—	749,112
Minnesota . .	6,077	—	6,077	162,022	—	162,022
New Hampshire	317,976	—	317,976	326,072	—	326,072
New Jersey . .	489,319	236	489,555	672,031	—	672,031
New York . . .	3,097,394	—	3,097,394	3,887,542	—	3,887,542
North Carolina	580,491	288,548	869,039	661,586	331,081	992,667
Ohio	1,980,329	—	1,980,329	5,339,599	—	2,339,599
Oregon	13,294	—	13,294	52,464	—	52,464
Pennsylvania .	2,311,786	—	2,311,786	2,906,470	—	2,906,370
Rhode Island .	147,545	—	147,545	174,621	—	174,621
South Carolina .	283,523	384,984	668,507	301,271	402,541	703,812
Tennessee . . .	763,258	239,459	1,002,717	834,063	275,784	1,109,847
Texas	154,431	58,161	212,592	420,651	180,388	601,039
Virginia . . .	949,133	472,528	1,421,661	1,105,196	400,887	1,596,083
Vermont . . .	314,120	—	314,120	315,116	—	315,116
Wisconsin . . .	305,391	—	305,391	775,873	—	775,873
	19,866,662	3,200,600	23,067,262	27,185,109	3,949,557	31,134,666
Territories:—						
Colorado . . .	—	—	—	34,197	—	34,197
Dakotah . . .	—	—	—	4,839	—	4,839
Nebraska . . .	—	—	—	28,832	10	28,842
Nevada	—	—	—	6,857	—	6,857
New Mexico . .	61,547	—	61,547	93,517	24	93,541
Utah	11,354	26	11,380	40,266	29	40,295
Washington . .	—	—	—	11,578	—	11,578
District of Columbia . . .	48,000	3,687	51,687	71,895	3,181	75,076
	19,987,563	3,204,313	23,191,876	27,477,090	3,952,601	31,429,891

THE END.

LONDON
PRINTED BY SPOTTISWOODE AND CO.
NEW-STREET SQUARE

Messrs. SAUNDERS, OTLEY, & Co.'s

RAP ANNOUNCEMENTS

THE VOYAGE OF THE NOVARA ROUND
THE WORLD. The Circumnavigation of the Globe, by the Austrian Frigate Novara. English Edition. Containing an Unpublished Letter from Baron Humboldt. With numerous wood engravings. Dedicated, by special permission, to Sir Roderick Murchison. 3 vols., 8vo.

THE MARQUIS OF DALHOUSIE'S ADMINIS-
TRATION of BRITISH INDIA. By Edwin Arnold, M.A., of University College, Oxford.

THE POLITICAL LIFE of the EARL of DERBY.

THE LIFE of the RIGHT HON. BENJAMIN
DISRAELI, M.P.

THE SPEECHES AND ADDRESSES of the LORD
BISHOP of OXFORD from 1841 to the Present Time. Edited by the Author. 1 vol., 8vo.

THE LIVES of the SPEAKERS of the HOUSE of
COMMONS. By William Nathaniel Massey, Esq., M.P., author of "The History of England," and Chairman of Ways and Means.

THE LATITUDINARIANS.
A Chapter of Church History, from the Accession of Archbishop Tillotson in 1691, to the Death of Archdeacon Blackburne, in 1787. By Edward Churton, M.A., Archdeacon of Cleveland.

THE LIFE OF THE RIGHT HON. W. E.
GLADSTONE, M.P. 1 vol., 8vo.

ECCLESIA RESTITUTA.
By F. C. Massingberd, M.A., Prebendary of Lincoln and Rector of Ormsby.

SEVEN ANSWERS to the 'ESSAYS and REVIEWS,'
BY SEVEN WRITERS IN SEVEN SEPARATE ESSAYS.

THE HISTORY OF THE CONSERVATIVE
PARTY, from the Defection of Sir Robert Peel to the Present Time. 1 vol., 8vo.

THE HISTORY OF THE CHURCH OF
ENGLAND, from the Death of Elizabeth to the Present Time. By the Rev. Geo. G. Perry, M.A., Rector of Waddington, late Fellow and Tutor of Lincoln College, Oxford. 3 vols., 8vo.

CHURCH RATE A NATIONAL TRUST.
By the Venerable Archdeacon Denison. 1 vol., 8vo, 10s. 6d.

THE CHURCHES OF THE EAST.
By the Rev. George Williams, B.D., Senior Fellow of King's College, Cambridge. 1 vol., 8vo.

THE AMERICAN CHURCH and the AMERICAN
UNION. By Henry Caswall, D.D., of Trinity College, Connecticut, and Prebendary of Sarum. 1 v., post 8vo.

PHILOSOPHY ; or, THE SCIENCE of TRUTH,
being a Treatise on First Principles, Mental, Physical, and Verbal. By James Haig, Esq., M.A., of Lincoln's Inn.

RECOLLECTIONS OF GENERAL GARI-
BALDI; or, TRAVELS FROM ROME TO LUCERNE, comprising a Visit to the Mediterranean Islands of La Madalena and Caprera, and the Home of General Garibaldi. 1 vol. 10s. 6d.

THE TRAVELS AND ADVENTURES OF
DR. WOLFF, the Bokhara Missionary. 2d. edition, 2 vols. 8vo. 36s.

AN AUTUMN TOUR IN SPAIN.
By the Rev. R. Roberts, B.A., of Trinity College, Cambridge, and Vicar of Milton Abbas. With numerous Engravings. 21s.

HISTORICAL MEMOIRS OF THE
SUCCESSORS OF ST. PATRICK AND ARCHBISHOPS OF ARMAGH. By James Henthorne Todd, D.D., F.S.A., President of the Royal Irish Academy, Treasurer of St. Patrick's Cathedral, Regius Professor of Hebrew in the University, and Senior Fellow of Trinity College, Dublin. 2 vols., 8vo.

THE LIFE OF GEORGE FOX,

The Founder of the Quakers. From numerous original sources. 10s. 6d.

THE PRIVATE JOURNAL

OF THE MARQUESS OF HASTINGS, Governor-General and Commander-in-Chief in India.
Edited by his Daughter, SOPHIA, the Marchioness of Bute. Second Edition, 2 vols. post 8vo, with Map and Index. 21s.

NAPOLEON THE THIRD ON ENGLAND.

Selections from his own writings. Translated by J. H. SIMPSON. 5s.

THE HUNTING GROUNDS OF THE OLD

WORLD. By H. A. L. (the Old Shekarry). Second Edition. 21s.

HIGHLANDS AND HIGHLANDERS;

As they were and as they are. By WILLIAM GRANT STEWART. First and Second series, price 5s. each; extra bound, 6s. 6d.

THE ENGLISHMAN IN CHINA.

With numerous Woodcuts. 10s. 6d.

LECTURES ON THE EPISTLE TO THE

EPHESIANS. By the Rev. R. J. M'GHEE. Second Edition. 2 vols, Reduced price, 15s.

PRE-ADAMITE MAN; or,

THE STORY OF OUR OLD PLANET AND ITS INHABITANTS, TOLD BY SCRIPTURE AND SCIENCE. Beautifully Illustrated by Hervieu, Dalziel Brothers, &c. 1 vol, post 8vo, 10s. 6d.

LOUIS CHARLES DE BOURBON:

THE "PRISONER OF THE TEMPLE." 3s.

A HANDY-BOOK FOR RIFLE VOLUNTEERS.

With 14 Coloured Plates and Diagrams. By Captain W. G. Hartley, author of "A New System of Drill." 7s. 6d.

RECOLLECTIONS of a WINTER CAMPAIGN

IN INDIA, in 1857—58. By CAPTAIN OLIVER J. JONES, R.N. With numerous illustrations drawn on stone by Day, from the Author's Sketches. In 1 vol. royal 8vo, 16s.

TWO YEARS IN SYRIA.

By T. LEWIS FARLEY, Esq., Late Chief Accountant of the Ottoman Bank, Beyrout. 12s. Second Edition.

DIARY OF TRAVELS IN THREE QUARTERS

OF THE GLOBE. By an AUSTRALIAN SETTLER. 2 vols, post 8vo, 21s.

RECOLLECTIONS of the COURT of NAPLES in
OUR OWN TIMES.

MOUNT LEBANON AND ITS INHABITANTS:
A Ten Years' Residence from 1842 to 1852. By Colonel CHURCHILL,
Staff Officer in the British Expedition to Syria. Second Edition.
3 vols. 8vo, £1 5s.

FROM SOUTHAMPTON TO CALCUTTA.
Sketches of Anglo-Indian Life. 10s. 6d.

THE TABLETTE BOOKE of LADYE MARY
KEYES, OWNE SISTER TO THE MISFORTUNATE LADYE
JANE DUDLIE. Post 8vo, 10s. 6d.

TRAVEL and RECOLLECTIONS of TRAVEL.
By Dr. JOHN SHAW. 1 vol, post 8vo, 7s. 6d.

LETTERS ON INDIA.
By EDWARD SULLIVAN, Esq., Author of ' Rambles in North and South
America ;' 'The Bungalow and the Tent;' 'From Boulogne to Babel
Mandeb;' 'A Trip to the Trenches ;' &c. 1 vol. 7s.

CAMPAIGNING IN KAFFIRLAND; or,
SCENES AND ADVENTURES IN THE KAFFIR WAR OF
1851—52. By Captain W. R. KING. Second Edition. 1 vol. 8vo, 14s.

THE RELIGIOUS TENDENCIES OF THE
AGE. 6s. 6d.

ADVENTURES OF A GENTLEMAN
IN SEARCH OF A HORSE. By SIR GEORGE STEPHEN. With
illustrations by Cruikshank. New and cheaper Edition, 5s.

THE LANGUAGE OF FLOWERS,
Elegant Gift Book for the Season. Beautifully bound in green watered
silk, with coloured plates. Containing the Art of Conveying Sentiments of Esteem and Affection. Eleventh edition, dedicated, by permission, to the late Duchess of Kent. 10s. 6d.

THE MANAGEMENT OF BEES;
With a description of the " Ladies' Safety Hive." By SAMUEL BAG-
STER, Jun. 1 vol., illustrated. 7s.

THE HANDBOOK OF TURNING,
With numerous plates. A complete and Practical Guide to the Beautiful Science of Turning in all its Branches. 1 vol. 7s. 6d.

TEXTS FOR TALKERS.
By FRANK FOWLER. 3s. 6d.

THE SUMMER TOUR of an INVALID. 5s. 6d.

ARMY MISRULE : BARRACK THOUGHTS.
By a COMMON SOLDIER. 3s.

FICTION.

WHY PAUL FERROLL KILLED HIS WIFE.
By the Author of " Paul Ferroll." Third Edition. 10s. 6d.

OUR NEW RECTOR.
Edited by the Author of ' Mr. Verdant Green.' 10s. 6d.

THE RECTOR'S DAUGHTERS.
A Tale of Clerical Life. 10s. 6d.

SWEETHEARTS AND WIVES.
A Novel. By MARGUERITE A. POWER. 3 vols., 31s. 6d.

AN M.P. IN SEARCH OF A CREED.
A Novel. 10s. 6d.

ROTTEN ROW. A Novel. 2 vols., 21s.

CRISPIN KEN. By the Author of ' Miriam May.'
Dedicated, by special permission, to the Right Hon. Sir E. B. Lytton,
Bart., M.P. 2 vols., 21s.

WHO SHALL BE DUCHESS? or,
THE NEW LORD OF BURLEIGH. A Novel. 2 vols., 21s.

THE LIGHTHOUSE. A Novel. 2 vols., 21s.

THE SKELETON IN THE CUPBOARD.
By Lady Scott. 2 vols., 21s. Cheaper Edition, 5s.

TOO LATE ! By Mrs. DIMSDALE. 7s. 6d.

HELEN. A Romance of Real Life. 7s. 6d.

THE CASTLE and the COTTAGE in SPAIN.
By Lady Wallace, Author of ' Clara; or, Slave Life in Europe.'
2 vols., 21s.

CYRUS. By Lady Julia Lockwood.

GERTRUDE MELTON ; or,
NATURE'S NOBLEMAN. A Tale. 7s. 6d.

RUTH BAYNARD'S STORY. 1 vol., 10s. 6d.

VANITY CHURCH. 2 vols., 21s.

MY WIFE'S PINMONEY.
By E. E. Nelson, a grand niece of the great Lord Nelson. 5s.

THE EMIGRANT'S DAUGHTER.
Dedicated, by permission, to the Empress of Russia. 5s.

MIRIAM MAY. 4th Edition. 10s. 6d.

WHISPERING VOICES OF THE YULE.
Tales for Christmas. 5s.

THE SENIOR FELLOW.
A Tale of Clerical Life. 10s. 6d.

ALMACK'S.
A Novel. Dedicated to the Ladies Patronesses of the Balls at Almack's. New Edition, 1 vol, crown 8vo, 10s. 6d.

NELLY CAREW.
By Miss Power. 2 vols, 21s.

MEMOIRS OF A LADY IN WAITING.
By the Author of 'Adventures of Mrs. Colonel Somerset in Caffraria.' 2 vols, 18s.

HULSE HOUSE.
A Novel. By the Author of 'Anne Gray.' 2 vols. post 8vo, 21s.

THE NEVILLES OF GARRETSTOWN.
A Historical Tale. Edited, and with a Preface by the Author of 'Emilia Wyndham.' 3 vols, post 8vo, 31s. 6d.

CORVODA ABBEY.
A Tale. 1 vol, post 8vo, 10s. 6d.

THE VICAR OF LYSSEL.
The Diary of a Clergyman in the 18th century. 4s. 6d.

GOETHE IN STRASBOURG.
A Dramatic Nouvelette. By H. Noel Humphreys. 7s. 6d.

SQUIRES AND PARSONS.
A Church Novel. 1 vol. 10s. 6d.

THE DEAN ; or, the POPULAR PREACHER.
By Berkeley Aikin, Author of 'Anne Sherwood.' 3 vols. post 8vo, 31s. 6d.

CHARLEY NUGENT ; or,
PASSAGES IN THE LIFE OF A SUB. A Novel, 3 vols, post 8vo. 31s. 6d.

PAUL FERROLL.
By the Author of ' IX Poems by V.' Fourth Edition. Post 8vo, 10s. 6d.

LORD AUBREY ; or,
WHAT SHALL I DO ? By the Author of 'Every Day.' A Novel.
2 vols , 21s.

THE IRONSIDES.
A Tale of the English Commonwealth. 3 vols., 31s. 6d.

AGNES HOME. A Novel. 10s. 6d.

LA CAVA ; or,
RECOLLECTIONS OF THE NEAPOLITANS. 10s. 6d.

ANSELMO.
A Tale of Modern Italy. 2 vols., 21s.

THE DALRYMPLES ; or,
LONG CREDIT AND LONG CLOTH. 10s. 6d.

INSTINCT ; or, REASON.
By Lady Julia Lockwood. 5s. 6d.

CARELADEN HOUSE. A Novel. 10s. 6d.

[illegible]

Sir E. L. Bulwer Lytton's Eva,
AND OTHER POEMS.

Sacred Poems.
By the late Right Hon. Sir Robert Grant, with a Notice by Lord Glenelg.

Eustace ;
An Elegy. By the Right Hon. Charles Tennyson D'Eyncourt.

Oberon's Empire.
A Mask.

The Shadow of the Yew,
AND OTHER POEMS. By Norman B. Yonge.

www.ingramcontent.com/pod-product-compliance
Lightning Source LLC
Chambersburg PA
CBHW020946030726
47496CB00005B/1382